Sacred Pathways

Divine Feminine Archetypes in You

By Cassandra Eve

with Illustrations by Pauline Burnside

Published 2020
Sacred Pathways – Divine Feminine Archetypes in You
© Cassandra Eve Whole Woman

Cover design by Cassandra Eve

ISBN: 9798574877722

Dedicated to women's journey in the awakening Sacred Feminine
and to the men who love them

Sacred Pathways – Contents

How to work with this book

Take it slowly. Pause in your reading. Absorb the essence of each archetype.

I suggest you read the introduction and the first two chapters initially. This will connect you to the Divine Feminine energies of Venus and Psyche as they express through the Sacred Pathways. Then move on to the other goddess archetypes with their shadows. Dip in and out as you feel drawn or read in chapter order.

Be aware some chapters may trigger you. Take in gently. Reach out for support where you need to.

Mythic Names: I have used the astrological names for these archetypes throughout - Greek or Roman - except when directly referring to the myths. There I have used the relevant archetype name from the myth's culture, together with the alternate astrological term. For example: when relating the Venus myths, mainly derived from the Greek culture where Venus is known as Aphrodite, I have used Aphrodite/Venus. Venus is both the Roman and the planet's name.

The Sacred Pathways Mandala

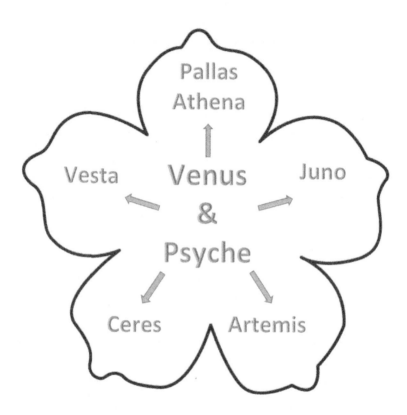

Venus | The Abundance Pathway
Feminine power for receptivity, attraction, magnetism & creativity
Psyche | The Soul's Pathway
Soul's yearning to express, embody & evolve on Earth
Vesta | The Authenticity Pathway
What's sacred? Growing relationship to yourself & the Divine within
Ceres | The Evolutionary Pathway
Nurture & growth through your changing rhythms as woman
Artemis | The Wild Pathway
Independence & inner connection. Nature & Moon as mirrors
Juno | The Intimacy Pathway
Keys to commitment in all seasons of relationship
Athena | The Purpose Pathway
Engaging & energising your unique contribution in the world

Introduction to
Sacred Pathways
Discovering Divine Feminine Archetypes in You

When life as we know it falls apart, we are called to discover new pathways. As our familiar safe ways of being are challenged, we must change and evolve. New life experience however it appears, requires new maps. 2020 is such a year and perhaps will go down in history as the year humanity finally woke up. Currently there are more questions than answers about how we may resolve our complex global dilemmas. So many aspects of our human lives are out of balance. We are facing the moment of truth. Having destroyed much of the environment and wonderful diversity of life on this planet, we now face the potential of our own annihilation. Confronted with the truth of our self-created predicament how do we start to instigate change? It is obvious. We must change our consciousness.

Emerging Feminine consciousness sits at the forefront of required change in these times. We can see women have been calling for liberation and equal rights for more than a century now. There's no doubt this is one aspect of required change, yet Feminine consciousness goes way beyond the movement for emancipation.

What is Feminine consciousness? How is She relevant to your life challenges and our current global crisis? What does She want to express, create and share on our beautiful Earth? Which doors is She opening within you, in your life? This book presents some possible answers to these questions. It reveals the potentials emerging through Feminine consciousness.

Clues to our emerging potentials lie in what I call her-story, the hidden history of women's lives. They lie in remembering (literally re-embodying) through reclaiming our divine nature as the Feminine. In exploring the themes presented in the weave of this book - her-story, astrology and mythological Feminine archetypes - the infinite potential of Her Mystery opens in your own intuitive and experiential insight. It opens in you, in your experience, in your life, in your consciousness. Connecting with each of these archetypes opens doors within that act as pathways to divinity. As you connect with each one, they emerge as facets of individuality that have always been there. Their unique qualities and energy begin to infuse your psyche, reconnect the

2

pathways to higher consciousness and feed your way of being here as a woman vehicle of the Divine Feminine. This is a guidebook to your core Feminine.

This book has been written primarily, but not exclusively, for women. Sacred Feminine is beyond gender. Its energy permeates all forms as does Sacred Masculine. Masculine and Feminine are genderless principles as in the Yin/Yang symbol of Chinese mythology. The Yin-Yang symbol represents complementary aspects of wholeness expressing through differing frequencies of energy. According to the Chinese, Yin and Yang were born from chaos when the universe was first created. They exist in harmony at the centre of the Earth and their balance in the Cosmic Egg brought forth the first human. In deepest truth we cannot separate Masculine and Feminine. As with Yin/Yang each contains the seed essence of the other. For the purposes of this book however I am focusing on Sacred Feminine as the inner qualities and life-sustaining holistic values that have been denied, denounced or dishonoured in the name of science, rationale, progress and materialism. We could describe that process with one simple term: patriarchy.

Just as Feminine and Masculine as principles of energy exist in both men and woman, patriarchy plays out in both genders too. What do I mean by patriarchy? The dictionary states that a patriarchy is a society where men dominate. Although that is a pertinent reality to explore that's not where I'm pointing in this book. Patriarchy is goal orientated, the ends justify the means, profit and greed. Patriarchy is inequality, privilege and supremacy (of any kind). In all its forms patriarchy is about power, its use and abuse. Is that true of just one gender? I would say no. Goal orientation, power, control, repression are aspects of our current paradigm that we are all familiar with. Whether we're using, abusing, over-consuming, controlling or being controlled, we're all playing patriarchal games to different degrees. It's a choice to use our power of creativity solely for personal advantage or with an agenda to stay safe.

Creative power is a healthy aspect of being human. In this book you will discover how it is a core principle of Feminine energy. You'll discover how Feminine energy is being used, how you, woman, are being used, and how to fully engage your evolving creative potential as Sacred Feminine. In our current collective culture creative power is being used for security, survival and competition. For the sake of the Earth, for all creatures, for humanity as a whole, we are being called beyond that way of life now. We are called to return to balance, to discover ways of co-creatively engaging our collective challenges. It is the embrace, caretaking and guardianship of all aspects of life on Earth that is needed now.

Feminine acting in unity with Masculine is the synergy required to evolve. The uplifting and embodying of form as consciousness will not only revitalize both our humanity and this world, its potential is to open the gateways to an utterly new experience of life on Earth. Given that, where we do find the guidance that takes us there? One place is astrology. It is the mirror for our universal consciousness and its evolution, both personally and collectively.

Astrology: It's not what you think it is

One might ask how can a system of esoteric knowledge based on a band of rocky bodies or gaseous planets in the universe resolve our current dilemmas? Isn't it here on Planet Earth that we need answers and solutions? Certainly astrology seems strange if not completely 'woo woo' to the scientific mind. Yet astrology has been informing humanity for more than five thousand years.

Astronomy and astrology were intricately linked until the 16th century. Ancient structures such as Stonehenge, the Pyramids and temple structures worldwide show us that ancient civilisations were connected to the rhythms of the planets in ways we have lost collectively. Our surviving tribal cultures retain this intimate link with the Earth and stars, the understanding of interdependence. The fact that everything in life is intricately linked and what happens to one aspect affects another.

The earliest wisdom of life's natural unity is now available to us through science. New physics reveals that matter can express both as form and energy, particle and wave, even appearing in two apparently different places at the same time, yet always unified at its source. The boundaries between science, philosophy and spirituality are blurring. Yet science will perhaps never discover the deepest truths, for as we now know, the beliefs of the observer influence the results. To discover the deepest truths, we must explore the consciousness of the universe. We must suspend rationale and belief to fall into the Mystery. We must learn to let go of focus on matter and discover the language of energy.

Astrology is an energetic language. It gives us a framework through which to explore. In order to do that we must look at *energy rather than form*. Just as new physics reveals that matter is both particle (physical matter) and wave (energy) simultaneously, so our universe is both physical and energetic, expressing on many different frequencies. Planetary bodies have physicality: material or gaseous. How they move through space, orbiting the Sun and aligning with other planets, creates diverse energy fields in which Earth (and humanity) is immersed. Science has known since the early 1940s that particular alignments of the Sun with Earth and other planets affect radio signals. More recent discoveries expand on that knowledge. Coming back to astrology, if we accept that each planetary body has an energetic resonance that we are receiving on Earth constantly, we begin to see how life here is not just a matter of physicality and the five senses.

Just as life on Earth has seasonal rhythms so does our universe. The energy of the planets is radiating at different frequencies, with different rhythms every day. We understand this through our physical connection to the Sun and Moon cycles. We see them moving through their phases caused by the Earth and Moon's rotations. We might notice these daily and certainly will recognize their longer rhythms: New Moon to Full Moon, or the flow of the seasons. We can also see the stars and planets Mercury, Venus, Mars, Jupiter and Saturn physically without the aid of a telescope. When we do so, the beauty of the universe we're part of astounds us doesn't it? What we fail to recognize perhaps is that we are experiencing their energies too. The ever-moving rhythms of the planetary bodies are an intricate aspect of our life rhythms, much as the Sun rising every morning. The only difference is the energies of the stars and planets are invisible to us. We don't yet fully understand collectively that we not only receive, but we *are,* the energy of the universe.

How does this work? We could use the phrase, 'as above so below'. Just as the Sun radiates as a huge source of light and life for our planet and humanity, so do other planets transmit energy. We are immersed in a universal field. We could consider this to be like walking through a field of invisible rays, much as we are living in background radiation, mobile phone signals, radio waves and so on without necessarily being aware of it. Then we have the energy of consciousness itself. Consciousness is still a mystery to the scientific mind. Generally it is defined as the state of being aware of and responsive to one's surroundings. It is seen as a product of the brain, but is it? Or is this merely a scientific theory yet to be verified. Spiritual belief systems suggest the opposite; that the brain is an instrument of consciousness. This larger definition suggests that consciousness is all that is, formed and formless. Within the field of infinite consciousness, we also have individualised consciousness. This is where astrology comes in, creating a bridge of language and understanding between the energy of the universe and every human being.

The innate connection between universe and individual is demonstrated through an astrological birth-chart. The chart operates as a map of individualised consciousness taken from planetary connections at the time and place of birth. When any human being is born clearly the whole of humanity is immersed in that energetic field. Yet for that newborn the energies of the moment inform their energetic make up as an individual. Having just taken physical embodiment this is their soul map for life. Not as a static or fatalistic way of being – for the universe is infinitely expanding. Planetary bodies, even our Earth, are always moving. For the individual being born the chart acts as a map of their ever-evolving way of response, expression and evolution through a lifetime.

If we look at collective human evolution we can see even deeper into the 'as above, so below' of these universal maps. The timing of the discovery of different planetary bodies gives us clear pointers to how life in the universe and on Earth all works perfectly naturally. Some of the 20th century astronomical discoveries point the way towards understanding how the energies operate.

Astronomers know of the existence of a planetary body long before they spot it. There are clues to its existence through the orbits of other planetary bodies. When they see a new planet physically through a telescope however something quite amazing happens. In 1930 Clyde Tombaugh of Lowell Observatory in the USA discovered the dwarf planet Pluto. Strangely (and yet not so strangely as you'll discover) this new planet was named Pluto, after the Roman mythological Lord of the Underworld. This naming demonstrates the synchronicity of the universe at work, for the correlation between planetary discoveries, their naming and events on Earth is more than coincidental. If we look at what was happening on Earth in the 1930's we can see this. This time period was the entry point into one of the darkest phases within recent human history, namely the rise of fascism, the Second World War and the holocaust. The physical sighting of Pluto paralleled a dive into Pluto's realm, the underworld, here on Earth.

There is an even deeper indication of this 'as above, so below' link to Pluto's energy. In 1932 scientists split the atom for the first time. Science presented human beings with the power for total destruction. This is Pluto's realm. With this radical act the need for understanding the consequences of such power became apparent. The mantle of responsibility for life or annihilation was birthed, for all human beings and for the Earth herself. It is a clear and crucial point in humanity's evolution. Pluto lies at the outermost reaches of our universe. This fact demonstrates how we are reaching our limits also. What lies beyond?

As Pluto's discovery signified a shift of consciousness for humanity and the necessity to ask bigger questions of ourselves, so does the discovery of all planetary bodies. We can see this clearly in the history of planetary discoveries since the 18th century. It's not relevant to this book to share them all here but there's one other clear correlation that's worthy of mention.

The discovery of a centaur planetary body Chiron took place in 1977. Chiron is the Wounded Healer archetype from Greek mythology. He represents how our suffering can be a profound teacher and healing tool; how we are animal, human and divine in one complex mix. The late 1970s saw the emergence of diverse holistic healing practices into the mainstream. This 'New Age' movement brought an increase in meditation and mindfulness as stress-busting tools and a deeper exploration of body-mind connections through spirituality. The idea of ourselves as consciousness having a human experience is becoming more widely explored. The differing needs of each aspect of our Being, divine through human and animal, how they operate differently and yet as a whole, is now a vast field of enquiry. Chiron's discovery awakened another layer of self-knowing beyond being simply human.

The mirror of 'as above, so below' operates despite our human rationale. How were Pluto and Chiron so aptly named? It would seem to be synchronicity indeed given hindsight into the events and development that followed their discovery. Yet there is intelligence at work on this planet far beyond our human capacity thus far, or indeed our understanding. Unity is at work in many ways in our lives. We may see it, yet when we try to understand it, we are bemused. We can only put it down to the Mystery of life or what we call 'The Divine'? Similarly, the naming of planets and zodiac signs after mythological archetypes is this mysterious principle at play. Whether we've heard them or not myths lie deep in our collective psyche. Archetypes too; they are aspects of the human psyche; the ways in which we know our self, respond, express, act and grow.

Patterns of being

Archetypes are inner symbols or images that we recognise. They are symbolic patterns of energy underlying our collective experience from which we derive meaning. For instance, if I use the word 'warrior', you may connect with the general qualities of that archetype. You would recognise the word represents a model of a certain way of being and behaviour. It works similarly with 'mother', 'villain', damsel in distress', 'wise elder', 'lover', jester' and so on. We could say the archetype holds the core energy of a particular form of expression that speaks to us symbolically.

We encounter archetypes in many ways. Externally the usual encounter would be through dreams, stories or fantasies. We all recognise when the wicked witch appears in a fairy tale there's drama unfolding for our hero or heroine, don't we? Internally we may be aware of an archetype as a particular response or reaction to stimulus, in other words, the pattern behind a particular behaviour. For instance, given certain circumstances we may always act as a rebel. Patterns operates much like a software program; press button 'a' and 'b' happens. Similarly, planetary energies are archetypal. They have a particular form of energy and expression. At some level we recognise them, even our language relates to them. For instance, the word 'martial' meaning warlike has its roots in the name of planet Mars. At Full Moon we might feel moody, unusually high or low, much as the tides of the ocean. Life activates different archetypes in us at different times, sometimes naturally, for instance in becoming a mother or father. At other times they operate seemingly despite our self, for instance when the 'victim' archetype is activated in us.

According to Jung who first used the word archetype for these collective symbols, archetypes are innate universal pre-conscious psychic patterns or predispositions. They form the basis from which the collective themes of human life and experience emerge. Archetypes are components of the collective unconscious, organising, directing and informing human thought and behaviour. The Greeks first developed theories about these patterns of human behaviour; Plato described them as ideas and forms that are imprinted before birth. Another way to describe this theory would be as

9

energetic frequencies and patterns that we live through. These patterns have a certain density, depending on how much validity we give them personally or collectively. They have both a personal and collective element. Similarly, the planetary bodies can be known as active forces within us, by which we receive the energy to experience life in different ways.

From the 1960s questions about our role as human beings within the cosmos, energy, extra-terrestrial life, fate, destiny and free will have become more common. Many individuals are now more aware that humanity is in a process of evolving consciously. There is both a greater understanding and more questions about the nature of our self through our psychology, religion and spirituality, philosophy and new physics. New physics now shows us the innate oneness of all life is differing interconnected frequencies of energy. It reveals that life is a synergy of possibility and probability and that our conscious perspective has influence in the collective field.

Nothing is certain in this new age, even though we might want it to be. The old view of astrology as predictive or fated has now made way to an understanding of the synergy between the universal energy we receive and are constantly immersed in, and how we respond to it i.e. free will. All with the purpose of developing greater self-knowledge, of bringing to awareness the unconscious factors underlying our life experience. It's to know and understand our inner and external worlds in greater depth and to discover interconnectivity. Yet more so it is to recognise that we actually *are* universal consciousness at play on Earth and to consciously participate in that unfolding.

What lies beneath
Jung's exploration of the human psyche and the nature of consciousness led to a great interest in astrology. His words 'Astrology represents the sum of all the psychological knowledge of antiquity' reveal his deep understanding of the inner workings of human beings and the universe. Jung likened the planetary bodies not only to archetypes but to gods and goddesses that loom large as symbols in our collective unconscious. These symbols act as guide,

mentor, protagonist, catalyst and so on within our inner world and in our relationships. They provide us with maps for ways of being and expression, along with our evolution in individuality.

We recognise core archetypes when presented to us through story, song, theatre and film, or through reading the ancient myths, yet many of the inner maps we need lie buried in the unconscious. This is particularly true of female archetypes that have been lost through patriarchy, denied by a world view that focuses on progress, control of nature and the Feminine. They have been forgotten due to a lack of acknowledgment of their relevance, let alone value, in our world. Yet all is not lost. For astrology (through the some of the less well-known asteroid archetypes), mythology and history support and deepen our connection to these hidden aspects of our psyche. They are mirrors for forgotten aspects of self. We are enlightened and empowered in our opening up to them.

Mythology is not solely comprised of stories of a fantastical past; it's alive. It came straight out of the unconscious as a means to express and describe human impulses and motivations. Then the storytellers, those who had no conscious knowledge of psychology or the unconscious levels of our humanness, wrote or related it to others. Just as in those times, we are living mythology today; it's fluid, a map for our expression and evolution. Myth provides us with the means of accessing the 'gods' in our unconscious. Those 'gods' are our drivers. They express personally and collectively. We project energy onto them. For instance, the ancient gods and goddesses are now expressed through the cult of celebrity. We worship them (if we do) in similar ways to the Greeks worshipped Zeus or Athena. We can see how they change through history; the goddess for one generation was Marilyn Monroe, now it's Beyonce. Similarly, Elvis morphed into Leonardo di Caprio. The characters may change yet in reading the ancient myths we can see how the magnetic play of energy within our self is timeless.

Myth provides us with maps of living frequencies that we energise and express both personally and collectively. Like archetypes myths are inside us, speaking to us symbolically. Myth bypasses the rational, logical scientific perspective. It's multi-layered; symbolic, both collective and personal. It denies the either-or, black-white perspective and takes us into the world of both-and. Myth belongs in the world of oral tradition, where there are many multi-layered versions with the same archetypal theme. We cannot neatly box and label these themes expressed through myth, but we can connect with them, for they are already alive within us.

Myth evolves through different eras of human history and through different cultures, many of which have creation myths with similar themes. The story of a Christ figure is presented in like ways in different traditions. Most of the myths underpinning the astrological archetypes arise from the Greek and Roman cultures. Figures of Roman mythology were largely appropriated from the Greek tradition and given new names. Yet if we travel deeper into history, before the Greek culture, we find these are based on even older stories. Not only that, we find that the Feminine archetypes as portrayed through Greek or Roman perspectives have been sanitised. Her-story has been changed. Understanding the rise of these cultures, the changes they brought to the lives of human beings, especially women, and what they destroyed in a quest for power, is vital to understanding our current gender power plays and politics. Deep in the unconscious we know there's been a takeover. The archetypes and myths of that time are still playing out. In connecting with them, understanding how they influence us still, deconstructing the patterns and receiving their gifts, we not only reclaim what's been lost, we evolve.

The Ages of Evolution

There are many ways that we learn about our history, personally and collectively. The means of historical discovery includes archaeology, genealogy and numerous scientific routes. There is also written documentation, the arts, tribal memory, myths and stories handed down through time orally. Yet if we look into our collective history it's pretty obvious that who gets to tell the story influences it, along with its focus and meaning. Everything is open to interpretation through the beliefs of the observer or explorer, especially through the conqueror. The lens we are looking through also influences what we see. A palaeontologist, no matter how knowledgeable can only see from the perspective of their experience as modern man. Then there is the fact that most history has been written by men. What actually happened through the ages lies buried beneath layers of interpretation or downright manipulation. This is never truer than when we look into the lives and experience of human beings. Yet we may find clues to other versions of what purports to be definitive.

Looking at the astrological big picture in terms of human evolution, what are known as 'the astrological ages' reveal some of the main themes of evolution for humanity and its cultures. The astrological themes of this system align with discoveries from paleontology and archaeology going back to the 10th millennium BC megalith temples in Turkey, even to goddess figurines dating back 35,000 years. For the purpose of this book however the time frame 4000BC to present day is particularly relevant. It is represented by the astrological ages of Taurus through Aquarius, that we are just entering. The astrological ages last approximately 2000 years with a transition period between each lasting several hundred years. As we can see each age brought a transition that changed culture and the lives of human beings dramatically.

Age of Cancer: 8000-6000BCE approximately
Humans began to move from nomadic to settled cultures and develop agriculture. This is the Age of the Mother. Human beings lived in participation mystique with the Earth as nurturer, sustainer and giver of life. Many Goddess figurines have been discovered from this era.

Age of Gemini: 6000-4000BCE approximately
Settled communities developed into cities in this era. Trade between cities began. The development of writing started. The first written texts appear from this time, in the form of stone tablets.

Age of Taurus: 4000-2000BCE approximately
A time of mainly peaceable creative cultures without weapons or armies, where matrilineal descent was the norm, the role of the priestess and temple

was central to culture, distributing food, taking care of the weak and elderly, as well as providing a focus for worship, ritual and celebration.

Age of Aries: 2000BCE-0CE approximately
During this age great military cultures arose and invaded the settled cultures. This is the time of the takeover of patriarchy where the 'right of might' rather than the good of the people began to take precedence. This is the age of the warrior and the hero. Dominating the power of nature and the Feminine. The separation of the divine from body, land, Earth Mother and sexuality began.

Age of Pisces: 0CE-2000CE approximately
This is the age of patriarchy and religion. Christianity, Buddhism and Islam appeared during this period. It was a time of suffering and victim consciousness, guilt and sin (promoted through control of Mother Church) This age saw 300 years or more of witch-hunts. Women were labelled within the roles of Madonna, mother or whore, natural healing arts became hidden and the true nature of sexuality was forgotten except by a few.

Age of Aquarius: 2000CE-4000CE
The era of higher consciousness, when innovation through technology and science may provide the answers to our global dilemma, working with and for nature. Potentially an age of individuality, equality and global community is dawning where technology becomes the servant to abundance for all.

Exploring this bigger picture of humanity's growth process, it may seem we have gone backwards in terms of evolution, particularly regarding our connection to the natural world. Yet without doubt our consciousness has evolved. We have moved through the states of tribal dependence and participation mystique into independence, from polytheism to monotheism and are now travelling towards interiorized spirituality. We have moved on from expressly solely as an instinctual self to an egoic self and the emerging potential is for our sense of self to be derived from soul and spirit. Collectively our knowing of power received from connection *to* nature (Great Mother) that during patriarchy became power *against* nature, is now called to evolve towards power *with* nature.

Given that our consciousness is growing into its next shift, how we use the gift of emerging possibility becomes a vital question. Will we continue to use our consciousness for personal gain above collective need, or to serve our global culture and the environment? It remains to be seen. Now more than ever we have the power to evolve or destroy ourselves. Perhaps this is the true meaning of our life on Earth – that we become conscious with the power of free will?

The great takeover
For the purposes of this book the period from the age of Aries onwards is most relevant to our exploration of her-story. It is in this period that we find the main body of mythology through the Greek and Roman culture, with its roots in more ancient times. The systematic destruction of women's knowledge and power occurs in this timeframe. Our cultural conscious connection to the Divine Feminine was lost.

The split away from the Feminine led to an overt disregard of women's naturally sacred role as life-giver within the family and culture. Over centuries men totally denounced women's role within society in favour of control. The conquerors used and abused through force, or in some cases they simply took over and 'married' their own god to the existing goddesses, just as the Christian church built on pagan sites in later times. The incomers god was generally a single solar figure, masculine, a hero, that gave rise to the many hero myths of this time. Power was separated from the Great Mother and became centralized in a Solar Deity. Human beings began to look away from the Earth that gives us life, towards the heavens. This was mirrored in the rise of kings and male leaders from whom power was devolved in a hierarchical way.

The power grab of this time was strengthened through the ending of matrilineal inheritance and increased control of the role of the priestesses.

15

The temple system of caring for the community was overthrown in favour of male right to own, control nature and grow personal wealth. Over centuries the cultural shift to the ownership of property by males (including ownership of females and female children) became established as the norm. Women and girls came to be seen as the property of their fathers or the male householder.

The move away from Mother and Earth-honouring cultures that created a split between spirit and body, also shattered the knowing of sexuality as sacred, aa expression of divine union. In Roman culture the priestess retained her strong social and political role initially within the culture as Vestal Virgin. Yet the demand that she remained a virgin sexually also (on pain of death) grew the split between spirit and sexuality that we see so strongly marked in our cultures now. With the rise of the Christian religion the devolution of power to males and the dishonouring of women's sexual creative power was established. Women now tended to be identified purely as Madonna or whore, in line with biblical concepts. Women's original nature as the sensual being, creative vessel of the divine was demeaned as sinful. She was demoted from divine creatrix to an animal body for producing heirs or providing satisfaction.

Here we meet the myth of Eve and the serpent in the garden. Some sources state that this myth - Adam and Eve, man and woman created in pairs, with woman emerging from man's rib – was created for political purposes. Whether true or not we can see the results. The story of Eve and serpent power – a potent remnant from temple cultures - strengthened the idea of woman's nature as sinful, to be avoided or feared. Woman was thrown out of the garden along with her naturally sensual creative nature, to be judged, vilified, demonized and controlled. Ideas and concepts based in fear began to take control of the creative power – or to try to. This natural power is still raw, alive and potent in nature, despite mankind's attempts to control and abuse it.

The world as we know it now is based on these misunderstandings or outright distortions of the female role as creatrix. It has led to the abuse of our innate creative power and the decimation of our Earth and her creatures. A rebalancing must occur. A deep understanding of how we use creative power is crucial. Every aspect of life arises from that. The creation of children is an obvious one. Our disconnection from nature's creative i.e. sexual power is another.

Our understanding and respect of that power in ourselves as women is fundamental to the shift that needs to take place. The Sacred Feminine is calling to emerge in her purity. To unveil her we must travel through her shadows both personally and collectively. It starts with each one of us. In understanding the collective patterns that have arisen from that takeover and how they are operating through our consciousness now, we may transmute them. In transmuting them we also connect with their great gifts. We reclaim the innate power of Sacred Feminine wisdom, caring for each other and our Earth. In the reclamation of ancient wisdom, in the evolution of finer frequencies of consciousness, we engender deeper values. The potentials for the evolution of our collective consciousness are both potent and vast.

Consciousness rising and descending

The naming, blaming and shaming of women as a means of patriarchal control has permeated the last 3000 years or more. The use and abuse of nature has paralleled this denunciation of what is not only natural but fundamentally life-sustaining. What lies beneath this control is fear; fear of Her Mystery. For are not women and nature mysterious in their life-giving and life-destroying cycles?

Before the age of Aries it appears that human beings were deeply aware of, and in awe of, the natural mystery of life and its cycles of birth and death. Communities knew their reliance on and oneness with nature. Woman was seen and honoured as intricately connected to this mystery through her blood cycles and capacity to create, sustain and nourish human life. Nowadays the mystical knowledge held by the wise women and shaman has mostly been lost. A few ancient tribal peoples remain and are speaking to us with this earth-based knowing yet are we listening? Mostly we have forgotten this deep sacred knowledge; certainly we are disconnected from it. Yet the fact of life is obvious. Without woman what happens to physical life? Without nature what happens to humanity? Acknowledging this is not only clearly needed but is a sacred requirement.

To access the power of transformation of our ancient wounding is essential in our times. It is to reclaim the truth of who we are as Divine Feminine in bodies on Earth as women and as men. We are at the dawning of the Age of Aquarius, the age of higher consciousness. We are called to rise and engage evolving consciousness for the good of all. Yet without the body that uplift of consciousness has no real value to our lives or the Earth. In truth we are called to both rise and descend; to descend into the body but more necessarily, through our shadows of pain.

In exploring the mythology and archetypes of the Age of Aries to current times, particularly in regard to Feminine energy, we are given maps for the journey. There are many Goddess archetypes available through mythology. I have chosen the ones with strong archetypal and astrological themes. These themes are deep in our psyche already. We know them intimately. Yet we need to be reminded of who they are, so we can truly be who we are, as woman vessels of Sacred Feminine, as earth-connected men and women. The archetypes I present here have planetary bodies, namely planets, asteroids and dwarf planets. They are physical. This reveals their importance in healing the wounds of humanity and in growing finer frequencies of Sacred Feminine energy in us all. These archetypes encompass both gifts and shadow. The shadow wounds contain power to light up the world when we reclaim them. For they contain energy we have judged, denied or repressed. The shadow of our wounds is a power source for good when we allow it to transmute.

The Feminine reveals how to reclaim the gifts of the dark rich spaces within. Nature is our mirror for this process. Life begins in the dark – the dark of the soil or the womb. Darkness is where we are nurtured and replenished –

through sleep, through the dark days of winter, through rest and quiet. When we pause, rest and feel, we reconnect to what is essential to us; we renew our deeper values. Without the dark shadow of life in a physical body, with its suffering, there is no possibility of the development of empathy or compassion.

In exploring both the light and shadow within our self we are empowered in our wholeness; consciousness and body, ascending and embodying, embracing our role as Earth Guardians. We re-sensitise our self to our inner wisdom, to what is needed for the whole. That might be the whole of oneself, the family or tribe, or the collective. When we reclaim the inner darkness, we reclaim the natural process of alchemy.

Alchemy is the mystery of how nature transforms itself. Our body is this mystery too, naturally converting food to fuel and living tissue, converting breath to life force. This mystery, the multi-dimensional nature of reality, can be explored through science but ultimately it cannot be communicated through rationale. To know it we must know our innate unity with it. We must recognise the natural flow between divine and human, light and dark, Yin and Yang, Masculine and Feminine is the process of life on this planet and we are here to engage it all. In so doing the potential of a true 'New Age' becomes truly tangible. In so doing the already-innate-unity that we are becomes known here. In That, all life thrives, our dilemma becomes resolved naturally through higher consciousness. We are returned through sacred pathways to our original nature.

Chapter 1
The Divine Feminine at Our Core – Venus

There's an ebb
and a flow
tonight.
I feel Her pulsing.

The mysterious urge,
rhythm of life,
sensating,
vibrating,
pulsating me.

Venus
rising in my belly;
galaxies pouring from my breasts;
tide of sensuality rising;
the calling of intensity
running in my blood,
my body.
Every cell tingling,
mingling earth with universe,
colliding stars,
roaring through infinity,
with the scream of ecstasy.

It's all inside,
this passionate union of life.

It's in me, beyond me, through
me.
He & She entwined in cosmic
fusion
exploring
exploding
imploding
ecstasy.

It's here
from fingertips
to warm moist inner cave.
With each breath
I feel Her rising
and falling;
calling Her emptiness yet fullness,
her rhythmic sensating
running wild
through His silence.

I am the Lover
and His breath
Tonight.

I am Beloved.
I am loved.
I am Earth Moon Sun love tonight.
Cassandra Eve

Archetype: Goddess of Love

Symbols: love arrows and darts; a magic belt; swan; dove; myrtle; rose; cypress; apple; tortoise; swan; scallop shell; mirror; gold and golden energy

Message: I am Love. It's all about Love. I am the creative power in woman on Earth.

Expression: The core essence of feminine energy; the desire nature; magnetic attraction; reproductive force; creative power; the natural processes of fertilization; passion; beauty; charm; goldenness; self-love & self-worth; the capacity to give and receive freely; enjoyment; abundance. Venus also symbolizes our relationship with money.

Shadow themes: body and Earth disconnection; misuse of creative power; a lack of self-worth; transforming the bitch; the use of sexual energy; rejection and loss

Also known as: Aphrodite (Greek)

Venus Goddess of Love represents attraction, magnetism, relationship and abundance. She is the Goddess of desire, pleasure and fertility, married but with many lovers. To the Romans Venus was considered essential to the generation and balance of life. In their pantheon she is the polarity to the active and fiery male gods. She absorbs the male essence, uniting opposites in harmony, love or sexual union. Venus is responsible, with the mother goddess archetypes, for the continuation of life on Earth. She lies at the core of our creative potential as women, both for physical life and other forms of creation.

Venus holds central place within the Sacred Pathways mandala of goddess archetypes. As the receptive principle of creative power and potential in every woman Venus manifests the infinite possibilities of the Moon's cycle. It is her creative energy that carries the potential of fertilising an egg and growing it into the form of a child through pregnancy. It is this potency of Venus energy that expresses through all the Feminine archetypes. She represents the creative power of the universe appearing and manifesting through a particular expression or function here on Earth. In eastern cultures this creative feminine energy is known as Shakti. In our western culture, although she is personified in Venus and ancient forms such as Inanna, Astarte and Ishtar, she is not well known and barely acknowledged.

Venus energy is sexual energy; life's potential for new creation. The Sacred Feminine archetypes – each with different potential and strength within us - express Venus energy in unique ways. Venus lies at their core as the innate creative energy that moves through us into a particular process of self-expression or manifestation.   Whether expressing through the sacred devotion of Vesta, Juno's relationship commitment, Pallas Athena's creative intelligence, or any other expression, it is this energy – Feminine power and potential represented by Venus - at its core. She is life's desire to know itself through the physical flow of our life force into love, beauty, abundance and creative expression.

Her-story

The origins of Venus lie in the ancient legends and writings of Inanna, Ishtar, Astarte and Nana. As with many of our goddess archetypes, her origins are hidden in the mists of time. There are pointers to her in ancient eastern Mediterranean, North African, Slavic, Baltic, Arabic and Native American cultures. In her original nature she is seen as a goddess of both fertility and destruction, deeply connected to the rhythms of nature and the land. Her identity seemed to change over eons yet the Venus nature, with its underlying expression and meaning, remains constant. Also known as Queen of the Heavens, she is the embodiment of creative energy manifesting itself whatever her name.

The physical planet Venus appears and disappears as Morning and Evening Star. This reveals the pre-patriarchal understanding of her nature as both light and dark. Life's eternal cycling through day and night, light and shadow, summer and winter and its cyclical transition between these different modes of being. The Sumerian and Babylonian myths of Inanna and Damuzi, along with that of Ishtar and Tammuz, relate to this natural connection to natural cycles. The Descent of Inanna is the most ancient surviving epic tale, 4,000 years old. It reveals the natural sensuality and earth connection that was alive in pre-patriarchal cultures of the eastern Mediterranean. The feminine nature of the divine was known and acknowledged in nature and through our sexuality. Her cycles of birth, life, death and rebirth were honoured through ritual. In many cultures the goddess rituals involved the queen or high priestess taking a young lover as consort for a season to fulfil 'hieros gamos' the sacred marriage. He then 'died' (either symbolically or literally according to the culture and time) to be reborn in the spring. It was felt that his blood fertilised the land, much as menstrual blood is linked to the cycles of fertility and sperm impregnates an egg to create a child.

Venus was also central to the Mayan culture. She was interpreted as a goddess of war and strife depending on her astronomical position. Changes in her orbit gave rise to blood sacrifice, mirroring the link between fertility and woman's menstrual cycle. Blood sacrifice was an offering to the gods in recognition of how blood was an integral aspect of the creation of physical life. Venus's astrological positions dictated the placing of the Mayan windows and doors so they could sight her changing placement in the sky. Ancient cultures recognised and honoured this intimate relationship between nature, woman and life. It is only at the dawning of patriarchy that this natural connection, and the goddess energy in her many forms, becomes sanitised. Venus became known only as the Goddess of Love and connected to romantic love. Yet Venus has many aspects, including a dark side, as we shall see.

Venus's more recent roots lies in mythology as Aphrodite her Greek counterpart. Homer's version of her myth relates how she is the daughter of the sky god Zeus and the sea god Titan Dione. The more commonly known myth by Hesiod, depicted in Botticelli's famous painting 'Birth of Venus', relates how she was born of sea foam after Saturn/Cronos cut off the penis of his father Uranus/Ouranos during the war of the Titans. As his penis fell into the sea, it ejaculated, emerging as sea foam. Venus appeared from this sea foam and floated through it in a mussel shell to the island of Cyprus. As she shook seawater from her hair its drops became pearls. Wherever she walked lush grass and flowers appeared under her feet. Escorted by sea nymphs to Mount Olympus, the home of Greek deities, Venus/Aphrodite was immediately received as one of the gods. She was so beautiful all the male gods desired her hand in marriage. Interestingly this sea route from east to west was used by sea traders who may have brought her mythology with them on their journeys.

There are many Greek and Roman myths with Aphrodite/Venus playing a central role, especially when it comes to love and sexuality. She was married to Hephaestus/Vulcan crippled god of the forge, with whom she was always unsatisfied. Zeus/Jupiter had arranged their union to prevent a war amongst the gods for Aphrodite's hand in marriage. Despite her apparent lack of connection to him, as craftsman to the gods in some ways Hephaestus is Aphrodite's natural counterpart. He created thrones and weapons for the gods, automatons and sculptures made of precious metals. He created Aphrodite's magic girdle that was woven with irresistible powers of magnetism and love. He is a creator. The fire of Hephaestus's forge could be said to represent the fire of desire and how it transmutes everything. His workshop was at the base of a volcano, a fitting image for passion. There are also myths that relate Hephaestus ejaculating onto the Earth, impregnating Gaia with a different being each time. This is another link to the Aphrodite energy of sexuality and fertility.

Aphrodite and Hephaestus seem to be a well-suited pair, yet marriage did not stop Aphrodite following the flow of her desire. Her husband was married to his work, so she took innumerable lovers, both god and human. The two most favoured were her astrological consort Ares/Mars and Adonis. Homer suggests that Hephaestus and Aphrodite were divorced after he found her in bed with Ares.

Driven by the need to express love and desire, Aphrodite not only took many lovers but stimulated love amongst others. She had several children, the most famous is said to be Eros/Cupid. Eros has roots in more ancient times however as one of the primal forces of creation. Certainly the baby Cupid with his bow and arrows is a poor representation of the force of Eros desire nature. Where love was involved, along with romantic intrigue and love triangles, Aphrodite was usually found to be playing. Strangely she was fulfilled in love only momentarily. This reveals much about the ephemeral nature of love in both our human world and the realm of the gods.

Venus's Place in the Universe – Astronomy & Astrology

Venus is the second planet from the Sun and third brightest object in the sky after the Sun and Moon. It is sometimes referred to as the sister planet to Earth, because their size and mass are so similar. Venus is also the closest planet to Earth.

Venus's orbit with the Earth creates a beautiful Flower of Life/five-pointed star pattern over a period of eight years. Eight Earth years are roughly equal to 13 Venus years, meaning the two planets trace out this pattern with 5-fold symmetry as they orbit the Sun. Together they map out the points of an astounding but not quite perfect pentagram in the sky. This ratio of 8/13 is one of the Fibonacci numbers. The Fibonacci sequence lies at the fundamental core of nature and its creations. The anatomic structure of humans follows the ratio of these numbers, from the body as a whole, to the details of the face. Even our DNA shows Fibonacci number relationships. The shell of the Nautilus sea creature follows these numbers, as do many flowers and plants. It is interesting to note that implementing the Fibonacci sequence into the design of a musical instrument gives it the best tone. The correlations are infinite and form the basis of our universe. This symmetry also affirms Venus energy at the core of Earth life within our universe.

Venus is visible either as the Morning or Evening Star during her full orbit and disappears from our view completely when it draws close to the Sun. It rises ahead of the Sun for roughly 260 days as the Morning Star, then disappears, reappearing as the Evening Star for approximately 260 days.

Venus is one of the five personal planets in astrology, along with the Sun, Moon, Mercury and Mars. She rules both the earthy sign of Taurus and the harmony-seeking air sign Libra. Interestingly this dual nature is also reflected in her different forms in mythology as Aphrodite Pandemos - sensual Venus - and Aphrodite Urania – heavenly or spiritual Venus. In this dual naming we see the beginning of the split between sexuality and spirituality that was further promoted through Christianity.

Through her sign placement and aspects in a birth chart Venus reveals how we feel, how we love and the ease or challenges of our relationship connections and intimacy. Venus is also representative of self-love, self-worth, our capacity to give and receive freely and to create abundance. In women she represents the truth of our role as creatrix on Earth, the core creative power that expresses through the Feminine archetypes of the Sacred Pathways in unique ways.

My Journey with Venus

Do we choose who we love? Or does love choose us? This is a lifelong question perhaps. Can we make love happen, much as we might try? Do we create it; or is love a mystery that seems to descend on us?

What is it that calls a man and woman together? Certainly there is the pull of sexual attraction or the play of needs but isn't there more? Isn't there the desire to know the mystery of who this is? Isn't there the calling to discover some kind of fulfilment, wholeness or completion, through this possibility of relationship? Isn't there the desire to see where this calling to love takes us? Or to discover what is behind this mysterious magnetic allure of 'other'?

Love's mystery is calling me deep right now, as it always has. The arrival in my life of a man who is twenty-seven years younger is certainly a big mystery. Yet there was no denying when that calling to love appeared. The recognition of 'I know you' powered through my body from my soul. His pure Masculine presence poured in, holding space for a deep opening in this body, even without the physical bodies touching. I could feel his presence tangibly inside me as vibration. How could I not respond to this invitation from Venus?

In a connection such as this one there is plenty of fuel for the mind. Lack of trust becomes active simply because of the vulnerability brought about by cultural and personal beliefs of how love or a relationship should look. Yet I pay it no heed. I embrace the vulnerability that opens in me, knowing it is a door opening. Nothing in life is certain, especially in relating. I give thanks for the opportunity to love and to be loved. I recognise that when I stay out of the mind's questions about the future, or the need to understand, everything unfolds beautifully now. Who amongst us ever knows the when, where, why or how of love anyway? To think we do is foolish. When the mind kicks in with its questions, I simply celebrate each moment of this love.

As for him, his expression to me: 'I didn't see body; I didn't see age; I knew you as pure alchemy' revealed the vulnerability he also experienced on meeting me. I was as unexpected to him as he was to me. His honesty opened my heart to a bottomless depth of rawness. I see his struggle as a man to be much more than the man. I know his deep and full Masculine presence when he stops trying. I see his rampant mind try to control life, not fully aware yet that he cannot limit or label who She is.

This relating is not easy. But I don't call for easy. I am ready for a connection that is much more than that. He is also ready, or it wouldn't be happening. In the honesty with kindness we both commit to, there is ease. Often there are fireworks. Yet I am ready for all of it; for it is real loving with all its transformative power. He sees this too and is ready to break the boundary of what he thinks he knows. For the first time in this life I can say 'I trust him'. Not him the man but the presence of Masculine that comes through him. That is utterly real. As I open to That, the presence of Feminine within me pours through. My body comes fully alive simply through a brush of the hands. She awakens in me. This is Venus's mystery, what we call love.

Venus Message: I am Love. It's all about Love

I believe we are made for love. More than that, we actually are love at our core and we are here to realise love through all the appearances that seem to belie its presence. Traditionally the heart is seen as the centre of love. It has featured through the ages as the container of romantic attraction and expression. Why is that? We know through experience that the heart beats faster when we are attracted or aroused. We also know now, through scientific research, that the heart emits a signature electrical frequency thousands of times more powerful than anything else in the body. This suggests the heart's unseen magnetic field has an impact of which we are not yet fully aware. We do know it extends through every cell in the human body and beyond it, even affecting those around us. I have no doubt the mystery of the heart and its force field has much to reveal to us yet.

The Venus archetype represents our desire and capacity for love. She's about how and who, even what, we love. She represents what is deeply of value to us, along with the expression of our creative potential and the enjoyment of true fulfillment. In exploring our capacity for relating and experience in love we may recognise that our longing for love is the fuel that grows us. This longing – when we are brave enough to follow it – takes us beyond our self. It shatters our old boundaries and offers us the opportunity to become more of who we are at core, beyond our self-beliefs and structures. Venus, as the archetype of love, offers us her hand and leads us into the unknown. Her calling is threefold. Her magnetic nature expresses through the primal urge of sexuality – to experience union and fulfilment, with its potential to create new life in the form of a child. It is known through the calling of love – to fully express the heart in intimacy. It reveals itself also through the desire to express or create forms of beauty and artistry. Venus calls us to fully give and receive, to express, know and enjoy life's natural abundance.

Our magnetic nature

Undoubtedly we all know women who are magnetic. Who seem to magically pull in men like beautiful flowers attract the bees. Some women appear to exude a certain 'Je ne sais quoi'. It may seem to be beauty or an overt sensuality but often it's not obvious exactly what it is. There is simply a quality that is captivating. There are women also whose capacity for creativity or prosperity is overflowing. Like a many-armed goddess they spread bounty everywhere. Their capacity for abundant creativity and generosity seems infinite. This is Venus energy at play.

Everything in natural life is fueled by attraction. Like summer flowers in full bloom calling in the bees, attraction has a certain quality. If we look with a scientific lens, we might put it down to pheromones or hormones, to survival instinct, the necessity for life to continue. We see it in nature through pollination and animal attraction; we know it in ourselves in sexual chemistry. However we might frame it, attraction and desire are the catalysts for life's creative urge to fulfil itself. It's how life on Earth happens.

When we explore the nature of attraction one thing is certain, it's a mystery. It's the mystery that ensures the continuation of physical life. Yet Venus represents the wonder of this mystery at play too. She is the experience of life's beauty and abundance. She is the magnetic calling and fulfilment of our

31

desire nature. She is there in our experience of falling in love, where the desire to unite with another is compelling and enigmatic. She is present when we are being touched by beauty. When we are filled with the natural magnificence of a sunrise, the emotive rise and fall of music, the vibrant colour of a piece of art or the subtle flow of a dance form, we are moved by Venus energy. The potential is we experience union with that that moves us.

The pull of male and female towards each other is this flow of Venus energy also. Both males and females have Venus as an archetype within, yet woman is its embodiment on Earth. It is woman who conceives, incubates and births new life. She is creatrix. Humanity continues through her capacity to receive the seed of new life, to gestate and grow it and to give birth. She fulfils the desire of life to create itself in new forms of human being. The ancients both recognised and worshipped the fertile life-giving power of the Feminine in woman. The 4000- year-old Hymns of Inanna honour and celebrate this potency; the people serve it in their Queen by ritually preparing the marriage bed. These writings are not only sacred they are erotic, praising the ripeness of Inanna's vulva and her consort Dumuzi's ferocious leonine passion. They reveal an eroticism and sensuality that is not only perfectly natural but to be fully enjoyed.

The Venus energy within us is magnetic and receptive. It is the attractor in the dance of duality. Her attraction is the pull of receptivity, that which invites or pulls in to itself. Desire, pleasure and enjoyment are Venus's vehicles. She rides through all the senses, yet her pull is beyond them, coming from the Mystery and calling us back into its arms. She dances our bodies.

In truly deep conscious love-making it is woman who opens and pulls man in – in every sense. Her mystery is inner; she draws the male into her space while he penetrates her with his consciousness. Their flow is the dance of Masculine Feminine powers in the universe. Whilst on Earth a woman's vagina and womb, and a man's phallus, fulfil the Great Mystery's potential for creating life. This is the power of life itself. The sexual union of man and woman seeds and realises this potential for new life. This happens on every level of creation, not just in procreation. The interaction of Masculine Feminine energies IS life. Sexual energy is at the core of everything.

Magnetism expressing as sexual energy also has its shadow. We see it everywhere in our collective culture, overtly used to sell anything from cars to magazines. Or covertly, it's repressed, sometimes aggressively, hidden behind veils, concepts and beliefs yet seeping out through sexism, misogyny, victim blaming and revelations of abuse. Try as we might, through ignorance, lack of true understanding, embarrassment or repression, we can't keep sexual energy down. It is the driver of our world. In its purest state this dance of union is the Deep Sacred Feminine calling in the seed of the Masculine. It is pure potential expressing as an idea or desire in order to create forms of life. The Feminine (in a woman or man) creates life from the seed, however that seed looks. It could be an inspiration or idea, an art form, a child, or a business. Sexual energy (life-force) grows it, tends and nurtures it.

Whether we know it, feel it or acknowledge it in our self or not, we simply are the play of creation. As women we are the attractor and the creatrix. We are the Divine Feminine in the form of woman creating life. Perhaps our deepest purpose as women is to align with that consciously, to honour and acknowledge it deeply? Wouldn't such recognition of the sacredness of our nature change our relationship to our self, to our sexuality, to the men we connect with and to the whole of life? Wouldn't such a knowing change our world?

Receptive to our true nature

For life to fulfil itself there needs to be openness. Nature shows us this. A bee cannot fertilise a flower if that flower is closed. The creative process fulfils itself through the openness and receptivity of Feminine energy. She – the Divine Feminine - is naturally receptive. We are naturally That. Even our female bodies reveal this truth. In lovemaking we are the opening that receives. Receptivity is linked to openness. How may we receive anything – an idea, inspiration, a gift, connection with another or even love – if we are not open? We will probably not even see its being offered.

33

Consider profound lovemaking; the body opens effortlessly. Consider birth; the feminine intelligence knows what to do in the body if we get out of its way. Some of us know that our soul opens through these deeply intimate experiences too. It's totally natural. In the expression of love the heart and emotional field are open and love flows; during meditation our whole energy field opens up to finer frequencies we might name Soul or Spirit. The nature of feminine energy is receptive and open. Openness is key to life forming and expressing naturally.

Openness is profoundly attractive to the Masculine. Just look at the open-throated beauty of a flower calling in the bees. Nature is a divine dance of procreation. Venus in us as women is this openness, receptivity and abundant flow of potential for life. This openly receptive energy is also a natural giver. For it's the flow of life. Many of us women are confident in the Venus flow of giving. It seems natural for us to give, to flow where there is a need or desire. Women will give even when it seems there is nothing left to give. We may see this as foolhardy. Yet it is our nature to give and to express. We are inordinately creative. We make a baby from a sperm; we take a packet of seeds and make a garden. Somewhere in us we know we are the creative power of the universe. Not that we have the power; we are that power. Yet opening, receiving and trusting it fully are often a challenge. Being fully open can make us feel vulnerable. Yet Venus is not vulnerable; she is the pure open flowing of life's abundance. She knows she is That, without question. She knows the fullness of life lies in flowing with her desire nature, that there is nothing wrong with it. For it is desire that brings forth new life.

When we are consciously connected to the power of pure receptivity that we are deep inside, self-love and self-worth are our natural state of being. There is no question that we are Woman, held in the arms of our Feminine nature. Our true strength lies in trusting this innate knowing. It gives rise to the glow we see shining through a woman at one with herself. She truly is one with her Divine nature. She is receiving it in her openness. The shallow sexual perspective based on body shape and manufactured beauty is nowhere to be seen. The sensual creative energy of Venus is pouring through. When we are at rest with who we are, with all our seeming idiosyncrasies and shortcomings, we are an open door to the light of Her. Our natural openness magnetically draws in and expresses who we truly are. A state of rest is key here, not as a non-active state but simply as open surrender and flow, resting in our naturalness. When caught in the busyness of our cultural goal orientation we lose this connection. Or more accurately, we close it down in the mistaken belief that we need something other than our inner state of natural flow and desire.

It is this natural flow that we already are that deeply feeds us. It is food not only for our self but for those we love, even for our culture. For when we rest in this deep state of open beingness we align with the creative power of the universe. Our Feminine nature is the power, our femaleness as a woman more fragile. Like the flower it opens in gentle vulnerability, awaiting the seed of potential that arises either from an inner spark or from relating. To rest in the Feminine is to rest in the power and strength of self-knowing, to deeply relax in the state of being creatrix here on Earth.

Connectedness dancing the body

The archetype of Venus is about connectedness and interconnection. She unites us with the abundant earthiness of body and sensuality. She engenders harmony within our social world of relationships. When we fall in love, we are experiencing the Venus archetype. Everything becomes infused with the golden light of love. What usually bothers us somehow doesn't now; we don't even notice it. We see each other in our 'best light'. There is magic in the air; the intensity of it is powerfully erotic.

Whether she appears as a dramatic passion or a more slow-burning connection, Venus arrives to show us who we truly are, to reveal our potential as love and for love. To truly ride and engage her connective flow we must first connect with her in ourselves however. Without that inner alignment we fall prey to her ephemeral nature as she seems to flit fleetingly through a diversity of experience, one moment as pleasure, the next as pain. Like falling in love Venus's fickle nature seems not to have staying power. Yet it is simply that our knowing of her inner flow is not stable or grounded. We are seeing her in the illusion of external love or intimacy rather than knowing her as our natural state of being.

When we are aligned to our true state of being, we are the natural creative power of the universe; it's flowing through us. We are deeply fulfilled within. We experience the pleasure of being here in a human body. We know the potential to experience its flow through sensuality on every level. It's the satisfying shock of an iced drink on a hot day; it's the scent of fresh mown grass; the sound of your baby's laughter; it's the overwhelming flood of passion at the touch of a lover. To receive Venus's gift to our senses we need to believe we have value, hence Venus's affinity with self-worth. If we do not believe we have value we will not even notice our own inner beauty, or life's rich natural blessings. We'll be disconnected from the feeling of being truly alive. The power of creation that we are gives us choice to use our life energy to enjoy life, or not. If our energy is tied up in beliefs and concepts about who we think we are or how life is, we miss the constantly flowing renewal of life's gift to us in simply being alive.

To be here in a body on Earth is to potentially know a flow of fulfilment expressing through our lives. In her essence Venus is about intimacy with life. We may ride this flow of naturally connective creative power through any form of relating. It's the magnetic pull of desire, the longing to experience pleasure and the yearning to create that that fulfils us, whether in a loving partnership, a beautiful art form or a growing bank account. Venus dances the particles of potential into manifestation. It's happening all the time, not just through the sensuality of intimate connection, but the flow of paintbrush on canvas, or the stirring of the crockpot. Venus plays through our passion for life. She dances through our desire nature. She is the power of falling in love instantly, whether that's with an idea, a colour, a sunrise, a woman or a man. Venus connects us to the knowing that life is already abundant and yet there is so much more to know and enjoy. Her desire is to experience the beauteous potential of feeling connections on Earth.

36

Venus energy inhabits our choices through the power of desire. Have you ever had that sense of not quite knowing how you ended up in a particular friendship? That's her instinctively dancing through your cells. Her energy within us magnetises what we most need as well as what we most desire. It's the 'like attracts like' principle that acts as a mirror for our distortions as well as our inner love. It's the 'attraction of opposites' that causes sparks to fly. It's the 'out of control' feeling of being inexorably pulled in a particular direction. Venus's calling is to connection, beauty and harmony but she's not always pretty. She is simply the creative potential. We have choice in how we use creative energy here on Earth - to connect with our truly abundant nature or to carry life energy into distorted forms.

The transmutative power of the Feminine

Woman's womb is a power for creation. It's a sacred space of attraction, union, fertilisation, incubation and birth. It conceives, nurtures, holds and grows new life. The menstrual cycle is the physical representation within women of each stage of every creative process, not simply the state of pregnancy. The potential of New Moon - the fertilisation of a new cycle of creation - through to Full Moon then darkness, reveals the endless life-death-rebirth cycling of nature and every created form. Venus is the active Feminine principle that brings forth that cyclical potential into forms of life, love, art and beauty.

For the most part women have lost but are now reclaiming this deep understanding of our innate Feminine creative potency. The birth of patriarchy diverted attention and power away from the knowing and worship of the Feminine through fear of woman's sexuality, through the need for control as false power. The ancient power of the goddess as creatrix was denied and denounced and replaced with sexuality as sin. Woman's accepted roles became wife and mother. Woman as lover with all her sexual sensual potency was demonised whilst also used and abused. Her creative power was distorted to serve patriarchal ends. Strangely women allowed this devolution, unless we fought it. Over centuries, mainly through fear, we began to adhere to the patriarchal system, at least outwardly. It's a complex unfolding, involving the need for peace, safety and security. The demise of an existing cultural expression is also an aspect of life's larger cyclical nature, the wheel of life turning. The rise and fall of patriarchy, or any system, is part of the evolutionary cycle. Now the wheel is turning towards the Feminine once more. The potential is arising for an integrated balance of Masculine Feminine power sharing in service to the collective and our Earth.

A growing aspect of this evolutionary process is the need for women to claim their birthright as Divine Feminine. To do this we must discard the patriarchal ways and repossess the right to be who we truly are. We need to affirm our magnificence. This potentizes our being 'equal but different' with men, our partners in co-creativity. The process of change seems to be a long road, with many twists, turns and roadblocks, but it is a worthy one. We have much to realise, acknowledge and embody even in this so-called birthing of a new age. For whilst the function of the mind to visualise and create is being recognised and claimed by many, the potency of woman's womb as the vessel of creation still lies unacknowledged or is largely ignored. To go out-of-body to claim our spiritual birthright is at odds with how the divine arrives here on Earth. Clearly there's a vital connection being missed. Understanding Venus as representative of our creative potency is vital. She returns us to the womb. She returns us to the Earth, to our senses and feelings. She returns us to our deeply denied Feminine nature.

Being immersed in the natural flow of opening, receiving, incubating, birthing, nourishing, giving and letting go is the full expression of our Feminine nature. Venus shows us that we are the magnetic pull and abundant creative nature of the Feminine embodied as women. Our journey is to re-discover this, to claim it fully, to live it well. How may we do this? Practice openness; practice receiving, practice allowing, practice embracing, practice being the flow. Practice through letting go of the masks and false roles. It seems strange that we may have to practice being who we naturally are, does it not? Yet, just as we have done to our Earth, we have covered this natural state of being with the concrete of beliefs. It's time to reclaim Her dance as our dance. In recognising there is no out-breath without first there being an in-breath; in seeing that without the open receptivity of our woman bodies there is no human life on Earth, we are knowing Venus, whether we realise it or not. It's time to claim her.

The creation of harmony and beauty

Venus in us is the energetic flow of potential for feeling that informs both our connectivity and creativity. That relationship can be to anything or anyone. Who can say why we are attracted in one direction or another, or to create a particular form but not something different? Is an exquisite piece of pottery more beautiful than a flower? Is a harmonious connection to a lover more fulfilling than the capacity to design a striking piece of jewellery? Venus represents all these creative aspects of our lives Her underlying theme is attraction, connection, enjoyment and the potential of intimacy with any one or any thing.

The experience of beauty is ephemeral and deeply personal. When we know beauty or harmony there is a subtly intimate connection with whatever we are viewing or experiencing isn't there? There's an alignment or synergy that is somehow pleasing, aesthetically or sensually. It may seem to arise through touch, a beautiful view, an attractive piece of clothing or art, or the intensity of a piece of music, yet if we look deeper, we might see it is the always-ever-present flow of Being through form that we are experiencing. In the moment of connection we are pure life force witnessing its forms. In that moment we align with both the pleasure generated by the external attraction or beauty and what's beyond it, with energy at its source. If we pause, pay attention and feel the sensation of life in the body, we'll notice that it's not only the form we enjoy. That is merely the catalyst; it is the pure enjoyment of being aligned with the harmony of our original nature; aligned, moving, beautiful, even blissful.

Venus doesn't always look pretty though, as we'll discover in the section on her shadow energies. Sometimes her connectivity can be fierce and raw. We know that passion can take us over the edge of pleasure, even into pain. We know that the course of love doesn't always flow smoothly.

The Venus connection is about bringing harmony or balance to that which is also uncomfortable. The Mayans linked the Venus orbit, her appearance and disappearance from the morning and evening skies, to the death and rebirth process. Here we encounter her original primal nature as guardian of the cyclical nature of life. Naturally we are drawn to experience the enjoyment of life rather than its pain. Yet it's the awareness of simply being touched open that truly is at the root of Venus energy. That touch – however it feels – allows our energy to pour forth in response or reaction. It opens the dam we may put around our heart, our sexuality or any level of our Being.

Life is always calling us to open. We could say perhaps that it uses any means to open us in the recognition, expression and embodiment of our fullest nature. Whether an experience is pleasurable or not it contains life-force. What we do with the creative power it contains has the potential to grow us. Connection to Venus in the body as our sensational experience teaches us how to unite with the most challenging circumstances or the deepest pain. Despite its appearance or sensation, when we pay attention, when we relax into life as it is, she reveals the underlying harmony that is present in all life.

The Shadow of Venus

Venomous, venereal or venerating?
We've explored Venus energy in her creative expression and forms. When we explore the root of the actual word Venus, we also find clues to her shadow energies.

The stem of the Latin word Venus is 'vener', originally a neuter noun meaning physical desire or sexual appetite. There's also a language link with the Sanskrit 'vanah' meaning desire. The words venerate, venom and venereal all have these same stems. Perhaps they reflect the many current concepts about the natural sensual power of the Venus archetype. There is certainly a link to sacredness, sexuality and its shadow: venerate meaning to worship, venom being poisonous and venereal as relating to sexual disease.

The goddess Venus/Aphrodite emerged in Roman and Greek culture at the time patriarchy was being established. She's a goddess archetype that arises in the age when matriarchal culture was being systematically removed from culture and community. I explored this take-over in the Introduction. Now as we explore the Venus archetype, we may ask what aspects of her nature have been purposefully hidden, sanitised or denounced? What wounds lie behind the face of what claims to be beauty and the play of attraction? What shadow wisdom does she hold that supports our evolutionary potential and the growth of conscious relationship now? In exploring our cultural as well as personal shadow energy we may become more deeply enlightened as to the distortion of the Sacred Feminine within us all.

The body is calling

The body is calling us deeply in these times of challenge through change. We are facing disharmony and ill health at many levels of body-being. Disconnection from our bodies, from instinct and from the naturalness of our earthy sensuality is unhealthy. It lies also at the root of our disconnection from the environment and our Earth. We've created a world of plastic, pressure and the constant demand for more. Many of us have gone up into the head to avoid the pain of being human in our inhumane times. Technology as a tool is a wonder; it makes a poor master. Consumerism is no substitute for being connected to our naturally flourishing state of being and the abundant creative potential that flows from it.

The world we live in now is filled with fakes. We inhabit cultures with false values, unreal standards of beauty and contrived principles that lack depth. Our world is deeply unsatisfying and yet many keep stretching towards the next irresistible goal as if it will save us. Even some aspects of our new age spirituality are based on better, more sparkly, more enlightened. We're looking for fulfilment everywhere, within a world that carries the very real threat of destruction. Even nature is challenging us to get more real, to evolve, to take responsibility for our place on Earth. Let's face it, humanity as a whole is lost. Yet all is not lost, for many of us are asking real questions. Many are living authentic values that embody our role as Earth guardians.

41

Understanding and connecting with the potency of our Venus energy as women is a very real aspect of the evolutionary shift we need to make. Sexual energy is power. It creates not only children but is behind everything in our world. We create with sexual energy. For when male (the sperm, seed or idea) and female energy (the egg, the creative manifestation energy) align or unite in physicality, in values, goals, intentions and actions, manifestation is natural.

If we look into the core of this alignment, it's perhaps easier to see what's happening in our world. The control of women, the use and abuse of our creative energy (and our allowance of that) has and is creating this mess we're in. In this alignment it sounds like women are the victims. Here lies the paradox. We are and yet we are not. There is the reality of inequality, exploitation and abuse, sexual or otherwise. Yet in other ways we are not victims; for we have colluded with the power play. There are many reasons behind that – from fear, for the sake of security or comfort, for the protection of our children, because we naturally want to love, support and unite with our man, to give just a few examples. This is the complex play of evolution. Yet it's time now to recognize how collusion with and adherence to patriarchal values is not only bringing us all deep discontent but it is destroying our Earth. The growth of consciousness now supports our deepening understanding of these power plays, and of where we give power away. It is time for a profound change.

As we mature both personally and collectively the demand of evolutionary potential is to reconnect our senses and sexuality to the naturalness of our body-being, consciously aligned and grounded in true values of connection, guardianship and co-creativity. It's to recognise that when we connect authentically to our source, our lives thrive naturally. We feed our collective culture with conscious vitality and our cultures shift because we are rooted in what is of true value.

Rooting to our true values occurs when we consciously inhabit the body. We become the bridge of soul-body, conscious participation in life. To do this we need to slow down, listen deep and respond to what we know is true. When we're disconnected from body, senses and feeling, we cannot find what we deeply need. Instead we run around looking for fulfilment where it cannot be found.

How many of us are living in our heads? How much are you living in your head rather than inhabiting your body? We might see that the same crisis is happening with our bodies as with our environment. We might go so far as to say we are abusing our bodies when we don't listen deeply for what's real right now. The Venus archetype's connectivity to feeling, sensuality and to our creative power is our guide to inhabiting the body; to moving through different layers of disconnection. To do that we have to get out of the mind, feel what's happening within our body-being, heal distorted emotions and drop deep into our natural state of aliveness.

What does it mean to drop deep into our natural state of being; to actually inhabit the fullness of the body? It requires we lose our mind and that we feel to heal. To lose the mind is not to become foolish; it is to become mindful. It is to understand how the different aspects of the body-being work together, either in conscious alignment or distortion. It is to become consciously awake to the power of creation flowing through each of us. It is to learn to feel the sensation of the body and its flow through differing frequencies, both pleasurable and unpleasurable.

To feel in order to heal requires us to take response-ability for our experience, for what we've already created, and to transmute it. True healing opens and empties the body-being, releases the energy from our old creation, reconnects us to the life within and makes that energy available for creation now. Our own growth processes mirror the consistent flow of life revealed to us in nature. We are called to consciously connect with the natural flow of creative power that we actually always are.

Venus is our guide into what the body needs: to be loved, to be healed, to be whole, to express through loving connection. To live as loving connection, we are called to heal our disconnection from being and feeling in the body. This requires deepening understanding of where and how we've denied or projected pain, or judged and repressed emotions, labelling them as bad or wrong. It requires that we inhabit the sensational reality of the body in all its frequencies as our guidance system home.

She's not a projection

When we look at the beauty in nature, if we're being present, we see what is. When we enjoy a walk in a forest we appreciate each tree for itself, not for how we think it could or should look. Perhaps we appreciate its natural shape, strength and unique characteristics. We can see how each tree has been fashioned by nature's elements of sun, wind and rain.

In a garden, how may we say a daisy is less beautiful than a rose? Each has their natural loveliness. Yet when we look at male or female bodies we move away from this natural perception. It's a different experience. Why is that? Our bodies are similarly fashioned by nature yet our ideas about how they should look get in the way of natural appreciation. We've become distorted in our ideas of how a body should look. Then we project an ideal onto our self and others. It's no wonder we are dissatisfied. We can't see beyond a projection of perfection that we can never live up too.

Projection is a natural function of our consciousness. When an idea arises, if it's of value to us, we naturally project it forward to see how that idea might take form. When we become aware of a desire, we might also project it out mentally. We grow it with intention, or we simply act on it. We engage it in some way, or not. This process might happen in a few minutes or over a period of time. To put it simply, we create, through idea or desire, will and action. In that creative process we experience all the challenges, opportunities and gifts of learning to grow a mature self. It's a very natural process. This function of body-being operating as holistic intelligence is explored more fully in the Pallas Athena chapter.

When we project ideals onto our self as a goal to achieve - particularly the ideals of others, our partners, family or culture - we miss the natural quality of beauty or character that resides within the uniqueness of our self. It's the same when we project onto others; we miss their natural beauty. This does not mean ideals cannot inspire us to stretch and grow, or improve, but the key lies in starting from 'what is'. A piece of clay that has the potential to become a beautiful pot. We wouldn't judge it for not being beautiful. We must start with the raw material, exactly what's in front of us right now.

Projection is a naturally Masculine characteristic within a man or woman i.e. it's of the mind. It's also linear. Man's body naturally reflects this Masculine quality. It's external and projective - just look at the phallus and its orientation. It's obvious. Woman's body is receptive. It opens; it takes in the man. Again, look at the body. If we look at the brain, we may see the same.

The left hemisphere of the brain is projective, whether it's in a male or female body. Projective mind is goal orientated, rational, linear, driven towards achieving a goal, often in the shortest time possible. Whereas the right hemisphere is imaginative, holistically orientated, fluid and creative. As the brain has projective and receptive aspects, so does a human body. When you bring the projective and the receptive energy together the potential is to fertilise, incubate, grow and manifest form. That's obvious with a child. Once an egg is fertilised by sperm the natural process of growing a baby takes over, it has its own rhythm and stages that emerge beyond a woman's control. Life's natural creative energy takes over the process.

Projection and receptivity move from a natural union into growth. Our human desire to create, achieve and manifest move through a similar rhythm, from seed to form. We're always creating, consciously or not. We project an idea, a belief or value and we give it power through our will. When we give energy to an idea, belief or value we grow its power. We create with it. There can however be a twist in the process. The natural capacity to create can become distorted through ideal or agenda. Perhaps we want it now, rather than in its natural timing? Perhaps we try to use force to accomplish? Or we get stuck in self-doubt? If we're not rooted in self-worth and grounded in our values, we miss the highest possibilities of that seed. The collective values come into play here too. For instance, if we believe that the cultural standard of beauty requires us to look a particular way, and we struggle to attain that ideal when it's not deeply true for us, we're giving power away. We're projecting the cultural standard onto our self and then self-judging when we fail. It's no wonder we're unfulfilled. Yet more crucially, we're failing to see how projection can cause us unnecessary struggle or pain.

Understanding projection and its creative potency has a real value. The converse to idealised projection arises if we don't value our innate creative potential. Then we may fail to give any energy to our ideas, dreams and desires, or to move forward. We may not give our seed (whatever it is) the intention and action it requires to grow and form. Instead we give power to distorted beliefs, old patterns of fear or doubt. We believe in the family values instead of our own perhaps, or the cultural ones. Perhaps we project failure before even starting? Or we stay lost in mental possibilities rather than taking one step forward? We give our creative power away and lose the potential of our opportunities.

Everything we do has impact. When we recognize this, it changes everything. To be awake now means our use of creative energy must be questioned. How are you engaging the gift of life? Are you using and abusing Her? Are you growing consciously in embodying your true nature? Collectively we can see how in these times the creative process of evolution has become the drive for progress. The drive to be loved, or for fulfilment, has become distorted through greed, our need to be someone, or the need to belong. Awareness of what we project through mind and how we feed it through will, intention, action or non-action, is essential to bring us the true harvest of fulfilment. We are called to unwrap everything, to see its source. We are gifted an infinite flow of creative energy to play with. To consciously connect with this abundance, we need to first embrace where we don't feel abundant. For the distortion in our creative expression comes from this feeling of lack.

Lack of abundance disturbs us. For somehow we know deep inside that we are here to enjoy life fully. We yearn for it; we reach for it; we try to make it happen. All the goddess archetypes point us towards fulfilment in different ways. With Venus it's all about relationship and the expression of our creative urge for beauty or harmony, in other words our desire for enjoyment and fulfilment. When we cannot reach a state of feeling good, we become frustrated or depressed, projective in a different way. We project onto our self negatively or we point the finger. This way of projection is a pressure release. It discharges the inner stress of disappointment in some way. Yet it does not transform. Often it escalates what was simply a passing state into an issue. We compound a negative belief about our self, or we make another individual wrong.

The blame game in relationships creates problems from just the smallest interaction. When projecting shadow in this way, the key to release is found in the sensational reality of the body. This is Venus territory: to feel what we are creating, however unpleasant. Venus calls us to come down from the head. Feeling the body fully, embracing the sensational frequency vibrating in disharmony in the body, opens the return to harmony, to the source of love within.

The Venus archetype seeks harmony in relating with what's external, either as lover or life experience. Yet she also reveals how harmony is constant within, underlying all experience. It is who we naturally are. We cannot find who we are naturally are as a state of fulfilment when we're projective. We must inhabit the body. This is how we evolve – through being in our sensational reality and embracing how it flows from light to density, from pleasure to unpleasant, from harmony to discomfort. It's a dance, both within our self and in our connections. We seem to fall out of love so we may reconnect with our inner love. Then, having filled up, we express that love in our partnerships and creative flow. This is true fulfilment; the flow in which we become unified, again and again and again.

This flow may be discovered in our expression of sensuality in all its forms, through connection to nature and animals, through sexuality, through the enjoyment of music, art and creativity. Following the thread of our desire to express love or move in creative expression brings us fulfilment. Yet the wonder is we can experience pure enjoyment, full aliveness, within our sensational body. It's a natural state of being, available always. For it is what we truly are.

How we use the gift of our creative energy is the core solution to our current dilemma. It's important to become aware of the beliefs or concepts we give power to as true; to become awake to where we're stuck in the head; to see where we project. To realise our motivations and our responsibility for how we use energy is to be empowered to live differently. Venus gives us clues to this. The answers lie not in our minds but in the womb; in womb knowing. For women it's particularly important to bring our energy fully into the body, to learn to trust our deep knowing. Have we incarnated in female bodies to live in our heads? Are we living in female bodies to take on or engage just any old projection from our men? Do we want to live unfulfilled lives? Do we want to participate in the desecration and destruction of our planet simply so we can live a comfortable life, asleep to our true potential? I would say not. I would say it's our responsibility as women, particularly now, to live consciously and to be discerning about what we engage with.

Our creative energy is our sexual energy. It's vital we understand how we engage it, how and what we open ourselves to, and what we receive and grow, on every level. It's time to pull the plug on distorted projective living: blaming another, sexual game-playing; chasing the dream of love and then paying the price through disillusionment; not considering the consequences of our desire nature; allowing abuse. We are the creative power of birth and creation on Earth. It's time to stand in the truth of that. We must cease the game-playing; we have to claim that we're worthy. We must know self-worth as a given.

For the fairest? Owning the bitch

The most famous of the myths about the Goddess of Love is recorded in Homer's Greek epic poem, the Iliad. Here Aphrodite/Venus is portrayed as the instigator of the Trojan war by tempting Paris with a bribe in the contest of the golden apple. The apple was inscribed 'for the most beautiful' or 'fairest' and was disputed by Hera/Juno Athena and Aphrodite. Aphrodite's promise to give Paris (judge of the contest) the love of the most beautiful woman in the world, Helen of Troy, won her the apple and the claim to being 'most beautiful'. As Helen was already married to King Menelaus, this overt manipulation by Aphrodite was the cause of the war between Greece and Troy.

The mythology of the golden apple shows a shadow face of Venus revealed by Eris, Goddess of Discord. On Mount Olympus the goddesses were deemed to be beyond competition, each brightest in her unique realm of affairs. Yet Eris's action revealed the shadows at play even in their goddess nature: competitiveness, mistrust of each other and desire to be 'the star'. It revealed a surprising lack of self-worth behind the goddess façade.

Here we also see Venus's connection to glamour in its truest sense. Glamour is the weaving of illusion; it enchants; it attracts and magnetises. Often glamour creates a possibility that promises more than it delivers, as with her promise to Paris. It was a promise that created a war. Glamour is revealed here as a manipulation. Aphrodite/Venus's drive to be seen and acknowledged as 'the fairest' revealed a compulsive need to win.

Winning, especially when motivated by competition with other women, is a Venus shadow connected to lack of self-value. We've explored Venus energy as the calling to relate and create. She also represents self-worth. Her energy as Sacred Feminine represents our capacity to love our self as perfectly imperfect. When we deeply know who we are and value that, despite our apparent failings, we have no need to prove, compete or win. We have no desire to use glamour, pretence, masks or manipulation in order to be seen, acknowledged or loved.

Self-worth is essential for healthy relating and the fulfilment of our creative urges. It's naturally strong when we're connected to our innate value as a girl or woman, when the qualities and gifts of our individuality are acknowledged, when we learn how to be rooted in the body. Yet how many of us reach womanhood with the self-confidence to simply be our self? How many of us navigate puberty with ease, with self-assurance intact?

Opening to the Venus archetype within reminds us we are the creative power, that we need to do nothing other than be that in order to be valuable. Yet mostly our experience informs us differently. Our vulnerable receptivity makes us naturally receptive to what comes towards us, whether or not that's self-affirming. Here lies the vulnerable shadow of Venus displaying as lack of self-worth. It's a lack that colours every aspect of life. It's interesting that in her many of her myths and despite being the Goddess of Love, Venus was constantly seeking validation. Much as we might perhaps. This shadow shows us that to know deep self-love, we must constantly affirm our innate self-worth, our natural worthiness as a being. We need do nothing to claim that. We must stand strong despite our inner quaking; we must know beauty is always there even when it's not obvious.

For women the wound of Venus is both personal and collective. When it comes to love and sexuality, we're fighting our way through layers of inherited beliefs, concepts, experience and emotional wounding from our mothers' mothers' mothers. We're carrying judgments and condemnations, the experience of pain and our own closure against it. Even when we feel centred in connection to our core Feminine power any transition may raise that shadow of lack in our self again: illness or accident, separation and divorce, relationship experiences or abuse, menopause and its body changes. We are always vulnerable whilst in a female body, simply because at the core we are the receptive aspect of human nature and therefore sensitive to what is projected onto and into us. When 'not good enough' 'too fat/thin' and all those other mental measurements arise within or are reflected to us, we take it in. The reaction to this can be to diminish our self, or project it back but feel hurt anyway, moving to over-assert our worth with aggression, acting up to prove who we are in distorted ways.

The expression of jealousy, competition, bitchiness or vindictive actions is a sign of deep wounding. Where a woman is insecure in her authenticity, lacks trust in being vulnerable, or is attached to looking a particular (always attractive) way, the bitch may rise. She arises because we feel unstable or wounded. We lack the capacity, or are unwilling, to feel the vulnerability of that wound. Instead it gets projected out as a defence. We attack to keep the wounded self-safe.

In her myths the vindictive side of the Venus nature expresses through jealousy and revenge. For instance, the women of Lemnos became so confident in their own beauty they neglected to worship at her shrines. Aphrodite/Venus cursed them with a terrible odour that stopped their men interacting sexually with them, with ongoing repercussions. This energy of cursing another woman is clear in the bitchiness of one woman deriding or mocking another. This happens particularly in teenage years when stability in knowing our unique beauty may be lacking. Underneath the bitch lies self-disconnection and pain. Her vicious expression is a distorted cry for help. We must listen deeply for this cry. If we cannot hear her, we cannot heal her.

Spitting and splitting

The wounded face of the Feminine is always calling to be seen. It plays through attention-seeking behaviour, the need for approval, emotional games such as manipulation, obsession or repulsion, the demand to be acknowledged, or the desire to wound. Given a more introverted nature, the Venus shadow may express equally through 'playing sweet and nice'. Here the pain of wounding is turned inwards as self-hatred and self-abuse. We become the bitch to our self.

Whether we cannot embrace our pain and project it outwardly, onto other women as jealousy or onto men for failing to love us, or we don't fit the required measurement of beauty, sex appeal, or any of those other labels inherited from family or culture, the outcome is the same. Either we spit or we split. We become the bitch, or the self-abuser; often it's both. Then we compound our lack of self-connection through projection or self-hatred. Either way, in the disowning of our deep wounding, we become repulsive in the true sense of the word. We push away the very love we are dying for, through being defensive, self-deprecating, through fake sweet-talk or conforming. The pain acts as a barrier to the very love we're dying for.

Feeling the split in all the layers of our body-being is essential in these times. Not as story but as sensation. When we move our attention from the story of 'what happened' into the sensational feeling in the body we get to the core of our wounding without projection onto other or our self. It is through this deeply felt embodied experience that true healing takes place. It is here that we penetrate the layers of emotional and physical armouring to reach both the core of our pain and what lies beneath it – the truth of our nature as always valuable. That journey requires that we navigate the ebb and flow of our inner rhythms with consciousness. We allow it to lead us where we need to but may not want to go.

In the healing journey everything serves, if we allow it. We must learn to let go of controlling our experience and instead learn to flow with it. This may mean we rage or sob at times; we may rise with fierceness and descend with grief; it certainly means we are called deeper into the body and our pain. According to Hindu philosophy we are living in Kali Yuga, the age of strife. Discord is the means of our redemption. Embracing our darkness leads us to the rebirth of light. Personal and cultural dishonouring of the Feminine nature is a key transformational urge of this time. This includes what's happening to the environment and our Earth. How can it not, for we are not separate. Our bodies are from Earth; they were created in the nurture of mother and Mother. When we truly understand this, the power of profound transformational healing opens.

Life, love, our pain, feels personal and yet truly it's both personal and collective. Facing the illusion of our disconnection is key; embracing and transforming how we actually create disconnection is key. Embracing the truth of Venus – creative power within – is paramount. This requires us to be the power to ignore, discard or transmute any value judgments that come our way, to transform the denseness of locked emotions. It's to stand strong in the innate power that we are as creatrix, to allow the energy of negativity to heal and empower rather than project. We simply need to give ourselves permission to stand in the power of who we are at our core: Divine Feminine. There is nothing to be done to achieve this; it simply is who we are. Affirming the truth of this brings strength and potency to our unique creative flavour of the Feminine. Affirming the truth of this opens and expands it for us all.

When is enough enough? Saying 'No!'

There is a truth that underlies the Venus archetype that is key to the whole play of life on Earth. Sexual energy is power. It is power that can be used and abused.

If we look at human history – at least that which we are aware of, along with the elements that we know have been hidden - we can see a shift of power balance between male and female over eons. How this shift originated lies in the mists of time and perhaps it is part of the evolutionary plan? The astrological ages point towards this as we enter the Age of Aquarius. The shift towards global community is evident, as is the re-emergence of Feminine power, in both men and women. Aquarius is the sign of brotherhood, sisterhood, and global community. Potentially it would seem that we are evolving towards a place of balance and freedom of individuality. To attain this place of balance – a deep acknowledgment and honouring of the qualities of both Masculine & Feminine within us all – we need to transmute our sexual wounding. We need to reclaim the use and abuse of sexual power.

When we're rooted in self-worth, sexual power is the natural attraction and magnetism of nature. It flows, moves, expresses, unites and fulfils us. When we're lacking connection to our essence, sexual energy may be used to grasp, manipulate, control, use and abuse. This need to exploit or possess in order to fill the inner void is a strong motivator. The quest for enjoyment or fulfilment becomes obsessive. The need to feel powerful, or simply in control, to avoid the inner pain of powerlessness overrides any natural sense of what's real. The use, exploitation or abuse of sexual energy runs our western culture. It's about avoiding the void, sating the inner hunger, gratifying want or need, in order to create temporary satisfaction and an evasion of pain, or the fact of death.

In these times many people are running on empty. Want, need and greed are directing the world. Pulling the plug on this distorted way of being is the core transition we're involved in, if we're awake as consciousness. The key to this process is understanding our misuse of creative energy i.e. sexual energy. Our core disconnection from the abundance of life that we already are is at the root of all lack. When we're deeply inner-connected abundance flows naturally, both in our own lives and out to the collective. It happens naturally. We simple flow with what is true, healthy and wholesome, in that flow what we need comes to us naturally.

All exploitation and abuse, sexual or otherwise, come from our disconnection to the source of our self and each other. Does anyone who feels truly alive, with the wondrous touch of quiet inner joy in the heart, seek to exploit another in any way? I would say not. The experience of seeming so far removed from that state of being feels immense. Yet the truth is we are not. We already are it, at core. We simply need to realise it and claim it.

As women we are leading the way in saying 'Enough!' We are voicing our knowing of imbalance. Men know and are voicing this too. 'Enough!' is the point of power we all need to reach. Yet sometimes we must get desperate before we reach it. In my life I recall how much awakening it took to leave a violent marriage. Yet somehow I did. Was it divine timing at play; the hand of Grace? Certainly something shifted and awakened my consciousness. Finer frequencies of consciousness are far more available now than thirty plus years ago. Humanity is evolving despite what we may think. When we look at our world the healing shift seems like a huge task but it's already happening. It begins with each of us being courageous enough to say 'No!'

54

When it comes to sexual attraction becoming aware of where we're connecting from is key. As women we have the primary responsibility in this - simply because what we take into our bodies, into our wombs, manifests. It not only manifests as children, it manifests as a healthy creation or not, Personally and collectively. It manifests as deeper connection to the life that we are, or as divine discontent. It is truly vital to understand this energetically. How we connect sexually has power. Power for evolution, both individually and collectively. It's simple to recognise this. Reflect on how you feel after lovemaking or having sex. Look at what happens in your relationship and in your life. Our deepest intimate connections are here for us to know love. They're also here to open us up yet we have to be clear if we're opening for love, transformation and healing, or to abuse. Where there are power plays, manipulation or distortion, our 'No' needs to be clear.

Expressing an unreserved 'No' in any aspect of life can be challenging. When it comes to sexuality it's even more so. There are so many subtle energies and hidden agendas at play within any relationship, especially when a potential for intimacy is present. The core of these agendas is power – power for love, or power for control. This applies equally to a man or woman. A woman can hold emotional or sexual power over a man just as much as a man may hold physical strength over her. Much is made of man's sexual exploitation of woman and rightly so, yet we do not necessarily have the full picture behind all the energetic game playing yet. And it takes a lot of self-responsibility to be clear and honest about our own motivations.

The most potent awareness for women that is not generally recognised yet, is that when a man enters a woman's body, he leaves his energy inside her vagina and womb. This is a truly profound recognition for a woman and especially for pubescent girls. Clearly the question that arises then is: do you want this male's energy in your body? Is he truly worthy? Not in terms of judging him but simply in terms of the presence or absence of a core deep resonance of connection. One could describe that as a feeling of rightness, a natural respect for each other along with the attraction. There's either a deep natural bond in the moment or a misalignment. The potential for misalignment is there particularly when we're hungry for love, or simply for some kind of attention, even negative attention.

Sexual attraction is a tricky arena. At times our need and desire for love is so strong that we can manipulate the hesitation of a 'No' into a 'Maybe' that is easily overridden. To know this is empowering. To know the potential that we are wearing rose-tinted glasses is wise. The Venus archetype wants so much to express love that her call is compelling. To know our own hunger is to be discerning. For the awareness supports us in making a more conscious choice.

As we move into or away from an attraction; we fall into love or it fizzles out. To know what underlies the connection – without driving yourself crazy in over-thinking it – is to be curious, alive and open. It is to be open to the possibility, indeed the probability, of both love and pain and healing. The key awareness is to move as consciously as possible, for our own sake and for all women's.

When we allow our body to be used in any way, we are adding to sexual wounding. When we misuse our own body – by over-work, pushing past tiredness, or not eating well - we add to our self-disconnection. That's easy to say perhaps; less easy to do, especially sexually, for we are still learning about the energetic functions and interplay of bodies. Yet it's in having awareness of what lies behind our sexual connections in particular that we discover both the deeper wounds and the truth. It's a true voyage of discovery.

When we share a conscious deeply loving connection, coupled with loving compassion for our wounds, we realise the potential to heal. There is no right or wrong way. We're all exploring, learning and discovering as we go in this great experiment of loving connection on Earth. At core our power to say a clear 'No!' or even one with quaking knees, is key. Transmuting our fear of doing this in whatever way is needed is life changing. Embracing our fear of doing this is the healing balm that uplifts all women.

Total embrace - 'Yes!' to it all

There's no doubt that the Venus archetype's unrelenting desire for connection takes us beyond our boundaries. It's the invitation to drop everything and simply fall into love. In that pull both our capacity for a clear 'No' or an affirming 'Yes' to what appears is constantly being refined. The flow between both is a crucible in which we are being purified and called back to our original nature: one with Love. This synergy between a real attraction, the passive acquiescence to another's needs or demands for love, or an out-and-out refusal to take a risk on attraction, develops our awareness of trust in our self and life, if we allow it to.

Whilst we're in this evolutionary process we can swing between the heights of exhilaration and the depths of misery. All the while life is calling us towards integration of deeper self-love and its expression in relationships. Sometimes we may experience passion so intense it feels overwhelming. Love seems to compel us to obsess, to act in irrational ways, to risk all. It certainly requires us to become intimate with chaos. We may be surprised by the intensity in which we act. The greatest potential is we lose control.

Losing control is a key facet of love and loving. It begs the question: can we love and be in control at the same time? We desire the fulfilment of love yet know it may well kill off our unconsciousness – at least the current self we think we are. More than anything love is about being open: open to change, to both ecstasy and pain, to getting carried away, to falling again and again. Venus's expression is based on attraction and magnetism, sensual and sexual energy, and our overwhelming desire to be seen, acknowledged and loved. Yet love always has a price. It lifts us to the heights then drops us to the floor. For how else may we evolve? How else may we know we are held in love yet must also face our wounds?

The Venus archetype in us longs to create harmony and connection yet her shadow brings us inevitably to loss. When we deeply love, the shadow of loss is always present. It is unavoidable, for always the wheel turns. Just as women's cycles of physical fertility wax and wane, just as the moon waxes and wanes, the cycles of love ebb and flow. We cannot control love. Even Venus was touched by its ephemeral nature. Her myth with boy god and lover Adonis relates this unexpected aspect of the Aphrodite/Venus nature. It shows us both the necessity to fight for what we love and yet the need to let go too. It shows us even the goddess of love could not control love, its flow or outcome. Can any of us?

Baby Adonis was adorable and since there was no one to look after him, Aphrodite/Venus claimed him as hers. She became so obsessed with this new role she began overlooking her responsibilities as a goddess, so she decided to send Adonis to Queen of the Underworld Persephone/Proserpina.

Persephone fell dearly in love with Adonis too. She loved him so much she refused to give him up when Aphrodite came for him. There was a fierce argument between the two goddesses in which Zeus/Jupiter was forced to intervene. He decided that every year Adonis would spend four months with Persephone, the next four months with Aphrodite and the last four months alone. This way he may learn to take care of himself.

Adonis grew up to be very handsome. Aphrodite's heart opened even wider to him. This beautiful adventurous young man loved the thrill of the hunt and although warned by Aphrodite of its dangers, he loved to plunge deep into the wild forest. One day in his wanderings Adonis encountered a wild boar. Enraged, the boar attacked Adonis piercing him with its tusk, killing him. It is said that the boar was no ordinary beast but the god Ares/Mars, who jealous of Aphrodite's passion for Adonis, took the form of a boar and attacked the young man.

Hearing the screams of her beloved Adonis, Aphrodite flew into the forest, where she found him dying. Kneeling by his side, she sprinkled nectar over the wound and to ease his pain she sang gently to him. A smile on his lips Adonis silently passed away into the Underworld. The nectar that Aphrodite sprinkled on Adonis's wound turned some of the droplets of his blood into beautiful red anemones. As the rest of his blood flowed, it became a new river.

Persephone greeted Adonis with joy as he entered her realm, the underworld, permanently now. At the same time, Aphrodite, knowing that her Adonis was now in Persephone's clutches, rushed to the underworld to bring him back. Once again, Zeus had to intervene to stop a war. He ruled that Adonis would spend half the year with Aphrodite and the other half with Persephone. Both were forced to learn: there is no control or ownership of love.

This myth reveals that we lack any control over love ultimately – either its arising or its loss. All three involved in this love triangle were called into love's demand to let go, to fulfil the whole cycle of life, love, loss and its return. In this myth Aphrodite/Venus as goddess of love represents the heavenly heights to which we ascend; Persephone/Proserpina stands for the dark of the underworld we also must enter. Our knowing of this cycle lies at the very root of our fear of loving. It lies at the core of our disconnection from the potency of Venus's power in us. For we know to love is also to lose. That knowing may cause us to pull back from love when it appears. It's the hesitation that arises before the plunge into a new love affair, or its dismissal. How many of us recognise this shadow of fear that stops or delays us going there?

Loss and rejection both play their part in the shadow of Venus. The pain involved in relating can cause us to close down to its potential, not only closing our heart but doubting our trust in our self, in love, even in life itself. When we believe life is just about loss or pain, we may project our fear onto what is actually an opportunity. Fear of loss can influence every aspect of our lives, for if we give it too much value, rather than recognizing its place in the cycle, we close down life's natural flow. That natural flow always moves to renewal at some point, to the spring that follows the cold of winter.

An abundant life is deeply connected to the truth of this cycle. When we're in flow we are naturally moved in giving and receiving, opening and closing, contracting and expanding, no and yes. At the very root of our fear of loving lies the knowing that truly we have no control in love, that we are always vulnerable to its loss. This may make us wary. We open, but only a little. We test the waters perhaps. We give, but not fully. We receive, but not with an utterly opened heart. Then we wonder why loving is lukewarm, or it dies.

To live and love fully our 'Yes' needs to be full. Yet this can be tricky too. For our initial passion can become attachment to a certain expression of loving, or a particular individual. Desire may land in trying to control the when-where-how of relating, or in feelings of ownership. This doesn't mean we don't have preferences, can't make choices, or that we're not committed; it's simple about flow. When we're not in flow, passion can become obsession, the dream can become the nightmare. We become driven by the compulsive need to have, possess or control love, or a specific individual.

When we become driven by need or want, passion has met its shadow, the need to own or control in order to feel powerful. Yet love itself is the power. The mysterious allure of its power both attracts and compels. The gods and goddesses of Greek mythology demonstrate this play especially Venus. They demonstrate the many games of love from its deepest truth to its demise. Fickleness and fixation, rape and revenge, jealousy, rage and poison, their mythology is filled with intensity. There's nothing like love to draw out the deep-seated archetypes from our unconscious. Falling in love is an archetypal experience, sometimes leaving us reeling and wondering what happened. We behave in ways we abhor in others. We lose control. In recognising the games of love are here to reveal this – that love brings out both the best and worst in us – we can say a full 'Yes!' to it, and then let go into its flow.

Being love is a different story to falling in love. It requires the intention of both individuals to engage in co-creative relationship. Like the marriage vows 'for better or worse', it is mature in recognising that relationship isn't always a bed of roses. Or if it is, those roses also have thorns. Just as Venus's fire of passion draws us into love, those fires are also destructive, transforming what does not serve love, or a particular connection. Through it all, if we are to know deep fulfilment, love requires we give our fullest 'Yes!' to the whole relationship experience, not just the parts we enjoy.

60

The truth is love always requires our fullest 'Yes!' Yet it's not exclusive to relating. It flows where the calling is. A fulfilled life requires our complete 'Yes!', a full engagement of its limitless potential. To say yes to life requires our vulnerability. We do not know how life or love will unfold. Certainty is anathema to Love. Love is always a risk, as is life. Yet to be alive is to go there regardless, if the attraction is real. It's leading us somewhere. What stops us is simply the shadow - shadows around self-worth, self-trust, fear of pain or loss. Venus in us knows this is part of loving; it's a natural aspect of living. She goes there anyway. For her calling to love, her yes to intimacy, her need to express creatively, her desire for fulfilment, is her very reason for existence. She is Divine Love expressing itself. She is Divine Love expressing itself through us as women. Would you deny Her calling?

Chapter 2
Original Innocence – Psyche

Seeds
blowing in the wind,
we are seeds
flowing down life's stream
floating in Love's ocean.
In which field
will you fall?
What outgrowth of life
will you be?

Will you let the power
of life's call to grow
shatter you from within?
Will you let the touch
of Love's call
open you
through innocence
to inner-sense?
Will you leave the shell,

the warm protection
of your self-cloaks
to let your shoot unfurl?
Leave the known
to open out anew?

Though vulnerable,
fragile,
prey to careless feet
or nature's whim,
will you risk it all
to open as life's rich stream?

What flower of life
might your seed unfurl?
What wondrous treasure
might your innocence
hide?
Cassandra Eve

Archetype: The Soul

Symbols: Butterfly, a box, butterfly wings

Message: Your soul will guide you. Trust it!

Psyche themes: Innocence and its journey into maturity; intuitive knowing; attunement and bonding with another; conscious relating as a path to wholeness; trust in one's own evolutionary process; the gift of vulnerability

Shadow themes: Naiveté; passivity; victim consciousness; powerlessness

Also known as: Anima (Roman)

Psyche sits at the centre of the Sacred Pathways mandala with Venus. As Venus represents the creative power of the Feminine expressing through woman, Psyche represents the innocence of the soul and its journey in our human realm. Both are central to our consciousness in terms of evolving embodied maturity here on Earth. In the Greek language the word Psyche means breath, life or soul. It also means butterfly. These descriptions provide us with clues as to Psyche's way of being. Her myth reveals the soul's journey through experience into maturity. The young Psyche's sweet innocence is like the first breath of the soul newly arrived in a body. Her journey is that of a baby taking the journey into humanness and beyond it, into full soul expression. Psyche's myth reveals to us the stages of that journey. Like the development of egg to caterpillar to chrysalis to butterfly Psyche's story reveals how we have the potential to move through distinct stages of development in order to fully embody our soul energy. The journey of Psyche reveals there is no end to our potential for growth whilst in a human body.

Psyche's myth reveals to us the heroine's journey. It reveals the evolution of innocence to strength, authenticity, maturity and wholeness. Yet it's so much more, as we shall discover. Psyche's journey reveals the evolving integration of soul and humanness. It is a mirror for our own stages of development, revealing where and how we may get stuck in unconscious patterns of thinking and behaviour, and how we may move into maturity. In particular it reveals the deep inner processes available to us through relationship; how relating acts both as an invitation and catalyst for us to grow. It reveals how what we see as obstacles, either within or in our relationships, are in fact vehicles for the growth of maturity.

Nature's mirror is a wondrous reflection for our own human nature and the means of its growth. Butterflies and moths reveal to us the processes of transformation. Each phase brings different forms and unique requirements. The egg stage represents birth and the potential of growth. The caterpillar stage is where the work of eating and digesting happens; for a human being this represents our journey through experience, how we digest it and what we learn from it. The chrysalis represents the resting and developing phase that we have no control over, where hidden processes are at work. The butterfly is the emergence of that inner process where we begin to fly, to taste the freedom of being our unique self and living our soul's purpose. Yet the cycle continues. The butterfly both pollinates flowers and lays her own eggs; seeds for the future. It shows us how as mature beings we have the capacity to live our soul's potential through a life of fulfilment, even a legacy, through what we create and how we live. As Venus and Psyche are brought together in Psyche's myth so they are intimately linked in terms of the soul's creative expression.

Her-Story

Like many myths of the Deep Sacred Feminine, Psyche's tale centres on a descent into the underworld. This journey of descent is the making of her. The story came originally from Metamorphoses (also called The Golden Ass), written in the 2nd century AD by Apuleius. The tale concerns the overcoming of obstacles to the love between Psyche and Eros and their ultimate union in a sacred marriage. Eros and Psyche appear in Greek art as early as the 4th century BC so the Greek myth must have more ancient roots, as do many Greek and Roman myths. It has inspired poetry, drama and opera and is depicted widely in diverse art forms. Psyche's Roman name through direct translation is Anima.

Psyche was the youngest of three princesses and the most beautiful. The subjects of her father the King compared her beauty to that of the Goddess Aphrodite/Venus who had sprung from the waves of the sea. They said Psyche was so beautiful she must have sprung from a drop of dew. So they began to neglect Aphrodite's altars and worshipped Psyche instead. This angered the Goddess. As punishment she asked her son Eros, God of Love, to send one of his arrows to make Psyche fall in love with the most miserable creature living.

Psyche, despite her beauty, had no suitors. No one felt worthy of asking for her hand in marriage so her father, the king, made a pilgrimage to the Oracle of the Sun God, Apollo, to seek advice. Apollo's advice was to dress his daughter as though in mourning and take her to a mountaintop, where a hideous dragon would take her. It seemed Aphrodite's desire was to be fulfilled, either through the actions of her son Eros or the Psyche's father.

Thus, Psyche went to the mountaintop. Here she was simply to wait for the dragon to devour her. It seemed that Psyche was doomed to life with a terrible monster. Yet as we know from all the best tales, wicked plans are sometimes apt to fail.

Psyche was accepting of her fate. She did not blame her parents. Alone on the mountaintop she waited and waited but to her surprise the dragon did not come. Meanwhile Eros, who had been sent to punish this lovely maiden at the command of his mother the Goddess Aphrodite, flew onto the mountain. When he spotted Psyche, he was so surprised at her beauty that he accidentally pricked himself with one of his arrows and fell in love with her.

Eros fell so completely in love with Psyche that he asked one of the gentle zephyr breezes to bring her to his secret palace. Here invisible hands waited on her, fed her wonderful food, bathed her in rose water and then showed her to a luxurious bedroom. In the blackness of night Eros came to Psyche and having declared his love as if her bridegroom, made Psyche promise that she would never seek to discover his identity. He threatened that if ever she were to see him, he would disappear from her life forever, as would the palace and all in it. Psyche made the promise. Their union was fulfilled and so she enjoyed the splendour of the palace and its garden by day, whilst falling into the loving arms of her invisible bridegroom each night.

Eventually Psyche began to miss the company of other humans and asked Eros if her sisters could visit. Reluctantly he agreed but warned Psyche that if she told them about him, disaster might happen.

The sisters were brought to the hidden valley where Psyche was living. When they saw the splendour of the palace and its gardens they became envious. They plotted between themselves how they might harm Psyche. Gradually, by continuous questioning they discovered that Psyche had never seen her husband. On their next visit, having realised that Psyche was now pregnant, they questioned Psyche how the child might look if she, its mother, did not know the form of its father. They reminded Psyche that she was supposed to have a married a dragon. Although in her heart she felt her prince was a gentle, loving man, Psyche took on her sister's fears. She accepted a small sharp knife they brought with them, together with an oil lamp. The sisters encouraged her to light the lamp once the prince was sleeping and told her that if he were a monster, she should kill him with the knife.

In the darkness of night Psyche, knife in hand, lit the lamp. When she saw Eros in all his beauty lying at her side with the quiver full of love arrows at his feet, she was so entranced that she pricked herself on one of the arrows and fell irredeemably in love with him. Swooning with the love she felt, inadvertently a drop of hot oil fell on Eros's shoulder and burnt him. He awoke with a great cry and leapt up, his wings carrying him upwards. Calling out to Psyche that she would never see him again, he flew off and disappeared, as did the palace and everything in it. Psyche was left, bereft, in a wild valley with a torrent racing through it. In despair at her loss she flung herself into the river, which for love of Eros would not allow her to drown but flung her on the bank amongst the herbs. There the nature god, Pan, found her. Somehow already knowing her story, Pan encouraged her to seek out Eros rather than destroy herself. So began Psyche's journey, travelling about the country to seek her lover, Eros. She didn't know he had taken himself to his mother's bedroom to heal the wound caused by the burning oil.

Meanwhile Aphrodite, having heard Eros's tale of failure, was raging. She called her servants to bring Psyche to her. On her arrival Aphrodite beat her and declared that she could only win reprieve from her anger through service. Then she began to set Psyche a series of tasks.

For the first task Aphrodite took a great sack of grains: wheat, poppy seeds, barley, lentils and beans and poured them upon the ground. She instructed Psyche to sort them before morning, one type from another. Naturally Psyche was distraught at the complexity of this task, not knowing how to proceed. She sat and wept; she simply didn't know what to do. A small ant, witnessing Psyche's tears and taking pity on her, called all her friends to help. One by one the ants put each kind of seed in order and then went away. When Aphrodite returned in the morning, finding the task completed, she was furious. She thought that her son Eros had helped, so she proceeded to lock him up deep within her house.

The next day Aphrodite summoned Psyche and gave her a second task. She commanded her to collect the golden fleece of the wild, flesh-eating rams that grazed by the river. Psyche, overwhelmed by this task, decided again to simply drown herself. She was about to throw herself in the river when a green reed called to her and told her to wait. The reed told Psyche that while the sun was high the rams were most dangerous, but in the evening, when they refreshed themselves in the river, their fury would be spent. Psyche could then gather the fleece that had caught on the briars in the hedges. Psyche did this and then she took the fleece to Aphrodite. Once more Aphrodite was furious, being aware that Psyche must be getting help from somewhere, yet not knowing where. She decided to send her into even greater danger.

For the third task Aphrodite gave Psyche a crystal bottle, demanding that she fill it from the waters that flowed from the top of the mountain into the river Styx. She warned Psyche she would suffer great punishment if she failed. When Psyche came in sight of the top of the mountain, she saw that the task given her by Aphrodite was impossible. Fierce dragons protected the waters that were bounded by great rocks and deep chasms. Psyche stood as if turned to stone at the thought of the great danger she faced. But once again help was at hand. This time it arrived in the form of a magnificent eagle that took pity on her. Flying down from on high the eagle grasped the crystal bottle, flying with it into the centre of the river and filling it with water. As always, help had appeared through nature. Psyche was able to bring the water to Aphrodite, who now accused her of being a witch. She took a box from amongst her things and gave it to Psyche, demanding she go to the

70

Goddess of Hades, Persephone, requesting a day's worth of her beauty as a gift.

Psyche could see no solution to this final task, so she went to the top of a tall tower, intending to throw herself from it. Once more help was at hand however, as the tower warned her of the folly of taking her own life. The tower gave Psyche clear directions on how to find her way down into Hades and to its queen, the goddess Persephone. She was told to take with her two pieces of barley bread soaked in honey and to carry in her mouth two coins. She would meet a man with a donkey carrying sticks. He would ask for her help, but she should ignore him and carry on. Psyche would then come to the river of hell where she must let Charon, the ferryman, take one of the coins from her mouth. She should ignore all those who asked for help, as these would be the tricks of Aphrodite to make her drop the honeyed bread, each piece of which was needed to help her pass Cerberus, the three headed dog who guarded the gateway to Hades palace. Once before the throne of Persephone, the tower told her, Psyche should refuse all food except plain brown bread. She should then present Aphrodite's request that Persephone fill the box with a day's worth of her beauty. When Persephone had given her the box, Psyche should return the way she had come, giving the second piece of honeyed bread to the dog and the second coin to the ferryman, again ignoring all diversions. Above all she was told; do not be curious about the contents of the box.

Everything happened as the tower had foretold on Psyche's journey into Hades but as she returned to the light of day Psyche paused. Suddenly she was overcome with a desire to see what was in the box. She didn't hesitate. She knew she wanted some of its beauty contents for herself. 'Why shouldn't I just have a look?', she said to herself. Psyche lifted the lid but strangely could see nothing within it. Instead she was overcome by a deadly sleep. She lay on the ground as if dead.

Meanwhile Eros, being healed of his wound, had escaped from his mother Aphrodite's house and came upon Psyche lying on the ground. Overawed by her beauty and his love for her, Eros wiped the sleep from her face, waking her and telling her to take the box to Aphrodite, as she had demanded; he had a plan.

Eros flew to the great God, Zeus, to ask him to intercede with Aphrodite on Psyche's behalf. Accordingly Zeus had all the Gods and Goddesses called to the great banqueting hall, to discuss the matter of Eros and Psyche's love and Psyche's great quest. All agreed that Eros and Psyche could marry, and that Aphrodite must accept Psyche as her daughter-in-law. Not only that, as the great wedding feast was held, Psyche was given a drink of the god's elixir of immortality. Through her quest she had become a goddess. Everyone rejoiced.

In the fullness of time a daughter was born to Psyche and Eros, whom they called Pleasure. Soon their union brought forth more children whom they named Bliss and Ecstasy.

Psyche's place in the Universe – Astronomy & Astrology

The asteroid Psyche was discovered by Italian astronomer Annibale de Gasparis in 1852. It is one of the ten largest asteroids in the asteroid belt and contains a little under 1% of the entire asteroid belt material. Psyche appears to be comprised almost entirely of metal, just like the core of a rocky planet. NASA is planning a mission to Psyche in 2022 (to land in 2026) to study Psyche's metallic composition, in the hope of better understanding how planets like Earth are formed.

Psyche's astrological placement in a birth-chart reveals how we take the journey from innocence to maturity through facing the challenges life brings us, especially within relationship. She shows how we develop the mature skills needed to evolve our fragile and disempowered humanness into maturity. Psyche's myth is clearly the tale of victim consciousness finding its power and yet it is so much more. In relationship Psyche represents the initial experience of falling in love, with its veils of romance and mystery, illusion and unknowing, then the trials and initiations we face to bring that love to its fullest expression as pleasure, bliss and ecstasy. Her journey also represents the soul's calling to fully express itself within human form and the quest to embody that. Astrologically Psyche in aspect to Venus and other asteroids reveals the dynamics of the soul's journey from innocence to maturity, particularly within intimacy. She points towards the potential of evolving our soul's expression within our lives and relationship.

My journey with Psyche

In adolescence connection and friendship with boys or girls usually occurs naturally through family interactions or through school. It's a normal phase of development. When that is interrupted, for whatever reason, the gender dynamic becomes a mystery in one's life. This developmental gap breeds vulnerability. There has been no role-playing, testing out, relationships games and flirtations, and therefore no opportunity to learn. Innocence then may play out as naiveté, even well into adulthood.

For me the natural adolescent boy-girl friendships, teasing and flirting, embarrassments, first dating and crushes, never really arrived. When I left school at age eighteen, I was very naïve about the intricacies of relationships and sexuality. Getting married at twenty I thought I was in love, but he still needed a mother and I was happy to play that role, for a while. I learned little about conscious relationship at that time, but lots about co-dependency. Within five years we had parted.

The next relationship encounter brought forth the Psyche archetype in me, although I only knew this with hindsight. There was no doubt he was a man rather than boy; handsome with blue eyes, a Paul Newman look-alike, well-muscled, charming and yet edgy. On every level he shouted 'danger'. Despite a friend's warnings I was naïve to the potential. I was attracted to him; that attraction was taking me to the Psyche initiations.

The first blow happened within a few weeks of our meeting. It was physical. One night I voiced my disapproval at his late arrival. On leaving, boots on, he kicked my arm as I lay by the fire. Still I did not really see the signs of what was to come, or perhaps I chose to ignore them. I was simply glad someone had chosen to 'love' me.

Who knows the mystery of how the soul works? Yet growth through experience becomes clear with hindsight. Over the next few years I lived on a knife-edge of alcohol-fueled behaviour and violence with this man. Unless one lives it, it's difficult to describe how life wasn't terrible, only sometimes. This man had a sweet love of nature where we connected deeply. There we knew love, yet at times there was fear in me, very naturally, and the desire to escape. For a while the good times, the connectedness, outweighed the terrible times. His intention to heal his drink problem was strong yet time after time he fell. I could not help him even though I wanted to.

It was only with hindsight that I saw the purpose behind this intense experience. Like Psyche I was in the underworld. Naiveté and lack of self-worth were the tools of my growth. I was learning not to be distracted by another's need of help; I was learning to say 'No', and to affirm my own self-worth. Despite my strong desire to help him I couldn't. Eventually I made the choice to say, 'No more'. I opened the box. Like Psyche I had developed the resources and the will to say, 'What I want matters'. I left. Within a year he had died. But I lived. The victim in me was evolving.

Psyche's message: Your soul will guide you. Trust it!

Psyche's myth reveals to us the journey from innocence to maturity. It's a 'happy-ever-after' tale that has deep value to understanding the journey of embodiment. Each of Psyche's tasks provides clues to the focus of our maturing process at different stages of development, or even over a lifetime. As with many such processes we may pause, take time or get stuck in a particular phase. Viewing the tale as a whole gives us a unique perspective on both the parts and the whole of the journey to maturity, as well as the evolution of relating. This is not a goal-orientated process – for in truth we are already whole in our Being. The process represents the spiral of evolution on which we journey to greater wholeness through cultivating self-love and risking the journey towards a deeply authentic relationship. It's a paradox that encompasses both soul and humanness.

Like the soul, Psyche was the most beautiful and innocent. She was so perfect, so bright in her light, that no man would approach her. This quality was recognised in her by the people. They saw in her both the wonder and the potential she did not know in herself. They recognised the beauty of her innocence. No wonder they began to worship her, even more than the Goddess of Love Aphrodite.

Aphrodite's jealousy was the perfect catalyst for Psyche's quest. As Goddess of Love, mature in her self-knowing and expression of love, her tool was her son Eros, who represents both the birth and nature of desire. Along with the command from Apollo, God of the Sun, to marry Psyche to a hideous dragon, the stage was set for Psyche's evolution. Death was imminent, yet so was birth – for Apollo represents the light of consciousness. This myth relates the psychological death process that proceeds awakening.

In this tale, as in life, nothing is as it seems; everything serves a purpose. Psyche's apathy about her fate was a tool for the journey. What seems to be apathy was a shadow of her innocent unknowingness of the world. The young Psyche had no capacity for choice; it was undeveloped. Her innocence seems to be a handicap, yet it hid a natural wisdom that took her exactly where she needed to go. Soul was leading her, even through her passivity.

Psyche's journey unfolded perfectly to awaken her dormant capacity to meet life's challenges. She was on the brink of discovering her hidden strengths. Her distress, her playing of a victim was the initiator of her growth into maturity. As in the best stories, the helpers for her journey appeared just at the right time. In Psyche's journey we may see there is no right or wrong response, everything can and does serve the evolutionary process. Perhaps one purpose of this story is to shows us that in our own lives? Psyche, representing the undeveloped aspects of self in us, shows us how even naiveté may reveal a gift, if we don't judge its experience.

The journey into the unknown

A butterfly is the most fragile of creatures. Yet its fragility is its very nature and its beauty. Unwittingly through this whole saga Psyche's natural fragility, her lack of a sense of self, is the perfect quality for the journey. In following the unfolding thread of experience, not knowing where she was going, she was being led to exactly to where she could best grow and to what she was ready for, even if she didn't realise it. Isn't that the way of life? It brings what we need, not necessarily what we want or feel we're prepared for. Then it's our task, and often our challenge, to simply trust the process and step into the unknown.

Psyche's myth reveals to us the perfection of each stage of the maturing process. If her strength of will had been developed at the start of this journey perhaps she may have refused the growth that was being offered. Who wouldn't refuse the gift of fate at the hands of a monster? Yet Psyche simply flows with what's taking place. Not realising, as yet, that she has choice about what happens to her, her innocence expresses through unconscious trust in the process. She was trusting life without realising that she was trusting! Somewhere somehow Psyche was allowing her soul to lead. This is testament to her natural attunement to what she needs. The appearance of Eros - rather than the dragon that she thought was her fate – must have been a relief. And 'the gentle zephyr breezes' took her to the palace where she was nourished and taken care of. Her seeming fate, dealt at the hands of others, was changed. Her innocence allowed her to flow. Her lack of questioning Eros's appearance and his purpose simply opened a door for which she was ready. She seems to be a victim, yet somewhere in her being she's deeply trusting life's flow. In our lives we may also learn that in allowing our process, magic happens; we are taken care of.

Without knowing it, Psyche was clearly ready for this journey. She opened into Eros's embrace and in her promise not to look at him, was making a bond with love, a promise to trust. Psychically she was attuned to his being. Despite Eros's threat that in seeing him she would lose everything, Psyche was opening up, enjoying the pleasure that his love and being in his palace

76

brought her. In his threat did Eros want her to stay unconscious. Perhaps he did. Without doubt a promise in any relationship not to be truly seen makes an immature man's life easier. Or perhaps he wanted to remain in the dark to her, in his own unconscious. The journey to conscious relating that the Psyche and Eros myth represents takes us through all these masks. Meanwhile Psyche was simply enjoying this new life. And yet we all know the experience of falling into love's potential and promise. Do we stop to consider the consequences? And isn't that one aspect of love's allure. To not know what's coming and yet to experience the pleasure of love and being loved? As we shall see, the promise made – whatever it is - has to be broken. For love never stands still. Its calling is to evolve, or else it dies. Our task in that breaking of love's initial promise is to trust the process, as Psyche shows us.

The birth of consciousness

The innocence of love's first bubble always bursts. It must, for we are created to see and know more of our true nature, to travel deeper. Despite Psyche's bonding with Eros - and just as in our own immersion in a new relationship – life intrudes in love's bubble. Everyday demands come in, then we have a fall-out or get bored, or we go out to find a distraction. Opening our love connection from the love-bubble stage to full integration is the challenge. The next phase of opening beyond the innocent enjoyment of life's pleasures to a deeper reality simply happens, often when we least expect it. We reach different growth points where we're called to expand our experience of love and to live its presence in our lives. In Psyche's myth the growth point arrives in the form of her sisters. At this point Psyche knows through her psychic sensitivity that there is more love potential than she's receiving from Eros. Her sisters represent this aspect of herself that knows. Their voices of doubt and fear reflect her inner knowing. Perhaps she has an inkling of Eros's immaturity or his avoidance of being seen, of being fully with her. Perhaps she's simply knows there is more and is calling for it. She's in a place of paradox. In her heart she knows he's a gentle loving man; she has bonded with him in love; yet now she wants to take it deeper. The doubts fed her by her sisters reflect this desire to know more. The intensity of that desire to know him more deeply brings in the next stage of their evolving relationship. Isn't this true of all relating - unless we simply settle for comfort?

There's a similarity to the Adam and Eve story in this aspect of Psyche's myth; with the sisters playing the voice of the serpent. They are calling Psyche to question, in order to know more. Although their motivations may seem different to Psyche's, the desire is the same. Reveal him; see him; reveal your future. They are calling her to stop being a victim. Prior to this Psyche has never considered her future or fate. But now she is pregnant, there is an investment in knowing. Although carrying Eros's child physically, there is also a psychic element at play here. For unbeknown to her she is pregnant also with her own self. That new self knows there is a time to be passive and a time to take the risks of the journey.

In this phase of Psyche's myth love is taking its natural course. The fears and doubts sown by Psyche's sisters are the natural guardians of a new phase. The lamp is needed not only to see who her husband is but also to light the way into the next phase. It is the growing light of consciousness. The knife is required to cut away the initial stages of relating, to make space for a more authentic intimacy. When Psyche saw a glimpse of Eros for who he truly was, the seed of real love opened. Then, as happens in all intimate relationships, love's form (Eros) left. But in truth, love only appears to leave. Its apparent loss calls us to journey consciously back into its arms, perhaps with the same form, perhaps with another. We are called to face the feeling of despair at its disappearance and the question of 'what happened?'

There are always helpers and pointers on the path of love, if we are willing to see. In Psyche's despair Pan appears to encourage her quest and her growth. We too find allies or insights on our path to deeper love at the appropriate time. Pan is the nature god, earth-connected, sensual to the point of lechery. His appearance represents the calling to ground this innocent first love in maturity. Meanwhile Eros has journeyed back to his mother, Aphrodite, from whom he must gain his freedom, as must all men to be the fullness of their masculine power. At this point in the myth Eros has inner work to do; as does Psyche. They must go their separate ways, for a while.

Tuning in to what's truly of value.

Each of Psyche's tasks set by Aphrodite, although meant to be a punishment, are actually a means of developing maturity. Initially it seems the task is irresolvable, causing Psyche distress. Yet, like any quandary, the very nature of the task also reveals its resolution. This first task, sorting the seeds, one from another, is showing Psyche the necessity of discernment when faced with life's many possibilities. It reveals the nature of choice; that she must learn to sift, sort and choose rather than passively accept whatever comes along. It shows her everything has its rightful place and to place like with like. Without first doing that, she cannot proceed.

The accomplishment of what seems impossible always comes from beyond our current self. We are stretched to develop capacity and resources beyond what we know. When we are faced with a complex task like Psyche's our reaction or response naturally varies according to our previous experience and self-knowledge. Sometimes we may rise to the challenge and try to battle our way through a challenge, or like Psyche, we may fall into victim mode. We become overwhelmed with confusion or helplessness. It's not unusual to experience a combination of these responses. Their effectiveness clearly varies. Psyche's response to this first task was to weep. She was overwhelmed and did not yet have the maturity to know how to proceed. She simply didn't know what to do. Would any of us I wonder? Psyche sat and wept. It seems her response was from immaturity. She was overwhelmed. Yet it's precisely at this point that the soul can step in. We've reached the limit of our current capacities. Something more, or new, is required. Overwhelm can be a liminal space if we allow it; it's a space where previously undiscovered, or latent, capabilities may arise. It's a space where the mystery of life can operate, either through our self or the appearance and support of others. We need merely to allow our vulnerability in the face of what seems insurmountable.

Paradoxically the state of recognising that we don't know what to do - whilst making us feel vulnerable - can signify a point of maturity. It's the starting point for accepting we don't yet have the capacity to deal with this challenge. Knowing and acknowledging this is recognising the truth. If we do not judge our vulnerability as weak, if we do not label our lack of direction as inadequacy, we create a space of possibility. It is in this state of open acceptance to our lack that possible solutions appear. In openness a way forward arises from a place beyond our so-far developed humanness. This is where, if we allow it, soul steps in. Psyche shows us this clearly. She never judges her reaction. She simply reacts. Accepting her reaction, she listens. She is developing the capacity to find her way through the turmoil. In such open acceptance Psyche's natural attunement to her soul can speak and be heard through the forms of her helpers, however they appear. In Psyche's first task the solution arises through the ants. As we shall see in each of her tasks her helpers represent a quality she is developing inwardly. The solution to her issue appears externally but it mirrors a developing inner capacity. So what might the ants represent in terms of the maturing process?

Ants are very small, but they accomplish great things. They have a hierarchy; they work together and build large, structured colonies. Their colony comprises one or more queens, sterile females that act as worker or soldier ants, and winged sexual male and female ants. Each ant has its role within the colony with associated tasks. Yet amazingly ants also have the capacity to switch functions as the colony experiences different conditions. This change happens naturally through ant 'communication', the release of chemicals that convey what's needed through the entire colony. Similarly in our human body, different cells have different functions. Cells switch on and off according to the body's needs. Yet adult stem cells can also become whatever type of cell is most needed. There is intelligence beyond our human knowing constantly fine-tuning according to the body's requirements. Psyche's myth shows us this natural capacity to tune in is available to us psychologically too. It's what we might call 'psychic' capacity, truly meaning: of the psyche. To strengthen this capacity, we merely need to allow space for answers to naturally appear. That space is created by simply not knowing what to do and not struggling against that. In so doing we are naturally tuned in to answers that are ready to rise through the psyche.

How does this 'tuning in' process take place? The fact that ants are small and that they work together gives us clues. When faced with an overwhelming situation or challenge we need to value all aspects of our being. Rationale and practicality have their place yet intuition, 'gut feeling' and synchronicity are also valuable. They are where the magic arises. Worrying, trying to work a solution, micro-managing or conversely, trying to force a solution, are all ineffective when we are facing the initiation of maturity. We sometimes need to be 'hands off', especially in relating. What has worked before won't work when we're facing an uplift of consciousness. We need to wait, to make space, to allow the subtle nuances of the deeper self to arise or a way forward to emerge. If we're busy trying to work things out with our mind we may not hear the voice of soul. When our soul speaks – even if we're doubtful or uncertain - we need to move. It's in the earth element of action that we begin to see what's truly required. Even if our action is a step in a seemingly wrong direction, it's through stepping out not through worry and procrastination that we discover what works. There are no wrong moves if we learn through them.

In life each of us has our own assortment of seeds, ripe and waiting to be discovered. We're always in the act of sorting the seeds, whether it's everyday choices or more impactful ones. The ants, being small, show us smallness or humility as a requirement for solving the important choices. Humility comes from recognising and acknowledging that we don't have all the answers. It seems to be a powerless response yet in its honesty this response has power. Saying 'how it is' opens unexpected doors. It was Psyche's helplessness that drew the first ant in. The ant represents the unexpected solution, the hand of serendipity or Grace that simply arrives. Ants represent the wonder of working together, internally or with the support of those who can help us. Working together requires that we have the humility to ask for help.

81

Psyche's first task represents our growing capacity, as we mature, to actively allow all aspects of self to work together; to listen to the subtle inner nuances of self; to see holistically; to start small; to gather our resources; to ask for help and in so doing, accomplish great things. Ants live in the earth. The great thing they accomplish is building and maintaining a successful healthy colony. In Psyche's journey they represent the beginnings of her growth of a healthy integrated self. Psyche had committed to the difficult journey to maturity when she chose not to end her life. The ants, as soul helpers, were supporting her choice. They bear witness to and support her choice to reclaim the love of Eros. Whatever our quest, whatever our maturity process, whether in a relationship or not, the starting point is always sorting the seeds of possibility as best we can, from where we currently are, and then stepping into the journey with full commitment.

Claiming power wisely

Psyche's second task brought her a challenge with a strong element of danger. Facing the wild flesh-eating rams would generate terror in even the most heroic of us. It's a challenge that would seem to require a direct encounter. Yet such a meeting would undoubtedly need great courage, and more than a touch of strategy. How might Psyche gather the golden fleece without triggering the rams' aggression? Her response was as before, she felt overwhelmed. Does this serve her when it seems great courage is the capacity required? It would seem so, for yet again her vulnerability attracts the helper she needs.

This time Psyche's helper is a reed. The reed offers counsel to Psyche rather than completing the task for her. This is important, for it appears she is ready now to act on her own behalf and to do so with the discernment she has learnt through her previous task. The reed advises her to wait - to act but act wisely. It suggests she consider the whole situation and then decide how best to approach it. Psyche's growing ability to assess and bring together different aspects of a situation is being developed. She is slowly building on the development of discernment and choice presented to her in her first task, knowing when and how to act. This task is about claiming power wisely and developing patience in order to avoid danger. Now she's about to learn how to empower her choices through the fierce power of the solar rams.

To claim the golden fleece is to receive solar power, masculine energy – direct and pioneering. Solar power is the confidence to be fully oneself. The wild, flesh-eating rams are fierce guardians with self-assertive drive. They don't think; they simply charge. They are filled with aggression. To confront the rams openly would be foolhardy, with the potential for direct confrontation where Psyche could be injured or killed. The reed's wisdom of approach is necessary. To complete this task Psyche must take care. In essence she's discovering how to gather the directness of the ram's solar power but in an indirect way. This task is about discovering the appropriate way to act. Psyche is taking her first task a step further. Having developed the quality of discernment that she acquired through her first task Psyche now needs to learn to take action. In this second task she reveals to us that after sorting the seeds of possibility in our lives, we need willpower to initiate and act.

What might we discover from Psyche's helper in this task? Reeds have their roots in water, yet they reach into air. As such they are rooted in the watery element of feminine instinct and knowing. Yet they are also reaching and growing into air, the element of mental detachment that sees with clarity. The synergy of these two qualities represents a balance of intuition and rationale that make a holistic perspective. They emerge through action, the element of fire. This wider view is exactly what Psyche needs to transform her overwhelm. She's being shown to root deeper in water, her feminine knowing whilst connected more directly with mind (air), to activate drive (fire). She needs to cultivate a detached perception and capacity for action whilst also staying rooted in her feminine knowing. In not approaching the rams directly but collecting the fleece from the briars, Psyche is accomplishing what's needed wisely. She waits – the opposite quality to the ram's tendency to react. She waits for the right timing, at dusk. When it's becoming dark, she's less likely to be seen. The solar power that feeds the ram's aggression is dimming. The fading light is symbolical of moving towards feminine energy. Psyche is learning to use feminine energy to meet masculine force. This in itself is a profound integrated shift. Like the martial artist who meets a body blow with soft power, then focused response, Psyche is learning about the difference in active and receptive power and its appropriate expression. She completes her task with courage, and yet much more, she moves with both courage and wisdom.

In our own maturing process this task reveals the wisdom and understanding of timing, of using subtle means when faced with great challenges. This may mean us developing the quality of patience, staying with uncertainty until the right moment or action reveals itself. This capacity to wait requires great strength, for it involves an open approach to uncertainty. Uncertainty makes us feel vulnerable. Yet truly it's a great well of potential that we may tap into. Much like the reed's deep roots are in water, to anchor our self in not knowing is to be available for a new way forward to open up. There is real power in an open approach to not knowing. It's not a comfortable place but it's alive. As this task reveals, as we wait conditions change.

Taking a higher perspective
Psyche's third task seems insurmountable. Not only must she face the fierce dragons that guard the River Styx, somehow she must get into the rushing waters to fill her crystal goblet. Yet Psyche is growing, as is shown in her response. The thought of this challenge finds her turned as if to stone rather than overwhelmed. This paralysis is new. It's paradoxical. Numbness appears ineffective yet it shows how Psyche is containing her previous reaction of overwhelm. It demonstrates Psyche's ongoing development in terms of a mature response.

The River Styx is the river of life and death, flowing from the highest point of the mountain into the underworld. It represents the flow of every aspect of life from spirit to underworld, the collective energies of conscious and unconsciousness. Psyche's task to collect this water into a crystal goblet is symbolic of her growing capacity to hold all aspects of her nature as integral to wholeness. The crystal goblet represents the body and ego, which are the receptacles for life as a human being. The body and ego are both necessary that a soul may develop within its humanness. The goblet made of crystal stands for the soul's purity. Yet it also has edges that represent the boundaries and limitations of being human. The combination of the two - water from the River Styx and the crystal goblet represent Psyche's ability to engage the flow of consciousness and unconsciousness within the body from a new place. She is becoming embodied, more consciously whole, as she begins to develop self-knowledge and self-assurance.

Psyche's helper with this third task is the eagle. It represents her growing perception and also her need to call on her higher power's assistance. The eagle can fly high and has sharp eyesight. It gets the bird's eye view; it brings clarity. We might call this a spiritual perspective or witness consciousness. The eagle's gift is seeing the bigger picture with simplicity and precision. The eagle is one of the symbols for Scorpio, the sign that may transform its nature from the unconscious scorpion shadow energy to rise like the phoenix (another of the Scorpio symbols) towards the heavens. This shows Psyche is now developing the capacity to dive deep into the unconscious, pull out what's needed, to rise like the phoenix and yet also to recognise when she needs spiritual support. This is the capacity to traverse or call on all realms of her Being. In essence this task reveals Psyche's inner activation: the ongoing integration of all aspects of her soul in her self.

Our capacity to connect to the realms beyond our humanness is what gives us the trust and energy to go beyond our limitations. Psyche's myth shows us that when we trust the journey, and our growing capacity to meet it, despite our doubts and fears, we become empowered. As we go deeper, we also cultivate the capacity to go higher. Taking a broad perspective on a situation is not easy. It requires us to go beyond the personal aspects of a challenge into its archetypal nature. Every life situation has an ingrained pattern. When we take flight like the eagle and get an overview of a challenge, we have the potential to see with new eyes. We go beyond the pattern.

Psyche's response of numbness to this task, whilst not effective, reveals a development beyond her previous patterned reactions of mental and emotional overwhelm. She's learning to contain her panic and reactivity. She's meeting her own uncomfortable edges of growth. The goblet represents this growing skill of 'holding', a growing empowerment meeting difficulty. When this happens, chaos and reaction give way to the opposite pole – detachment. At this point it's an out of balance detachment that freezes rather than moves towards the bigger view. Yet it reveals the truth of any change process: that we often swing to the opposite extreme before integration.

The appearance of the eagle – detachment with fluidity – shows the growing potential. The eagle simply soars above the issue, pinpoints the core of it then acts. Without the eagle's gift Psyche may have remained stuck with this task. In our own lives without the capacity to take the impersonal wider viewpoint we stay limited, held in our problem orientation. Worry, mental turmoil, and trying to work out a problem through the egoic mind never works. When we're more detached clarity arrives. We then have the potential to fly.

The deepest journey
Psyche's final task is her journey through the underworld, the culmination of all the others. It brings together a new challenge and the opportunity to use the qualities she has been developing. Psyche's response to the underworld journey is similar to that in her other tasks; to kill herself. And who amongst us does not quake with fear at a major life transition? Yet help is at hand once more in the form of the tower she has just climbed. It brings her the counsel she needs. Even the act of climbing it shows us Psyche has grown the wisdom to go to the 'high place' of greater awareness. For this reason alone, the tower speaks.

In tarot the Tower card represents danger, crisis and liberation. It is a fitting symbol for this final task. The Tower stands for the connection of earth and sky, earth and heaven. We could also see it as symbolising the chakra system within the body. It represents Psyche's evolving connection to soul and body, the energetic frequencies within her own system and how they flow. Her initial response to the task, although seemingly suicidal, represents her knowing that this final task means the death of her old self. She is willing to give herself totally in surrender to this task, to die to who she was. The journey to the underworld always requires this willingness to completely let go. Psyche's previous task took her higher, into witness consciousness, now she must directly enter the river of life flowing from high on the mountain into the underworld. This final journey will equip her with the necessary skills and qualities to live fully and consciously; to embody and express the love she has touched with Eros. The three other tasks have been nothing but preparation for this daunting final mission.

Thankfully Psyche is given precise instructions to undertake this journey. She has not entered the underworld before so requires the map and instructions the tower provides. Strangely, or so it seems, her developing will is being sublimated to what is required to travel safely down and back again. This is necessary for the underworld is full of distractions and old energies that may trap her. She does not know how to navigate it without getting lost. The tower, representing her capacity for wholeness and for uniting heaven and earth, is her helper. In our lives these guides to the underworld process are essential. They appear in many forms; through myth and story, music and theatre, or by means of esoteric systems, religion, spirituality and philosophy. They also arrive through people: the friends, guides and mentors who support us through the toughest of times. Our inner world is also a rich source of support for this journey. When we are faced with such a journey, we can be assured we are ready, and help is at hand, even if it may not feel so. Such was the case with Psyche.

Psyche takes the challenge, equipped with the necessary information and aids for her journey. She knows she must remain focused, go beyond her old habits and patterns of emotional overwhelm or numbness. She must stay clear on her mission and complete it, for the sake of herself, the growing child within her and her love of Eros. She is to ignore anyone who needs her help. This means she is called to have full clarity about her purpose and strong boundaries. She must remain focused, retaining the coins she needs to pay the ferryman and the honeyed bread for Cerebus.

On her way through the underworld Psyche meets the potential distractions or catalysts that engender yet more maturity. The distractions of the underworld represent different aspects of her old nature. Even given the tower's warnings, Psyche somehow knows she must face them in a new way. This new way involves remaining clear and focused on her quest for the box of beauty. This gathering of energy towards the true meaning of her underworld journey is the culmination of her previous tasks. She is finally empowered in supporting herself in conscious choices, to set clear boundaries and maintain them, trusting the wisdom to know and engage her resources fittingly. By retaining what she needs until she needs it, rather than getting distracted by what others might need, she maintains both the strength of purpose and the aids she needs. Having stayed true to herself (and what the tower has instructed) she has both the inner and physical resources to complete her journey as easily and quickly as possible.

Descending into the underworld to claim the box of beauty from Persephone represents entering the mystery of the inner feminine; connecting to the dark goddess. Psyche is activating the power of transmutation within. Her need for humility when facing the Queen of the Dead Persephone is her growing understanding that she is a soul in a body and that her soul, her higher power, will guide her as she stays vulnerable, which means connected. In developing herself, her power of conscious choice, she is also empowered with letting it go, for the purposes of evolution. Gone is the passive girl, instead we meet a growing woman; this new Psyche is beginning to know the power of will and what lies beyond it. Without will, both the need to use it, and the need to drop it, her soul cannot guide her. She has gone beyond her old self-habits and patterns and is claiming the power of soul – innocence aligned with a growing fluid sense of herself. She is becoming authentic.

Yet there is one more shift to come. Psyche's quest was not activated through her own volition. She's made the journey, but she has yet to claim its power. In facing the underworld consciously Psyche has moved towards wholeness. Yet she must claim the power of desire and choice to fulfil her quest. So Psyche paused. Perhaps she mused, then realised the box of beauty held a key. How was she to forego the reward of the box of beauty when she had made the journey? Was it truly for Aphrodite? Was not any part of it for her?

Claiming wholeness

Psyche's final act is the culmination of her whole journey. It's also the whole point of her quest. This is the first action Psyche takes fully of her own volition and without guidance from elsewhere. It represents a point of choice from which there is no return. Choice and action are arising from her desire nature. She is claiming Eros, the god who represents our desire nature.

'She wanted some of its contents for herself. She didn't hesitate.' What a change from the Psyche we see at the start of this myth! 'She wanted'... choice is being born. 'She didn't hesitate' ... no emotion, overwhelm, panic or numbness, simply action to fulfil her desire.

Psyche chooses to open the box, despite every warning not to. She is making a conscious choice despite the potential repercussions. She is saying 'Yes!' to desire. Strangely it seems her action has failed - for there is nothing in the box. Instead she is overcome by a sleep like death. She has completed the journey. She has trusted her soul in its maturing of herself.

Process need 'hands off' inactive time and space for the new form to emerge. There is an innate magic to the process that we, as human beings, have no part of. Nature gives us signposts to this magical process, for somehow the new forms are already there, held in the process even from the start of it. Amazingly each part of the process already contains the whole. Psyche's symbol, the butterfly, shows us how this works.

The journey of egg to butterfly reveals the mystery of wholeness emerging. It is a potent reflection for Psyche's journey within us. Caterpillars, even in the egg, grow imaginal discs for each of the adult body parts needed as a mature butterfly or moth. Our development is similar. We might see imaginal discs as the potential of our mature form already being contained within our genetic material or our soul. In a caterpillar these imaginal discs begin to take the shape of adult body parts even before the caterpillar forms a chrysalis or cocoon, much like a female foetus already contains the eggs that may one day develop as her own baby. Some caterpillars walk around with tiny rudimentary wings tucked inside their bodies, though you would never know it by looking at them. Isn't this amazing? The immature expression already contains the potential of the mature wholeness. Psyche's myth and energy reveals this process within us. Our full maturity – not only our physical but also our soul expression - is already waiting, simply ready to emerge in right timing.

A caterpillar eats and processes, eats and processes. It's taking in and digesting the nutrition it needs to become a chrysalis then a butterfly. We are similar physically, but our food of soul growth is experience. We need experience to mature. The caterpillar stuffs itself with leaves, growing plumper and longer through a series of moults in which it sheds its skin. It is constantly transforming itself. Don't we have the same journey, with expanded potential? Yet for the caterpillar the biggest transformation is yet to come. Actually it's not a transformation; it's transmutation – a phase where the caterpillar disappears completely from its old form. One day, it stops eating, hangs upside down from a twig or leaf and spins itself a silky cocoon or moults into a shiny chrysalis. Within its protective casing, the caterpillar radically transmutes its body, eventually emerging as a butterfly or moth.

This transmutation process is a radical reinvention. It requires the caterpillar to digest itself. Cutting open a cocoon or chrysalis at just the right time, we'd discover caterpillar soup! There is no trace of the caterpillar. Don't we all feel like this at times. Especially when the pressure of change is upon us? But within this soup **imaginal discs** survive. These imaginal discs are the template for the future form of what was once a caterpillar. In humans we know this future form is contained in our genetic material; it's also influenced by our current choices and experience. Yet perhaps we could see imaginal discs as also representing our innate connection to our soul's purpose, held within our consciousness as a constant reminder of who we are beyond our humanness.

In the caterpillar the imaginal discs use the protein-rich soup all around them to fuel the rapid cell division required to form the wings, antennae and all the other features of an adult butterfly or moth. One study even suggests that moths remember what they learned in earlier stages of life as a caterpillar. Everything in nature, including us, is made to make this evolutionary journey. Even mountains are growing.

Returning to Psyche; at this stage of the myth she has faced the death of the girl in her. She will never be that girl again. She has been desire-less and now desire, the capacity to choose and act of her own volition, is born. It is strange that her love is Eros, who is the very nature of desire. There are no coincidences. Everything in myth is multi-layered, as in life.

Psyche has made the journey of transition but is not yet fully able to express or act from the new self that has already formed inside her. She's akin to the caterpillar soup with imaginal discs activated. Her sleep provides the space needed for transmutation to occur. She's in the Void – her old way of being is dead, the new one not fully here. Yet life is never static. At the appropriate point Eros steps in. He has also been through a maturing process. He has left his mother's house. Both Psyche and Eros are ready for the new life heralded by his kiss.

The kiss of Eros awoke Psyche from her death-like slumber. In our own lives the kiss from Eros represents Grace, the kiss of consciousness. It's always perfectly timed. In our own maturing process we cannot move through this Void stage of awakening by our own will. We must await the kiss of Grace, however it arrives. Each arrival will look different. The penetration of our psyche by new consciousness could arrive as a partner or an event; it may arise from within as an impulse or desire; it can appear in any form. Without doubt, it will see us changed beyond recognition. A new embodiment has arrived. In Psyche's myth this new embodiment is gifted and affirmed by the gods and goddesses. She is given the elixir of immortality. Now she is one with her innate divinity. Her children with Eros, named Bliss, Pleasure & Ecstasy, are evidence of this transmutation. They are our birthright too. Psyche's journey provides us with keys to reclaiming our original innocence and conscious unity with our innate divine nature.

Innocence and vulnerability as trust

Psyche's myth reveals innocence and vulnerability as gateways to growth. Yet how many of us remain innocent as we mature? Innocence is seen as more of a handicap than a gift. Yet it provides us with clues to a different type of maturity through Psyche's journey.

Innocence is vulnerability without knowledge of that state. Does a child feel vulnerable; or is a child vulnerable without knowing it is so? Innocence is trust until it is shattered. Once shattered we naturally become aware that we are vulnerable to life's apparent whims. We become afraid; we begin to recognise how vulnerable we actually are. We begin to lack trust in life and certainly in our self. We begin to step away from the power of open trust in life that is our natural state of being. We begin to become powerless. Or more truly, we begin to believe and affirm a state of powerlessness in respect to life's unquestionable flow of change.

What is powerlessness really? At its core it is a reaction to fear; it's a reaction to the fact that we are vulnerable. Powerlessness is actually a belief rather than a state of being. It's the belief that creates the illusion of feeling powerless. Powerlessness is based in past failures, perceived flaws and self-judgments. If we believe we are lacking in some way, or simply wrong, we are clearly handicapped before we begin. Naturally there are situations where we experience our vulnerability, in particular physically. But we always have inner power available at our core. Psyche's myth shows us the potential for support is always available. That is our power. For just as life changes despite us, and sometimes it seems in spite of us; it also flows towards us, and more importantly, through us. Psyche's apparent powerlessness, as ours, could be seen as a lack of knowledge of the growing capacity within to respond a challenging situation. It's a lack of trust in our own power for change, of our inner resourcefulness. It's a lack of trust that we are supported, that there is always help available if we remain open to possibilities other than our victim stories. It's only when we are challenged that we find what we are truly capable of? If we stay open and trusting, life's magic happens.

Psyche shows us a different meaning of vulnerability, where vulnerability and powerlessness are not weaknesses. They are the very guides we need for growth. Psyche's apparent lack of ability to meet the changes coming to her is key in the process of meeting challenge. She shows us that in merely staying open to the challenge of change, we receive what we need to meet it. It's the very act of allowing vulnerability that brings us what we need. It's openness and trust in the process that opens the magic. What a turnaround this is for our human need for control.

Openness is the key in this process - openness to not knowing what we need to do, or how to move. When we are vulnerable, we are open, and when we are open, we are naturally vulnerable. When we don't know – as long as we stay in the not knowing - we are open. That openness requires great trust yet it's a trust we are capable of, even if we believe we're not. For openness **is** trust. Psyche's emotional and despairing responses to her tasks, and her allowing of that response, are the very fuel for her journey. Psyche needed help. Her vulnerability drew it to her. At no point does she judge, criticise or blame herself for her reactions to her tasks. She doesn't invent a story about how weak she is. Her breakdowns are not seen as failures or labelled as pathetic – or any of those judgments we use to beat our self. Psyche simply emotes then accepts what she is given. Her vulnerability is trust in the process that her soul, not her need to be in control, is bringing her. She trusts what comes and through that process she learns and matures. In the myth it seems each of her helpers are external but actually each one was called in by her open acceptance of her vulnerability. They are her soul's gifts to her self. Each one is a mirror of her growing internal strength and maturity, opened up through her vulnerability.

The truth of life is we are vulnerable. We are always vulnerable. Life constantly reveals this to us. Yet many of us live as if we're not. Human beings try to control experience to avoid feeling vulnerable. Yet it doesn't change the fact that change is always finding us. The experience of change can be unexpectedly joyous or confrontational. To fully engage with life's inevitable changes is the reason we're here perhaps. Psyche shows us that everything we experience has its place within a natural growth process. She allowed it all, despite her apparent powerlessness to meet the challenges brought through her tasks. She responded with joy to Eros's appearance and grief at his loss. She allowed the natural growth process to take her where she was ready to go. She didn't know she was ready, but she allowed vulnerability to guide her; that is trust.

It may be difficult to countenance that our darkest most challenging experiences have a purpose - the purpose of growing us. Yet such depth of understanding shines a light that will take us from victim to creator, if we allow it to. Psyche teaches us that in this willingness to experience the journey, in the vulnerability to engage with it, even though we may not know exactly where it's leading us, we are supported. It may not feel like we are supported yet if we can open and accept, the Mystery appears as guide and support. Psyche's journey takes her from innocent girl to goddess. Each player in her myth has a role in that. Aphrodite played her part as antagonist to bring Psyche into maturity, just as others play that role within our lives. It seems Aphrodite was working against Psyche yet in truth the journey was for them both – goddess and girl, divine and human. In this synergy the soul's desire to experience and express itself is fulfilled, whilst the human evolves both for itself and for the collective.

Soul help is always available to us. The journey is, as Psyche's, to allow our human experience, stay open and vulnerable, to trust our deeper self and to attune to our own subtleties. The wondrous quality of Psyche's gift to us is contained within her acquiescence. Although seemingly passive it's this very quality that allows her soul to grow her. Vulnerability, which is a return to innocence, to inner-sense, to natural trust, is the key.

Vulnerability is wholeness

It seems strange to human consciousness to state that vulnerability is wholeness. For this is where we enter the world of paradox.

As human beings in the main we experience a sense of wholeness from the illusion of control, from maintaining our sense of self as-it-is, our identity, our 'I've got this', feeling power-full within life circumstances. This is true only to a point, for we cannot possibly be or stay in control. We all know experience happens despite us. In staying in control, in living from a fixed sense of self, we actually limit our self. We separate our self from the flow of life that we are. We think we know - our self, the other, life, the answers, the only possibility etc - and in so doing we put our self in a box of separation. It's the box of separation that has us living seemingly in control but with the constant underlying fear of its loss.

This myth shows us what happens when we let go of knowing who we are as a fixed self-identity yet allows the existing self to act as foundation for a growth process. Psyche's integration comes from opening the box. It appears to be the box of beauty but it's the box of herself. It's the box of the self that leads to the box of beauty – potentially. Opening the box of beauty was the final action that led to the reappearance of her love Eros, the acknowledgment of her divinity and the birth of Bliss, Pleasure and Ecstasy. In opening the box Psyche opened the fullness of her Self with all its gifts and shadows. It seemed to contain nothing, but it contained the everything; it contained the whole. Her vulnerability and trust bore the gift of her maturity.

In openness, which is vulnerability, we are empowered with the possibilities of the entire universe. We go beyond our existing self; we open. In openness we are whole. For it is only in open vulnerability that we have access to the flow of life's infinite potential that we truly are. It's only in open flow that we know we are already whole. Yet it is wholeness with a potential to grow.

Living wholeness

Psyche's four tasks lead to her being empowered in her capacity to discern and choose (task one), to act wisely (task two), to take a higher perspective (task three) and to go through an underworld journey (task four). In her myth we see her developing these qualities through a linear process. This provides us with the archetypal map for our own growth processes. In practice within our lives, if we are awake to our fuller potential, we will be constantly evolving our differing capacities. Yet clearly at times we are called into a deeper transition to maturity, through crisis or personal challenge. Either way Psyche's map acts as a guide for the most demanding aspects of our own quest for maturity.

Number four pertains not only to the number of Psyche's tasks but delivers a deeper esoteric meaning to this myth. Four represents a square; it is the box; the most stable of all symbols. Whichever way you turn a square it remains unchanging, firm and constant. Yet as we know a box can be opened; it can be filled, and it can be emptied. It is a container, just as the body is the container for life, for soul, expressing through the four human vehicles of body, mind, emotion and will. There are further clues to the deeper meaning of the number four within our earth's wisdom teachings.

In some Asian cultures the number four is associated with death. Fitting for the death of the girl and birth of the woman soon to become goddess. In Aboriginal culture the number four relates to earth; four seasons; four stages of life – infancy, childhood, adolescence, and adulthood; four directions– north, south, west and east; four types of life on earth – the four-leggeds, two-leggeds, winged ones and water life. The First Nations cultures of the USA honour the four directions and seasons; the four times of day—sunrise/dawn, midday/noon, sunset/dusk and midnight with its intense lack of sunlight. There are four sacred colours linked with these times; as there are also four elements; earth, air, fire and water. The Zia Pueblo Indians also have Four Sacred Obligations: develop a strong body; develop a clear mind; develop a pure spirit; develop a devotion to the welfare of your people. Even when we step beyond earth-based thinking we find there are four cosmic elements:

suns, moons, planets, stars. It's unsurprising therefore that the number four features strongly in the myth of Psyche.

Numerology gives us yet more affirmation of the purpose of Psyche's journey. Number four is a number of Being or soul. It is the number connecting all-that-we-are with the physical world of form. Psyche's story shows us the journey to becoming a complete human individual. She represents our capacity for wholeness. Strangely, we are always whole. Yet wholeness is not completion, not whilst in a body. We are always evolving, or at least this is the potential, for us as individuals and as a collective. As Psyche shows us, we have to claim it! We have to dare to open the box of beauty, to evolve and express our innate right to birth Bliss, Pleasure and Ecstasy through our relating with the nature of desire, Eros.

Psyche's Shadow Themes

The wounds of adolescence

In its simplest form Psyche's journey represents the transition of adolescence, the journey from the innocence of childhood into maturity. It's a rare individual that leaves adolescence unscathed, or even having developed a good level of maturity, especially within relationships. It's a lifelong journey.

During adolescence changes in the body, hormone surges and the arising tension of sexuality create a cocktail of turmoil. The vulnerability of having to leave behind our sense of belonging to family – however supportive or challenged that may have been – creates or deepens the wild teenage swing between needing security and demanding independence.

Adolescence is about developing a sense of belonging to oneself, having awareness of one's strengths and growing a capacity for maturity. In an ideal environment this is initially held within the safety of the family structure. A teenager can push against this security, testing their emerging adult muscles, but can still run back to safety when they need to. Who lives in an ideal scenario though? Some individuals experience this transition long before the physical onset of adolescence. They never know security, let alone safety. Some are thrust into independence well before they are ready. Sometimes we are catapulted into the underworld then must find our way through, even as children. Rather than the innocence of childhood entering the natural process of maturing, it is ripped away. Whilst other individuals are held too securely in the family nest and find difficulty leaving it. The square shape that represents stability is never formed, or it becomes a prison. Whatever the circumstances surrounding this transition, at some point, we must leave our known world behind. Life demands it.

The natural teenage phase of maturing is a journey in discovering who one might become. It's full of possibilities. With the engagement of those possibilities there's a growing demand to be self-regulating. The pressure of these two demands along with hormonal chaos creates a melting pot of crisis. It's somehow strange that evolution brings all these elements of maturation together at once. Innocence is so assaulted with the demand to learn, grow and move forward that it's no wonder we become lost in the surging tide of change. A healthy journey of maturing takes us from the vulnerability of innocence through a well-supported experience into self-knowledge and self-response-ability. But there are no guarantees we'll make it to adulthood. The body does, yet many of us get psychologically stuck along the way. The dynamic tension between who we might become, what parents want of us and what's actually possible, can leave us paralysed at certain stages. Just like Psyche we acquiesce because we don't know what else to do; we haven't yet developed our own set of values or the capacity to uphold them. Or we may take the opposite tack and rebel, sometimes just for the sake of it rather than from conscious choice. As we mature often it's a combination of both.

With openness and support we grow through the experience of adolescence, or we stagger into adulthood half-formed. By some means we continue to stretch our self into further development and mature in self-knowing. Even if we don't consciously seek to realise our fullest potential, life's flow of change finds us, encouraging or compelling us to grow. Change may be a subtle process or brought about in one traumatic event. Innocence is destroyed or we move beyond it. Either way, as in Psyche's tasks, we are challenged to somehow develop the capacity to discern and choose, to act wisely, to take a higher or broader perspective and to go through an underworld journey, maybe more than once. This development may begin in adolescence, or we may be so traumatised in childhood that it takes a lifetime to gain some maturity. We are all wounded in some way. Yet, try as we might, we cannot avoid any or all of the necessities of being mature, despite our innate vulnerability and lack of any real control.

Thankfully, whenever we approach another growth stage of maturity, there are maps, guides and helpers. Psyche, through her myth, is one of these. She reveals to us a framework for this maturing process. We could call it a map of the soul's journey incorporating full acceptance of 'what is' and embracing our vulnerability. Utilising her myth, we may enter the realm of transformation more consciously, holding the map her myth has provided. As we begin to explore Psyche's shadow qualities we are further informed of the focus of that transformation. To become a fully functioning human being is enough of a task surely. To bring in the gifts of soul, the fullest expression of Psyche's journey, is yet another journey.

Weathering the storms

Initially we encounter Psyche as the ungrounded princess archetype, with no sense of self and therefore no resistance to being led. She simply adheres to what her parents, and then Eros, want of her. At the start of the myth Psyche was purely passive. She had no desire nature of her own. Perhaps she didn't realise that she had a choice? It would certainly seem so. However, Psyche's meeting with Eros opened a door. She tasted something sweet and she wanted more. Desire was awakened. This is a crossing point in maturity. Desire would take her forward. Furthermore Psyche very soon became pregnant. She had a compelling reason to mature. As she was left on her own following Eros's departure, she was in a new place. For the first time in her life, she was alone. Then through a series of initiations presented as Aphrodite's demands, she was guided into maturity. Psyche's myth provides the road map for this ever-evolving journey in our own lives.

Psyche as an archetype of maturing shows us how to live our innocence, our inner-sense, whilst weathering the storms of life. She reveals how this is possible in the face of what seems impossible and also in terms of our reaction to what seems impossible. Each of Psyche's tasks shows us the evolutionary potential available through the challenge of that particular task – to choose well, act wisely, discover a higher perspective and emerge from the underworld transformed. It also reveals the potential of getting stuck in shadow qualities that are all based in powerlessness.

Through her myth Psyche's shadow seems to have just one expression - overwhelm. Overwhelm expresses as a reaction of emotional helplessness or numbness. It is based in feeling powerless, a seeming lack of capacity to meet what is before us. Change often makes us feel powerless. Yet, just like Psyche, we are invited or forced to change, through life's unrelenting opportunities and circumstances. For Psyche, Eros's departure meant she had not only to change but she also had to choose. To find her way back to Eros she had to meet Aphrodite's demands of her. The pressure was on.

Overwhelm expresses in many ways. Sometimes it arises as emotion; often we become confused; we simply don't know what to do. Feeling overwhelmed may push us into premature action, or we may simply freeze and do nothing. Overwhelm is based in a lack of trust in our capacity for change, or its development. We fear we will fail, or something worse. Maybe we don't understand, or don't want to acknowledge, that life is always calling us to change and grow, for change is its nature.

To get to the root of overwhelm it's wise to recognise firstly that energy within us is always seeking movement. This is mirrored in the fact that our moment-to-moment experience of life, and our experience of our self, is constantly changing. We feel different from day to day; our thoughts are constantly shifting, our moods too. Life is constantly moving; time is flowing; nothing is static - unless we make it so, through holding on, or trying to hold on to a particular moment, feeling or perception. Energy is always flowing and changing form. In that movement there is release and emergence, the potential of revelation and change.

Most of us face overwhelm at some time in our lives, often when life throws a curved ball our way. We know its chaos or numbness, the desire to deny, avoid or control what is already happening. Through her way of being with overwhelm Psyche demonstrates a key learning for us all. At no point does she make of an issue of her reaction to the tasks set by Aphrodite. She's simply overwhelmed. There is no story attached to it; there is nothing added to her emotion. It is not seen to be about herself or her ideas about herself. Her reaction is simply innocently expressed. Perhaps we all know this possibility? When emotion or reactivity can just flow freely? Simply because we are not becoming involved in a story that 'It's about this, or that, or the other', or 'That's down to my relationship with my father, mother, sister', or 'Oh no it's my lack of … again'.

The innocent expression of overwhelm frees up the static energy of a challenge, then new possibilities may emerge. What we tend to do however is energise the state of overwhelm with thoughts, judgments, or emotions such as panic. When we meet overwhelm with self-judgment, closure, or numbness we maintain its state of being, or we lock it down. Lock down arises from the desire to be in control. It may be a necessary reaction, for a time at least. Yet numbness as the inactive reaction to overwhelm will, if we allow it, lead to numbness in all aspects of life. When we clamp down on our reactions, on our personal expression, that closure remains in the body. Before we know it, we may be missing a sense of aliveness, lacking a joyful response to the good things in life as well as the more challenging. Eventually our closure to free-flowing responses, even reactions, may create ill health as the body becomes blocked with old energy.

None of this is wrong; it merely allows us to see how overwhelm diminishes or grows through how we respond to it. Making it a problem expands it. When we do that we are actively creating more overwhelm. Whereas in allowing our natural response to life's storms to simply flow, through feeling it as sensation in the body, overwhelm opens up. Once it opens up, it can release and flow.

When experiencing overwhelm we may weave between feeling emotional or shutting down, depending on our conditioning, what we've seen and learned from others. Our natural tendencies to be fully expressive or more inward are relevant too. Some of us are more reactionary and vocal, some calmer and self-contained. No matter what our reaction, Psyche shows us that the key starting point of a growth process is allowance and non-judgment. When we judge how we react we add a layer of shadow to whatever is already happening. We box it, label it and compound our erroneous self-beliefs, judgments and failings. We layer and reinforce the box of self that is calling to be opened. We are always choosing – either to open or control, to allow or resist, to accept or deny and fight. To be aware of where we choose from is vital. To recognise - I am choosing to hang on, to be emotional, to resist, to shut down. To allow or accept the energy of this reaction is powerful, for it is freeing. Psyche reveals to us the gift of fluidity, in being free and receptive to whatever is emerging in us.

To give free rein to our reactions doesn't mean being irresponsible. It simply means freeing up the energy of our reactions as sensation in the body. When we allow ourselves to feel the energy of a reaction, it changes. When we block ourselves from feeling it as sensation in the body and close it down, numb out, give it a story or judgment, or project it onto someone, it sticks. As it sticks it creates imbalance that may eventually lead to ill health. Freeing up the flow of energy in our bodies actually grows us in self response-ability because we naturally grow in subtle awareness of what's happening in our energetic field and in the body. We begin to notice the tightening of reaction even before it happens. As we grow in awareness of our energetic field, developing the psychic awareness that Psyche represents, a conscious response arises as a natural quality of maturing rather than a reaction of imposed self-restriction. It's a matter and process of embodying; this is the feminine path of bringing full consciousness to our humanness that Psyche's myth reveals to us.

Let us explore Psyche's tasks as a mean to uncovering the varied faces of powerlessness. Her first task — to sort the seeds - reveals the most common thread in any challenge of growth. That is the need to discern and choose, and the potential results when we abdicate our capacity for choice. Choice at this stage is not necessarily about the particular challenging life scenario and its solution. It is about choice in how we respond to the challenge. In effect it's not about the challenge itself, however it might appear. It's about growing our self, so we are transformed by the challenge. In that process we naturally discover new capacities, just like Psyche, and the challenge itself moves towards resolution, simply because we're opening up.

Our conscious choice of response to any challenge dictates how the flow of a potential resolution to the challenge itself emerges. We may believe that our emotional response has no choice in it but that is a powerless perspective. Reaction does seem to be choiceless when it happens, yet at some point we do recognise that we're being emotional or reactive, and that's the point of choice — to see what we are doing, even with hindsight. Opening, accepting, allowing our reactions and responses to open and move, empower the process at any point of the process. Getting lost or stuck in beliefs, ideas and concepts, confusion or 'poor me' emotional story-making, makes the process sticky. There is nothing wrong with that. Inevitably we all face our reactionary habits as we engage life and our experience of it. We cannot avoid it. To grow in consciousness is more about willingness. Through the spaciousness of willingness, if we simply allow what's happening, we get to see what we're doing. As we discover how we are reacting or responding new capacities emerge as a function of the process working through us. As we allow ourselves to free-flow our way through this stickiness and trickiness the energy of the soul is working away in the background to provide exactly what we need to mature. Sometimes that manifests as magical support in the form of insight, a guide or helper, an unexpected change that resolves the situation, or all of those. The ants are an indicator of this magical element at play.

Overwhelm is only a shadow quality if we energise it or stay in it. Looking to nature we'll see overwhelm is actually an aspect of energetic flow. Waves seems to overwhelm the land at times; the wind becomes too much for some trees; fire burns beyond where it's wanted and get eventually it engenders renewal. Earthquakes change the contours of the land. Inevitably the natural flow moves and changes, sometimes with speed, sometimes not. Life is always moving, changing form, giving birth to new potentials; so might we.

Overwhelm is a temporary state. It always moves on or it gets pushed into unconsciousness. We cannot sustain overwhelm. It takes too much energy. Inevitably we reach a point of choice. We are called, encouraged or forced to move on. Even if that choice is to abdicate from making a choice, it's a choice to remain static. Yet change will inevitably find us again. Sometimes the choice to remain static is to choose suffering; it is to choose against life. We have to take a step forward in trust at some point or remain a victim of circumstance. Psyche shows us this clearly, and its process. Trust is a choice. Do we ever fully know we can trust our self, another, or a life process that is truly unknowable? To trust is to live fully. To trust is to know 'I am vulnerable. I don't know what will happen.' but to step forward anyway, to weather the joys and the storms of life.

To our conditioned self, trust is not simply a matter of choice. Yet Psyche shows us it can be. By remaining in innocence (inner-sense) trust becomes simpler. We choose not to trust because we have knowledge of past experience we label 'bad', or 'wrong'. We choose not to trust our self because we feel we have failed before. We may have guilt or shame about that apparent failure. There are many layers to our beliefs about life and our self. Here lies the quandary. For past experience calls us to be wary perhaps, or only take it so far, to find some kind of certainty that things will work out. But is there ever certainty? And don't we sometimes wish there were?

The truth is we cannot make trust happen, except through making a choice to trust. When we do, life moves, as Psyche's myth shows us. The key factor is to trust that. That life will move when we do – because we are life - and that with each movement we will have another point of choice. To trust that even when we don't know the way, simply in making a move, we will be shown. To trust that even if we stumble, we will discover the capacity to pick ourselves up, or someone will appear to help us. To trust that the process will bring us exactly what we need whilst we reach towards what we desire. To trust that no matter how it appears to our self we are innocent, trustworthy and worthy. It is only in living as if that is true, that we make it true. It is only in choosing then acting that we make it real. To choose and to trust is to be an active co-creator with the natural beneficence of life. To choose and to trust is to fully engage the maturing process of a soul in a body.

'How we do', not 'what we do'
Our capacity to rise to a challenge is a positive human quality. There are times we all need to bring forth the qualities of determination, grit and tenacity. The task of sorting the seeds of possibility i.e., determining a course of action and its possible outcomes, will provoke a variety of responses from us as individuals. Some of us react just like Psyche's shadow and dive straight into powerlessness. For some individuals a challenge activates their fire energy. Just like the solar rams they may simply act or react, trying to battle their way through. At times a fiery response of simply acting is just what we need. The fighter response of 'I can do it, I will do it' is not always useful though. Just getting stuck in, using effort and exhausting oneself may not accomplish the challenge. It may even be dangerous. At a subconscious level Psyche knows to charge in when faced with task two – her encounter with the solar rams - would be foolhardy. Similarly when our intuition or gut feeling is activated, even though we may not know what it's saying, we are wise to listen. Recognising our inner signals, as well as how we react, or act, is an act of maturity.

Faced with Psyche's second task, we see the need for courage and action meeting the fear of the repercussions. The solar rams are a fierce challenge. They represent the energy of fire at its highest peak. To meet fire with fire can cause a conflagration. When we meet a risky challenge with force of will, courage can tip into foolhardiness. Some of us like this edge of risk but is it truly useful or effective? Is its cost too high, especially to the growth of our feminine energies? There is a different way, and this is what Psyche is showing us.

Acting rashly can come as much from fear as does feeling powerless and not acting at all. Behind it lies the same feeling of inadequacy. Impulsiveness can come from lack of self-knowing, from the arrogance of infallibility, the denial of vulnerability. It is short on the wisdom of understanding the many potential outcomes from such an encounter. It comes from ego's need to succeed without having to face or feel vulnerability, or the potential benefits of growth that come from embracing it. When we 'feel the fear and do it anyway' we act from wholeness. Moving in such a way opens up and grows deep-seated courage and steadiness. It enables us to bring higher consciousness into action. Whereas when we wing it, we may get away with our action but sometimes we miss the possibility of growing deep trust in our self. In recklessness we leave our body rather than fully inhabiting it.

In task two Psyche is learning to use feminine energy to meet masculine power or force. She still reacts as with her first task, becoming overwhelmed. In deciding to simply drown herself once more she is overwhelmed by emotion. Yet the call of the green reed – that which has roots in water and its head in the breeze - tells her to wait. The wise understanding behind this command is the core solution to the task. 'Wait!' Psyche's growing feminine maturity rooted in the water of intuition and knowing inside herself, combined with rationale and the detachment of mental acuity, reveals the way. It's to accomplish the task indirectly and in appropriate timing. This is wisdom in action. Psyche was learning to use her growing integration of inner masculine and feminine qualities to accomplish what initially seems impossible. Isn't that a wise teaching in this quest for maturity?

The truth in any challenge is that we are called to act. The key lies in recognising right timing. When we act from fear, or hold back in passivity, there is no growth of maturity at that point. In her first two tasks Psyche reveals to us the wisdom of discerning what's appropriate and then acting with wisdom. Moving in this way develops our capacity for insight, the understanding of the right boundaries, self-support and courage. The key is to wait, then act. When we wait without acting, we are powerless; we become stuck at task one, in trying to choose, or in making a choice but not acting upon it. When we act without the gift of task one's developing discernment, we put our self at unnecessary risk, or we waste energy through force, without necessarily reaping the gift of growth. We may think we're being courageous but in truth courage is the capacity to act from recognising, as best we can, the full implications of an act despite them. Or at least to understand we cannot know the full implications, but that we have explored them. That process may happen in an instant – such is our natural beautiful intelligence - or it may require reflection and the capacity to wait. Knowing where our actions come from – from an underlying fear and powerlessness, or from empowered vulnerability – is a key aspect of this task. The maturing of trust in our self and life is its gift.

The subtle traps of higher power connection

At task three – filling the crystal goblet with water from the river of life and death - we see a change in Psyche's reaction of feeling overwhelmed, or at least we see it manifesting differently. Psyche's reaction of numbness is the opposite pole to emoting. Yet it is also a bridge revealing that she is now able to contain her emotional reaction, to hold herself, albeit too tightly. When we are changing, our responses and reactions tend to swing from one extreme to another before finding balance. Numbness is a different response to the shock of this next task, but we could say at least that Psyche did not want to kill herself at the prospect. Perhaps she was recognising on a subconscious level that help would be at hand, or that she would find a way somehow. Perhaps she was slowly beginning to trust that this apparently extreme challenge could and would be resolved in some mysterious way.

Numbness is a protection. We see it in animals when they freeze. It's a natural response to danger. When danger has passed animals shake the fear response from their bodies. We would do well to do the same. In this task we witness Psyche freezing too. How was she to negotiate the dangerous rocks, face the fearsome dragons and fill her crystal goblet with water from the river? It was an impossible task, well beyond her human capability. Often when faced with such overwhelming challenges we might freeze too. It's natural and it's good to be aware of that. When freezing becomes resistance however, we face a different challenge. We have locked away or held onto fear and shock rather than allowing it to be a natural temporary state. Resistance can then become a habit of overwhelm. We become immoveable rather than openly allowing a response to arise either from inside or through an external source. Resistance means often we cannot see help even when it is at hand.

In this third task Psyche's development through the previous ones becomes clearer. Her numbness was a developmental stage rather than a resistant state. For life moves in response: the eagle appears. Once more Psyche's soul supports her quest. The eagle flew in to complete the job for her. Psyche's connection to her inner soul power is now manifesting at a finer frequency, that of the eagle who soars towards the heavens. A higher power is available to her. In our own lives, when faced with what seems to be impossible, it is that connection to the higher frequency of spirit that accomplishes or supports us in discovering a resolution. We may need to ask, to pray, to call for light yet help is assured if we trust it is.

This connection to spirit gives us clues to yet another manifestation of the shadow of powerlessness: the danger of spiritualising. Spiritualising is the tendency to use our spirituality as a means of escape from our human challenges. We could say it's 'rising above' the challenge without engaging it, whereas to rise above then engage is an expression of integrated spiritual connection.

To connect with and trust the bigger picture; that we are spirit in a body, is healthy. This is one aspect of Psyche's myth: that trust in something beyond our self provides the keys to our human dilemmas. Psyche is learning that, as do we. She's learning to trust the unseen, unknowable aspects of herself. Without our faith in a higher power, whatever we might call that, we are lost, especially when faced with major life challenges or transitions. There is a difference however between faith in our source and our innate connection to it, represented by the eagle, and abdicating our responsibility for life **to** that source. For are we not here to create, to co-create with the life that we are?

The tendency to simply hand over our power to fate, the universe or a god who controls it all is disempowering. We are it! Yet there's a fine balance between that knowing being egoic, with its danger of 'I'm in control' and its polarity, victim consciousness. Here we come to paradox; for in truth we do need to hand everything over to our source, for everything, including our self and all we create, comes from that. To have appreciation and deep gratitude for life is humility. Yet we are also here to co-create, to act, to take full responsibility for the gift of life we have been given and to live it well. To ask our higher power for guidance is healthy but then we need to respond, to move, to act. For we are here to live consciously. When we act with growing maturity of consciousness we are constantly led towards and by the source that we are. The shadow of Psyche's numbness reveals that when we simply freeze through fear then resist, or wait for a sign, we are abdicating our true role of co-creativity. We remain a child rather than maturing in our growing of soul essence expressing through a body. We have left our body with its power of consciously living as Source here on Earth.

Task three reveals that Psyche is moving towards more challenging endeavours and their resolution. The wild river represents the overwhelming emotional realm to which we may react with outright fear or numbness. The dragons guarding this have two clear meanings. They represent both the old habits and victim stories that may devour our power if we allow them. Yet they also act as the guardians of gold at the gates of higher frequency. The power of eagle is necessary when faced with such a task. Its capacity of far-seeing clarity enables the shadows of potential dangers, old beliefs, fear and vulnerability to fall away. Its ability to simply soar above the landscape of challenge opens a finer perspective where challenges fall into proportion with the truth of infinite possibility. The eagle reveals how we may live as the flow between human and divine, soul and body, finer and denser realities, rather than getting caught in one or the other as either victimised or disembodied. It reveals the synergy of detachment yet willingness to get stuck in that is key to empowered conscious living.

Death as a requirement of new life

Task Four of Psyche's myth reveals the truth of our maturity processes – namely, that they require an underworld journey. We all face these deep transitions even though we may not fully recognise their necessity or the potential of their gifts. Immaturity thrives on the belief that we are not going to face challenge or pain at times in our life, that we not going to experience loss. As we initially encounter her Psyche is the perfect mirror for this undeveloped aspect of the self. She's a princess, innocent, sheltered by her parents and protected from experience. To mature she must willingly step out or be pushed by circumstance. It is the same for us. The process of change is intense, but we have to go there somehow.

Intensity is a requirement of being fully alive. It is the pressure of living on a growing edge. Life is always full of the potential for dynamic growth and risk. No flower ever bloomed through fear of being battered by a passing rainstorm. Intensity lives in the saying of 'yes' to the risk of being fully here, in being vulnerable to experience all of life's passing moments. Psyche shows us the openness that says; I am here to know it all, to be the fullness of myself despite my fears, reactions and seeming lack of capability. Her transition into the underworld is bringing her to the culmination of her journey – the death of her old self.

The price of life is always death. It is the only certainty. What expresses falls back to silence; what emerges or is given birth, grows, flowers perhaps and dies. The cycle is eternal. Our acceptance of this cycle is maturity. The underworld is always there, awaiting our next spiral of growth; sometimes our sojourn there is brief, sometimes a major transition. We pass through it even as we simply let go of an idea, a hope or expectation. Death's requirement is to embrace the letting go without which we remain half-full of yesterday's projects, without space for the new to gestate. Psyche was ready for this

110

death, as are we at the right time. When the underworld appears it's always the right time. Her growing inner capacity to trust herself, her psychic attunement and budding maturity now faced the major transition for which she had been prepared.

If we don't allow the experience of the underworld, we suffer. It's somehow strange that in avoiding pain we suffer. Yet resistance to the natural processes of life not only causes, but is, suffering. In resistance we're escalating pain. We prolong the darkness of what is only ever a transition. Resistance comes from fear. It arises through the lack the knowing that when we allow the whole experience of life, renewal is certain. For life's calling to renewal is incessant. Or perhaps we lack trust that we will make it through. Yet we are the life that always flows into new creation. Experience teaches us this, but we make it through only with our own willingness; one could say, only with choice to willingly keep letting go and moving on. Awareness of the cycle and our place in it is essential. Trust in the natural processes of life is key. We never know exactly how spring will look but we do know it arrives, and that it brings a bounty of fresh new growth. Our cycles are the same. Through her tasks thus far Psyche has developed this innate trust. Her naivete about what the journey entails is contained in her capacity to retain her innocence. She retains her innocence by not giving energy or credence to mental projections about herself or making a catastrophe of what is taking place, she simply faces it in her full acceptance of 'what is'.

Human nature at its current stage of development generally tries to avoid the dark side of life and its attendant pain. Yet we cannot avoid what collective experience is showing us, as collective experience shows us. Even when we're in it, subtle avoidance or resistance to the full experience of what we are experiencing can keep us stuck there. In the main our family or collective culture does not prepare or equip us with the wisdom to go through the underworld well. Yet this is the journey of feminine embodiment, the growing of consciousness in our humanness. There are guides and signposts everywhere if we are open to see them. Psyche clearly has reached a deeper point of open willingness to take the journey. The appearance of the Tower as her guide and mentor shows us this. The Tower gives her clear instructions. Yet she must be humble enough to take them. She must be willing to go it alone too.

Having to go it alone may make some of us feel vulnerable. As we have seen, one of Psyche's gifts is her vulnerability. Vulnerability stems from not knowing whether we are capable of fulfilling a task. In full acceptance of this, and the emotions it may generate, a door opens. When we don't allow ourselves to feel just how vulnerable we are however, when we don't acknowledge our lack of skill or ability, when we don't accept that we don't know or need help, that lack of open self-honesty can tend towards arrogance or bluff. We do everything to avoid facing our challenge, or we resist and control, or we kid our self that we think we know, rather than remaining open and listening deeply. When we aren't willing to be humble enough to ask for help and receive what we need to take the journey, we fail ourselves in the journey to maturity.

The shadow of humility is arrogance. Arrogance is thinking we know, yet it arises from a deep-seated fear that we are not really up to the task. It's a bluff to cover vulnerability. It's the egoic response to a lack of grounded sense of self. Arrogance can be subtle. Inevitably it leads either to failure or the feeling of having failed, for we have not been fully open in our approach. We're attempting the journey from what we think we know rather than in openness to its potential. The antidote to arrogance is humility: humility as an acknowledgement of not knowing, as a capacity to listen. Listening is a skill of openness. To listen to our deep inner self, or to another who has taken the journey, requires that we die to what we think we know. Psyche shows us this in her open willingness to take on and follow the Tower's instructions to the letter. She knows she is entering virgin territory. And in truth isn't that always so in our lives? Nothing is ever certain, much as we would like it to be.

When we transit the underworld, it is essential to stand alone. Yet paradoxically in this standing alone we are equipped to receive the most help. In saying a clear 'No' to others, we are stating a clear 'Yes' to our self and the essential journey at this point. This does not mean we become selfish. It makes us cleaner clearer beings, equipped to truly support the needs of others at the appropriate time. When we are attached to fulfilling those needs, when we get distracted or scattered through lack of intention towards our true task, we fail the journey and our growing self. Our capacity to tune into what we most need at any given point is also diminished.

Psyche's mission was to obtain the box of beauty from Persephone, nothing else. The Tower's clear instructions equipped her to succeed in this task without becoming unnecessarily side-tracked. There are times in our lives, particularly when facing major internal change or life transitions, that our energy needs to stay contained to our own process. Meeting the needs of other's in our lives can seem to be a necessary aspect of our life's journey, particularly if we are a mother. Yet it's clear that the shadow can manifest here also, as getting involved in other's issues unnecessarily. This acts as a distraction to our own process. It can be avoidance; isn't it sometimes easier to support another rather than face our own vulnerability or fear? We all know busyness can be evasion of something we must do but don't want to do. Saying yes to our self in itself is often a major life transition.

To embrace our aloneness and face the journey births a great gift. It makes us resourceful; it calls up strengths we may not find whilst walking with another. When we're forced to call on our own resources; we discover gifts we may not find otherwise. We discover our inner depths. Being alone may scour us clean but being stripped to our core we're opened to qualities we may not have experienced before such as appreciation for the smallest glimmers of light, simple gratitude for being alive, hope, and faith in our renewal. At its heart aloneness, just like the underworld transition, is calling us to self-love, to self-connection that is unwavering, hearty and strong. It's calling us to acknowledge our resourcefulness and the promise of unshakeable self-fulfilment to come on the other side of our transition.

In Psyche's myth it seemed the box of beauty must be the fulfilment at the end of her journey. Strangely it appeared to contain nothing of value, yet it demonstrates the ultimate reward. Psyche's journey is not a goal-orientated process. Neither is ours. Beauty is not a thing that can be claimed like a prize. It is not a given except in the process itself, in what that process opens, grows and grounds within. For beauty is Psyche's accomplishment of true self, consciously connected to soul, manifesting as Bliss, Pleasure and Ecstasy. Without the shadow there is no journey to unveil that. Without knowing the darkness how may we appreciate the light?

For us to mature, both as humans and souls, the fixed knowing of our sense of self and its apparent competence or lack needs to make way to the vulnerability of our infinite potential. Psyche shows us the way to navigate the unknown and reach towards an ever-evolving synergy with our divinity. In the deepening of our conscious connection with that which is already intimately connected, we discover the ultimate fulfilment – to be fully oneself; to be whole.

Chapter 3
I Find My Self within Myself – Vesta

Profound intimacy
sits
in 'alone'.
The ache
that belief calls
lonely,
pierces
the veil of 'me',
opens the heart
and bows low
for Love.

Pen meets
paper
and sighs
"we are One'.
'

Senses meet
fragrant open rose
and know
dissolution
into beauty.

Eye meets
countless forms
and knows
there is only
this One,
Alone,
calling,
calling
all beings Home.
Cassandra Eve

Archetype: The Priestess

Symbols: A flame; a sacred temple fire; torch; the hearth at the centre of a home; a circle

Message: I find my Self within myself

Expression: Authentic; devotional; self-regenerating; focused; inward; alone; a path of service; the divine connection between sex & spirit; inner fulfilment and ecstasy

Shadow: isolation; burn-out; sexual disconnection; trauma in the body

How Vesta expresses Venus's energy: as authenticity, focus and devotion through the heart. Her link with sexuality differs to that of Venus in that the sexual act is performed as a sacred devotion.

Also known as: Hestia (Roman)

Vesta is a Virgin Goddess. She stands alone in her authenticity, focused on what is deeply sacred in her Being. Her capacity is one of wholeness and autonomy. She keeps the sacred flame alight in herself and ignites it in those with whom she connects. She is wholly herself, devoted to her heart expression and focused on her passions. Priestess Vesta reveals to us the ancient links between spirituality and sexuality, where the body with its sexual expression was revered and honoured as a pathway to the divine. A priestess was guardian of the sacred fire within the temple environment and acted as a vessel of the divine through her opening in sexual connection.

Her-story

In Roman culture the goddess Vesta was the guardian of the temple fire. Her name gave rise to the term Vestal Virgin. Vestals were priestesses who entered the temple at a young age. Their function was to represent the goddess, to tend the sacred fire and perform sacred ritual. The Vestal Virgins were honoured within the state, also holding positions of power within society. At this time, the term 'virgin' meant 'owned by no man'. It applied only to the Vestal Virgins and prostitutes, giving an indication of the ancient link between spirit and sexuality that was disappearing at this time. The Vestals were free of paternal control and could own property. Yet these priestesses were not truly free for they were required to be celibate; to control their sexual desire on pain of death. Intimate relations were forbidden as a desecration of the purity of the goddess. If caught in any sexual act the priestess was imprisoned underground without provisions until death released her. This covering with earth suggests the putting out of a fire. It's a clear indication of the growing control of women's sexuality by men at this time.

Through history it's clear how the Vestal Virgin function further devolved into the role of the medieval nun, where celibacy was a key requirement. In secular society control was also rising. Women who challenged male control were cloistered in nunneries or deemed mad. Being ducked in water or burnt at the stake was the response to any woman sharing her gifts, or the gifts of nature and the Earth. The sacred function of the Feminine expressing through women as sexual power, fertility and connection to nature was slowly being eroded.

Hestia is Vesta's counterpart as one of the Olympian Goddesses of the Greeks. Hestia was guardian of the hearth, the sacred centre and sanctuary found in every home and settlement. Hestia swore to remain a virgin although wooed by her brother Poseidon and nephew Apollo. Her virginity brought her the capacity to sit impartially at the centre of every home. In this we see the same theme of anonymity and service that was carried by Roman Vesta and later by the religious institutions of the nuns. When travellers went in search of new lands, they took Hestia's fire with them as a symbol of home, comfort and security, and to bless their homes. Another Hestia ritual occurred at weddings when the bride or bride's mother carried a flaming torch from their home to light the fire in the newlywed's hearth. This act was a blessing for their union and home.

Looking further back in 'her-story', into matriarchal times, we find this blessing has its root in more primal sexual rituals. The hearth fire is a watered-down symbol for the fires of passion and transmutation honoured in the temples of matriarchal times. There is also a clear link with the Beltane fires of Celtic traditions. At Beltane special bonfires were lit. Their flames, smoke and ashes were felt to have protective powers so sometimes people would leap over them for protection and renewal. Household fires would be doused and then re-lit from the Beltane fire, much as Greek or Roman newly-weds took the flame for their domestic hearth from the temple fire. The Beltane ritual gatherings were accompanied by a feast and often involved sacred sexual rites with anonymous partners to ensure the fertility of the earth for the new season's growth and harvest.

If we go further back in time, we discover the root of the Vesta archetype lies in ancient times when the role of priestess was both a sacred and sexual devotion. Sexuality was known and honoured as a cleansing sacred ritual, as a pathway to the divine. Men and women were connected to the eternal cycles of life, death and rebirth through the natural cycles of the Earth, Moon and planetary cycles. They were in direct participation with these natural cycles through ritual. There was a natural living intuitive connection to the Earth and her rhythms of abundance and scarcity. The sacred ritual of renewal through sexual union was celebrated within tribal cultures. In the matriarchal temples the priestess served openly and sexually for men to connect with the goddess energies. Soldiers returning from war would visit the temple before going home to their family. The sexual act was a cleansing; it removed the aggressive energy of war from the soldier's body. The priestess transmuted these coarser vibrations through the sexual act and her devotional service. The soldier went home to his family in peace. Sexuality and the sacred were unified and connected to deep understanding and honouring of our Earth connection; the fact that we are souls experiencing through animal bodies. In the more naturally connected rhythms of these ancient times, woman was known as a vessel of the Divine Feminine through her sacred sexual opening.

In the introduction to this book I have written about the takeover of patriarchy that occurred over hundreds of years. This is a period of time when many myths appeared in Greek and Roman cultures that transmit symbolically what was happening in the western-world cultures of that time. They include pointers towards the demise of the priestess cultures. The story of the sun god Apollo's role within the history of the ancient temple at Delphi pertains specifically to the control and denigration of the role of the priestess.

Apollo is the Greek sun god of light. He is known as the god of healing and medicine, archery, music and poetry. His main function in the Greek culture was as a god of prophecy. His Oracle at Delphi was very important to the Greek world; it was the site of the Pythia, the priestess at the sanctuary dedicated to Apollo. In Greek myths dating to around 510BC, Zeus (chief of the gods on Mount Olympus) determined the site of Delphi when he sought to find the centre of his "Grandmother Earth" (Gaia). He sent two eagles flying from the eastern and western extremities. The path of the eagles crossed over Delphi where the omphalos stone was sited. This stone was considered sacred and was located at Delphi after Zeus threw a stone stating where it landed would be Gaia's navel. Omphalos stones have been discovered at other ancient sites such as the Acropolis in Athens, Thebes and Karnak in Egypt. They often cover wells or caves where it is thought rituals involving prophecy were held.

What we know about the site at Delphi points us towards the change that happened over hundreds of years with the priestess cultures. If we look back to before the patriarchal take-over earlier myths reveal Delphi as the site of an important oracle. Originally the temple at Delphi was dedicated to Gaia and shared with the god of the ocean Poseidon. In more recent mythology Apollo was said to have slain Pythia a serpent or a dragon that lived there and protected the navel of the Earth. This serpent was guarding the Castalian Spring and the oracular energies of the site. Apollo was punished for this act but nonetheless the temple was rededicated to him and served as the major site for his worship during classical times. Apollo named his priestess Pythia after the original serpent energy. Greek classical scholar Erwin Rohde wrote that the Pythia was an earth spirit, who was conquered by Apollo and buried under the omphalos. As is often found with sacred sites it seems to be a case of one deity setting up a temple on the demise of another. In this case it was the patriarchal movement towards light and power overthrowing the existing wisdom of earth-connection and natural rhythms.

The esoteric meaning behind serpent energy gives us clues to the deeper meaning behind the Greek mythology at this time of patriarchal takeover. Serpent energy is widely known in esoteric circles through Hindu philosophy as kundalini. Kundalini is primordial cosmic energy within the body. Historic symbolism depicts Kundalini energy as a coiled serpent resting at the base of the human spine, at the muladhara or root chakra. It is also illustrated as two serpents intertwined as they climb the spine. Interestingly, the shape of the serpent coupling is nearly identical to the design of our double helix DNA. Some yogis consider kundalini to be the flow of energy within the network of the energy body and that there is no anatomical equivalent. Others relate the flow of kundalini to the flow of messages along the nerve fibres in the physical body. Most agree however that kundalini is a spiritual-psycho-physiological power that is centred within the sushumna, an energetic channel that connects along the spinal cord.

Whilst an individual is not consciously awake, kundalini energy is the static form of creative energy that serves to vitalise the whole body. When awakened and uncoiling, this electrical power moves in a spiral; hence the symbolic description of 'serpent power'. As kundalini is aroused (through spiritual practices or sexuality), it steadily increases the vibrations within the physical body and all its subtle bodies. This vibratory activity cleanses and transforms stuck energies in the bodies whilst also energising the consciousness of the evolving individual. Hindu philosophy states that kundalini practices raise an individual's level of consciousness towards enlightenment.

The symbol of the serpent or snake is sacred to cultures and religions globally. It has long represented life, health and renewal. In religion, mythology, and literature, snakes often represent fertility or a creative life force. The ancient Chinese connected serpents with life-giving rain. Traditional beliefs in Australia, India, North America and Africa have linked snakes with rainbows, which in turn represent fertility, or the union of heaven and earth. The spirituality of the Eastern Mediterranean and more recent Mayan culture had snake gods and goddesses. There are snake temples in Buddhist Myanmar where the snakes are considered to be protectors of the temple. The Hindu religion of India has snake temples too, where snakes are associated with fertility and rebirth.

In the Greek culture serpent energy is associated with medicine. The ancient Greeks considered snakes sacred to Asclepius, the god of medicine. He carried a caduceus, a staff with one or two serpents wrapped around it; this has become the symbol of modern physicians. For both the Greeks and the Egyptians, the snake represented eternity. Ouroboros, the Greek symbol of eternity, depicts a snake curled into a circle or hoop, biting its own tail. The Ouroboros symbol originated from the fact that as snakes grow, they shed their skin, revealing a shiny new skin underneath. This is the reason snakes have become symbols of rebirth, transformation, immortality and healing. Their association with immortality and as guardians of the underworld links them to the realm of death and the Great Mother goddess, giver of life and death. They have come to represent hidden wisdom or sacred mysteries.

Snakes were a valued part of ancient temple culture, as was snake venom to induce a state of trance whereby prophecy came forth. Snakes or serpents are also portrayed as symbols of death or evil, perhaps related to the fact that some are poisonous. The serpent that tempts Eve and Adam into disobeying God is seen as such. But if we explore deeper there is another meaning to this biblical myth related to sexual power. Some Christian saints are said to have driven away snakes as a sign of miraculous powers given to them by God, for instance St Patrick in Ireland. Yet this could be symbolic of the powers of the patriarchy, particularly in the Christian religion, controlling women and sexuality through the concept of 'sin'. The Nagas of Hindu and Buddhist mythology reveal this dual nature of serpents, that they symbolise renewal and evil, hopes and fears.

The myth associated with the Delphic site speaks of the Pythia as either a dragon or a giant serpent. Dragons have a similar esoteric meaning to serpents yet are connected to the body of Earth rather than our human body. Throughout history and more recently through ley line exploration, dragon energies are purported to be energy lines running through the Earth, similar to veins or meridians running through our human bodies. The concept of Earth ringed by meridians is based on Chinese medicine. These Earth energy lines are also known as Dragon lines and are the pathways of electromagnetism across the surface of the planet.

Magnetic images of Earth reveal veins of energy beyond our normal perception. They create an energy matrix much like the one in our own bodies. The ancients were drawn to these lines, especially where the currents intersect and energies are heightened. This is unsurprising given their deeply intuitive connection to Earth, their reliance on and honouring of her cycles. Many ancient sites such as Stonehenge or the Pyramids in Egypt and South

America are on these intersections, as are more recently built sacred places such as medieval churches. Yet again this indicates the takeover of ancient wisdom by patriarchal control. As patriarchy moved into the world of the mind, progress and expansion, our cultures lost connection with the true meaning of these ancient sites. They were literally hidden beneath the cold stone buildings of Mother Church. Our balanced intuitive and intimate relationship with nature, our knowing of the movements in the stars and their synergy with earthly life, the 'as above, so below', or 'as within so without', of our ancient cultures was being superseded by ownership, ambition and progress.

The takeover of the temple at Delphi by the cult of Apollo was just one aspect of the patriarchal control that was subtly, and sometimes more forcibly, taking power from the matriarchal and temple cultures over centuries. At Delphi Apollo was believed to speak through his oracle, the priestess. She had to be an older woman, pure in heart and deed, chosen from among the peasants of the area. Once dedicated to the role of Priestess of Apollo, she sat alone in an enclosed inner sanctum where a spring flowed beneath the temple, creating a cleft that emitted chemical vapours. According to one myth, when Apollo slew Pythia its body fell into this fissure and fumes arose from its decomposing body. Yet other ancient sources describe the priestess using natural means to inspire her prophecies. The priestess may have chewed oleander leaves or inhaled their smoke prior to her oracular declarations. The toxic substances of oleander result in symptoms similar to those of epilepsy which was known as the "sacred disease" in the early eras of Greek culture. The Pythia's physical spasms would have been seen in a similar way perhaps: as possession by the sacred spirit of the god Apollo. Later archaeological investigations revealed that the temple exists over a geological fault line from which toxic gases may have risen. Lacking understanding of the chemical components involved the Greeks would see the priestess become intoxicated and fall into a trance. They believed this indicated Apollo was in possession of her spirit. In this state she prophesied.

The Delphic oracle exerted considerable influence throughout the Greek world. She was consulted before all major undertakings including wars. She also was respected by countries around the periphery of the Greek world, such as Egypt and Rome. In a time and place where women's roles as priestesses were disappearing, the role of the Priestess of Apollo at Delphi stands out. Her position was at the centre of one of the most powerful cultures of the ancient world.

There are records of several women known by name who held the prophetic role at Delphi, including Phemonoe and Aristonike. The site became so busy at one stage that three Pythia were appointed to serve in the role simultaneously. The oracle prophesied to the powerful figures of the ancient world on a wide range of political and cultural issues, as well as personal questions. It was a position powerful enough to change the course of history. Yet over time efforts to deprive the priestess of her power prevailed. Some ancient sources suggest that the Pythia actually babbled gibberish and that her words were later put into deep and meaningful verse — by male priests. Whether this is true we will never know as other sources suggest differently. It seems clear that the priestess at Delphi is regularly named as the one and only source of the prophecies delivered there. It may be that over time the role devolved from one of being the Pythia Prophetess to Priestess of Apollo and then into being a priestess under the control of patriarchal influence. However it took place, over time the original role and sacred function of Priestess disappeared. History relates how the site at Delphi was raided and plundered and the 'unquenchable fire' at the centre of the temple was stolen. One wonders if this fire originated from the centre of the Earth. For in 381AD there was a major earthquake that closed the fissures at Delphi, destroyed the temple and changed the local landscape.

Vesta's place in the Universe – Astronomy & Astrology

Vesta was discovered by the German astronomer Heinrich Wilhelm Matthias Olbers on 29 March 1807. It is the brightest of the asteroids and one of the largest. It can be seen from Earth with the naked eye. Numerous fragments of

Vesta have been ejected through collisions with other asteroids millions of years ago and have been found on Earth.

Vesta's astrological placement in a birth-chart reveals how we connect to that which is sacred within us and where we place our devotion. In a mundane sense she is about authenticity, our capacity to stand alone, to be centred and focused. Her links to the ancient goddess rites and role of priestess, then Vestal Virgin, show our perception and attitudes towards sexuality – our openness and our fears, where we may judge or repress the natural flow of sexual energy, along with our capacity to serve and/or sacrifice. Vesta is happiest in retreat from the world or in service to that which she loves.

My Journey with Vesta

Meditation was my regular practice. Not only did it replenish my connection to stillness and peace, often I would receive profound guidance within a meditative space. This particular time guidance arose in the form of an image – an ancient stone gateway. I knew I had to pass through this gateway and that it would manifest in my life as an opportunity, an initiation. In my meditation I walked through.

Over the following days my meditations changed. Every time I closed my eyes, I would see a man. I had heard of this man, a spiritual Master, but had not met him. In this inner space I knew profoundly that we would meet and make love; that this lovemaking would be a profound initiation, the next step on my path. Understandably this inner opening seemed crazy, for I had no physical connection to this man. Yet every time I closed my eyes and went deeply into meditative space, this knowing appeared. It would not leave me and I could not deny the truth of my inner clarity. It had always led me well. Eventually I decided I had to act on what was being shown. The inner images stopped at once.

When the time is ripe life moves fast. Within hours of my inner shift towards action I received a phone call from a friend. 'Do you know this Master is giving a talk near your place at the weekend? Are you going to go?' I was not surprised. My commitment to follow through was being called.

The following Friday I went to the talk given locally by this Master. It was such an awakening, opening a powerful connection. As soon as this Master began speaking, I knew he was speaking as if from my own heart. The resonance of his words poured through me, moving me deeply. I was hearing the truth of my own journey, the conscious learning and growth that sat behind it, spoken by another. Following the talk, heart in mouth, I approached him and spoke of my inner knowing. His words 'Do you know I'm a Tantric Master?' meant nothing to me. I was innocent of that particular spiritual path. Nonetheless he revealed to me that lovemaking was a path of awakening. He had been graced in Realisation of the Divine Feminine. This Realisation gifted the capacity of opening a women's body into the truth of Divine Love. We agreed to see what unfolded. Yet life was already setting the path. We discovered we were both sharing workshops in the same town the following weekend. The inner gateway I had passed through in meditation was appearing. I had no idea of the profound awakening that was arriving.

Over the next months I connected deeply with this Master and the women in his life. Very soon I was living in the small spiritual community we created together. I didn't know it then but over this time I would be changed irrevocably.

I spent the next thirteen years living in this spiritual community with the Tantric Master and his partners, my sisters in love. My devotion to that path was total. It was my dharma. Although deeply true for me it was hell for my personality. Many awakenings arrived, taking me deep into the knowing of who I truly am, who we truly are as Beings on this Earth. I realised consciously and directly in my body that there is only one Divine Feminine in many women's bodies on this Earth. My courage at speaking my inner knowing had opened the door. The gateway was entry to Priestess Vesta's realm; she was awakened in this woman's body.

As I lived in the growing community that grew around this Master's teaching, the Vesta archetype continued to open in both my sexual expression and spirituality. My devotion to uncover and understand the truth of divinity within our humanness was fierce. I would question this Master again and again in terms of what he was sharing on that evolutionary process. With hindsight I can see how I was in a process of deepening integration. My questions were pulling down the enlightened perspective into the reality of our human realm. When our humanness was deemed 'an illusion' I would be ferocious in defending my deep Feminine knowing that form, matter, our bodies and human experience are as valuable and sacred as any enlightenment. I know now that I was healing the split that seems to exist between Divine Masculine as profound empty awareness and Sacred Feminine as matter. I was endeavouring to create a living bridge of understanding and integration between what I experienced in the pure infinite formless space I entered so deeply and an ordinary human life. Sexuality continued to be a potent aspect of that integration. It opened the gates of consciousness in this body.

Vesta's message: I find my Self within my self

If Vesta stands for the ancient priestess energy where might we find her in our lives now? It seems our world is devoid of devotion in the sacred sense of the word, especially when it comes to the acknowledgment of women's wisdom and the truth of our sexuality. Yet there is a grassroots revival occurring. Spirituality is coming out of the closet; the practices of yoga, meditation and tantra are opening doors to a reconnection to the sacred in every aspect of our lives. The roles of both men and women are changing as we step up, speak up and demand change. This revival is essential in the face of our cultural mayhem, environmental crisis and challenges of a pandemic. Yet any true change must be rooted in a movement for, rather than a protest against. It is only when we connect deeply to what is true within ourselves that we open the gates of understanding what is truly sacred in our lives and how that may be brought to life in our culture.

The Vesta archetype is the calling inward to deep self-connection, to the rediscovery of the divine within. Any time we close our eyes and allow the world of physical forms, self-expression, thoughts and emotion to drop away we are in the potential of connecting with her archetype. She is the calling within us that connects to something beyond, something that rests at our core. Vesta takes us into the truth deep within ourselves. Although her energy expresses predominantly through that inward pull, Vesta is also known in the movement to bring what is sacred to us alive in our lives through authenticity, devotion and focus. In sexuality she is the bridge that consciously unites physicality with spirit as a living union.

Authenticity comes from within

What does authenticity mean? And how do we know that we're being authentic? For me authenticity is about the truth of this moment. It's about connecting deeply within to discover 'What is deeply real for me right now?'

What is deeply true depends on where we focus. Attention to our physicality, thoughts and feelings might reveal a layer of what is true. Yet when we choose only from the mind, or our humanity alone, we may not be being fully authentic. Beneath the surface of experience lies our heart knowing of what is deeply true; this is Vesta territory. In the devotion to keep diving deeper within, our true knowing opens. It encompasses all we are experiencing on the surface with acceptance and brings it to wholeness.

Authenticity implies being aligned with oneself. This involves a willingness to enquire, reflect and deepen, in order to discern what's really behind our thoughts, feelings or perceptions. In our current cultural climate re-aligning often requires that we retreat or withdraw from the world. To become centred we need to stop the noise and cease the busyness. We need space, for space is an opening that allows truth to arise. We need to reconnect to our core truth in order to commit to what is deeply real for us.

Authenticity requires deep honesty – first to our self, then perhaps to another. It is only in honesty that we unveil our beliefs, agendas and resistance, and how relevant they are right now. It is only in honesty that we recognise a feeling of disconnection from our self and how we may be maintaining that. Honesty simply means owning up. Owning up with complete acceptance for what one sees is a key to authenticity. If we can see our own agendas with kind-heartedness, we naturally open a deeper space of connection within. Complexity makes way for greater simplicity and clarity.

Authenticity doesn't require us to be perfect or to get it right; it's simply a state of unity within unveiled through acknowledging our own complexity. Authenticity arises naturally in recognition of all aspects of oneself. It arises through the inward journey of discovery. Vesta is this inward journey; she is the pull to discover the truth of our heart's calling. She is the fire of authenticity that burns within us.

The pull inward

The pull inward to connect with our self may not come naturally. It may need to be cultivated. We may need to give it time and space in our busy lives. Sometimes it is life's circumstances or a crisis that calls us inward to reflect or connect deeper with ourselves. Sometimes it comes at a point of choice. We must weigh up options or find a consensus within. At times this is not an easy task. Pulled this way and that by conflicting needs or desires the only real way through is to go deeper. This is where connecting to the energy of the Vesta archetype is crucial. Vesta brings us to synthesis; towards a place where sacred really means 'What's vital to me?' 'What is it my heart is calling for?' or 'What serves the whole of this situation?' The fire we go through in the quest for synthesis is Vesta's fire, burning through the dross to discover what's at the core, to reveal what's truly sacred in us, to discover what we value most.

Making regular space in our lives for this inward pull supports us when a crisis calls. Touching the quiet inside on a daily basis gives us the capacity to more easily connect when we're stressed. Turning our consciousness inward then becomes a natural pull in any quiet moment. We build a foundation of stillness and presence that supports daily living and whatever it brings. Withdrawal from the world replenishes us. The ancient sacred rituals may

130

have gone from our lives in the main but what they represented is still alive in us. In withdrawal from activity we may re-connect to that ancient knowing, in essence if not in form.

Vesta represents our individual connection to divinity within, the divinity that we already are and may be endeavouring to live. That divinity will look and express itself uniquely for each of us. For some it may arise through nature, for others it might be to teach or nurture children. In others it may be through word, song or the creative arts. It literally is the calling to connect with and express from the soul.

The fire of devotion

Whilst living in community it stunned me that on the occasion I felt most at odds with myself or another, yet surrendered in acceptance to that experience, I would hear 'You look so soft and radiant'. What was going on to make the way I felt and the way I looked seem so different? One simple word; surrender.

Surrender opens the self-sustaining light of radiance that is Vesta's fire. It's the fire of acceptance of the whole experience in that moment. When we surrender our personal preference of how life should look, when we let go of thoughts and judgments about what we think is taking place, when we tenderly hold the sensation of our emotions as they vibrate in the body, we connect with what lies beneath all our vehicles of perception and expression. We connect to ourselves as a field of experience and something more. We connect to our innate sacredness. We burn in the fire of our own wholeness. This shines through as radiance. This consumes the inner dross in its fire of transmutation. This is Vesta at work. It is devotion to that nameless space within.

It seems like surrender means giving up or giving in. In truth it's the giving *up and in* to our Being, that which holds us through all experience; life itself. It's the quest for a deeper meaning to what's taking place, but without struggle, questioning or effort. It seems like surrender takes practice, but it doesn't; it takes willingness. The willingness to drop resistance, to let go of what I think I know; to be vulnerable; to discover what lies beneath and beyond what I'm currently knowing. It takes the willingness to drop my small self-concern and fall into something larger – myself as consciousness. In that more connected space within, the magic starts to happen - synchronicities occur, solutions naturally arise, opportunities open and transmutation miraculously takes place. Whereas when we struggle or resist that very energy blocks our way to healing and renewal.

We have a potential of knowing this 'letting go and dropping in' within sexual connection. Have you ever considered what deep surrender it takes for a woman to open her body in trust to a man's penetration? The sacred opening that can occur through such vulnerability is profound. Our capacity to let go everything simply into this moment of openness and connection can be truly transcendent. Here we may touch upon the true mystery of sexuality as the vehicle of Creation itself. We may recognise the inherent truth and beauty of sexuality, how it can be a voyage of discovery that takes us beyond the illusion of separation. How when man and women are truly devoted to sexuality as a sacred practice, they may know themselves as One, cleansing the physical and subtle bodies of the lower frequencies of energy. The passion of sexuality in its pure form is the fire of transmutation burning. This is Vesta's fire at play, cleansing and connecting all frequencies of self as One. It's as natural as breathing. Yet through our lack of real knowledge of her-story and the distorted beliefs we've formed about sexuality, such deeply transformative loving may be a rare experience.

Just as truly sacred sexuality takes us beyond our egoic self, cleansing the physical and subtle bodies, deep inner self-connection brings us the potential for renewal and regeneration. Dropping our sense of self into the pool of consciousness within ourselves we may discover that which deeply nourishes us – life itself. As we arise from this inner state back into self-expression, we are lighter – not just in what we carry and have let go, but in that reconnection with our essence. We rediscover our Self and bring the light of that back into the world with us.

The capacity for regeneration, either alone or with another, lies at the core of Vesta's energy. Whether we self-connect or whether we love, the connection we create opens our potential for renewal; it's a commitment to what inspires and nourishes us. What inspires us motivates the quality of devotion and our capacity for commitment.

Devotion in a mundane sense is focus. Like the fire of a laser beam Vesta's energy can take on focus when we find the truth of our heart. Devotion is soft and warming, whether through the silence of meditation or the joy of a chant sung out loud, its expression is full of heart. Or focus may be intense; it may involve mental concentration, acting like a laser beam. Behind both devotion and focus lies the truth of what is of true value to us. When we act on what deeply matters Vesta is expressing her sacred calling.

Embodiment as our birthright
The calling of the Vesta archetype is towards an embodied spirituality or service through our heart's devotion. Her Priestess energy points us back towards the body as a sacred vessel and the container for spirit. She opens us to the knowing of our natural purity as spirit in body. She represents our birthright to experience fulfilment and ecstasy within a human body.

When we give energy to what is truly sacred to us through focus or devotion, whether that's a sacred practice or a worldly task, we open up the potential for fulfilment. Fulfilment occurs when we feel complete in what we are expressing, sharing or doing. It's a state of fullness; body-connected, Earth-connected and spirit-connected.

Patriarchal thinking with its external goal orientation and endless pursuit of success or more, fails to bring fulfilment, or if it does it does so only briefly. This focus on success actually draws us away from fulfilment. It can also lead us away from our heart's true focus. Success means nothing if it's not connected to our core values. It can sometimes be the ultimate failure to live our lives in a meaningful way. The difference between success and fulfilment is our agenda; either towards external recognition at the cost of inner peace, or inwardly towards authenticity where we feel fully alive, yet we also rest in peace with our self and our source.

Being at peace does not necessarily mean we will not burn with passion or aliveness. Often to discover peace we must burn through layers of superficial comfort to discover the deeper rest. It's about becoming truly alive in the acknowledgement of that little voice arising from the heart imploring you to live in your deepest truth. It's filling up from the direction of inside-out rather than seeking fulfilment from the outside in.

Vesta reveals where we have potential to be truly fulfilled. Tending the temple fire was a priestess role. We can experience this inner fire anywhere we lose our self in expressing the calling of our inner passion. Artists and musicians know this fierce flame of manifestation; lovers express this living passion, as does anyone living on the seeming life-death edge of their creative expression. To be fully alive is to burn, sometimes quietly with the warming heart flame, sometimes with fierceness.

Our capacity for ecstasy

There is a state of being beyond fulfilment where the fiery energies of passion may take us beyond our small self. When we ride the emerging waves of our authentic desires, the potential for ecstasy arises. Aspects of ecstasy include delight, joy and rapture. We become completely intoxicated with the experience of pleasure and fulfilment coursing through mind and body yet taking us beyond mind and body.

The intensity of ecstasy takes us beyond body, yet it's also held within the body. It rises from root to crown chakra and beyond. The connections with serpent energy described earlier in this chapter are clear here. The kundalini energy coiled at the base of the spine unfurls and rises. Whether the catalyst is through creativity, spiritual practice or sexual opening the fundamental effect is the same. As energy courses through the physical and energy bodies, old skins are shed. The body becomes infused with light, renewed and reinvigorated by a surge of spiritual and creative power. We become 'enlightened' by our own passion and longing to express.

The partner to ecstasy is longing. At times the inner fire may be stoked more from a sense of lack, the feeling that something is missing, than from a need to express a passion. That seeming lack, when allowed to burn in its rawness, opens a longing for the ultimate fulfilment: love. Love of the divine, love of oneself, love of another. For love to open, the heart must be open; we must allow this feeling of lack to pierce us. When we do so we recognise our smallness in the face of the longing for that faceless nameless 'something more'. We become humble; we recognize the only true power we have is in surrender to 'what is'.

Longing can be the doorway to ecstasy, yet that is only possible when the heart is open, when we are actively surrendering; when we are open, vulnerable and raw. Strangely it is the honest acknowledgment of our lack that heals us. When we are humble, when we are empty, Vesta stokes the inner fire; we awaken, and we are filled. Humility is a key to ecstasy. When we are humble, the heart is at rest, awake to receiving. This openness heralds a capacity to serve what lies beyond the normal experience of self-expression, creativity or sexual connection. The longing for the numinous experience of being filled can then pour in, elevating us. In humility we are a channel for the profound blessing of spirit touching body.

A key to ecstatic experience is the penetration of the body-being by a higher frequency energy. For penetration to take place, openness must occur; or there must be willingness to allow an opening. When there is openness, penetration is an act of pure creativity that opens a new frequency of consciousness. Every artistic masterpiece, moving piece of music or creative genius carries this signature. That is why we are touched in our connection with it, whatever it may be. We are touched by the transmission and expression of an utterly new vibration of pure creativity.

This blessing of spirit touching body is spoken of in many esoteric and spiritual traditions. It is the Mystery descending on our humanity. Yet less is known of the ancient links between spirituality and sexuality; this knowledge has been hidden. In western cultures the history of the priestess and temple cultures was purposefully destroyed yet there are threads that point towards the intimate connection between sex and spirit in both Hindu and Buddhist tantric traditions still. In these spiritual traditions women were involved in tantra as teachers and guides in the art of sexual ecstasy and transformation. Here the conscious link between spirit body was kept alive. The knowing of key points on the body, how they activate neural pathways and connections within and beyond the body, is core to this knowledge. There are devotional rituals and practices that serve to open these channels within oneself and in sexual connection.

In these traditions the body is acknowledged as the vibrational instrument of the divine. The vagina is known to be alive and responsive, with agency. It opens in degrees like a flower opening in the sun ready for the bee to penetrate and pollinate it. This is diametrically opposed to the passive way it is viewed in the western mindset. Yet many women are touching on these mysteries through experience. My own experience of this is of my vagina opening and vibrating with pleasure simply sitting in the presence of a conscious man, even one I am not in sexual connection with. It is simply delightful, literally light-full. When a woman is open and ready in this way the vagina returns to its natural potency. In lovemaking it draws in the phallus, as the phallus also penetrates her body. Ecstasy is utterly effortless and spontaneous. There is nothing more natural.

This open way of ecstatic being is our birthright. When we are graced to open and be opened in this way, all forms are infused with light in pure flowing aliveness. All concepts dissolve. The belief in sin vanishes in knowing the purity of life. Sin is not sexuality as we have been taught. If there is such a thing as sin it lies in our disconnection from the naturalness of our sexuality and the blessing of its function as an avenue of expression and transformation for spirit in body.

Virgin territory

When we close our eyes, we enter a space of aloneness. When we fall into our inner world, beyond thought, feeling, vision and impressions, there is simply that – aloneness, spacious and pure. We could choose to see aloneness as wholeness. For when we dive deep beneath our surface experience what is there to see or know except a spaciousness that is whole? What is there to see or know except union with something more than humanness?

If we look at the original meaning of 'virgin' as meaning 'owned by no man' we get a sense of this wholeness. In Roman culture the Vestal Virgins and prostitutes, although split from the original knowing and unity of sacred sexuality, were women on their own. Men did not own them as fathers owned daughters and husbands owned wives; they had authority over their own lives. They had power and agency. And yet the split of spirit and sexuality had begun. The Vestal Virgins sexual energies were ruled by male control, on pain of death. Women's power and agency as Divine Feminine was being curtailed. It's a denigration and control we see growing through history to current times.

Go deeper into 'her story' and we touch the truth of the Vesta archetype as the connector of sacred sexuality and true virginity. The priestess in the matriarchal temples was the vessel of sexual service and devotion, the power of connection to the Holy. The knowing of the cleansing fires of sacred sexuality was alive, as both a renewal and purification for man and woman, of true benefit to the whole community. The priestess was self-contained and self-fulfilled in her devotion to the sacred rituals of body and soul. She cleansed and regenerated herself through her inner devotion. She remained centred through her dedication and commitment to the inner flame as well as the temple fire.

This theme of centredness remained even as the inner fires, the heart's devotion, became externalised symbolically in the hearth of temple, home or community. Yet its demise was perhaps inevitable, especially at the inception

137

of patriarchy. The Vesta archetype – as representing the link between sex and spirit held by the priestess - was replaced by Hestia, Goddess of the Hearth. As the original energies of sacred sexual purification and centredness became subdued into Hestia's hearth, a vital part of 'her story' was dying.

Reclaiming the Vesta archetype now renews our capacity to stand in our centre, to stand alone, yet with the potential for sacred connection through sexual union. In both states of being our energies may be renewed and replenished. The key lies in being fully open and connected to the source within oneself and also open to being penetrated by that same source in another. Vesta represents our capacity to bridge the intimacy of sacred union both within and without. To know ourselves as alone within and all-one in connection. It is only in this all-one-ness that we truly know our self as embodied spirit and we discover what is core truth. Through resting here, we get to know our self ever deeper; we discover what's deeply true both in our self *and* in any sexual union we're engaged in.

It is only the truth that will set us free. Vesta's devotion to uncovering that truth is a fire. It's the purifying fire within, in the temple, in the hearth, in sexual union and in the heart, at the very centre of our being.

The Shadow of Vesta

Too far inward? Too far out?
The Vesta archetype reveals to us how our connection to the inner world of divinity wants to express itself through devotion as service in the external world. Inner connection expresses authentically as outer focus. One of Vesta's shadows is imbalance in this flow. We can go so far inward that we fail to come out in expression of our true purpose of *being and living* from that deep inner space. When we go too far inward the danger is that we don't come out. The world becomes a fearful place. We isolate our self or we alienate people; we feel alone rather than all-one. This can lead us to feeling cut off and lonely, disconnected from the full authentic expression of our self and

therefore from real fulfilment both within and in our lives. Vesta's flame goes out when we dive into too much solitude.

Vesta's imbalance externally is revealed when we get stuck in outer focus, pushing and driving rather than truly serving from the deep inner well of connection. This happens when we misuse Vesta's fire of passion, creating burn-out. We become dry from over-doing, overly focused externally and failing to refill ourselves from our inner source. There are times we need to dive inward and away from the world in order to replenish. There are times we will be led by our deep inner passion into expression. In the healthy expression of the Vesta archetype both are aspects of the flow of living a connected life. This inner/outer flow is represented in the female body through the female reproductive system as a mirror for the natural pulse of life. Its functions of receiving and taking in through the vagina; fertilising through the release of eggs from the fallopian tubes; incubating, nourishing and growing in the womb; then either birthing or expelling through the pulse of contraction and expansion mirror the pulse of life and death in different creative rhythms. Much like the breath, there is a flow of life from source to body and back again, in and out, expressing and releasing, appearing and disappearing. Both are an essential aspect of the whole that the Vesta archetype represents.

A lack of this authentic and totally natural inner/outer flow is reflected in the challenges of our current world. Many people are exhausted in simply managing their lives. Finding the pause in the momentum, reconnecting inward to authenticity, refilling and moving from that deep inner connection, brings real aliveness to our lives and our world. When we pause to engage what's is authentic, our lives become our dharma, our sacred work. They serve our self and those we connect with. They serve the collective, simply because we are pointed in the most valuable direction; our focus is on being true.

Detached and disconnected

Vesta's energy expresses through being centred in the connection to our divine or true calling, yet it is something more. It encompasses the whole of life in its expression, including our sexuality as a sacred function of being human.

Wholeness is truly holy but how may we be whole if we are not being conscious with our natural sexual energies, which in truth are the source of creation on Earth. When we are cut off from the power of our sexuality, we are divorced from the totality of our life force. We aren't fully alive and awake; our fullest connection to body and earth is not active. When a deeper sense of aliveness or fulfilment calls to us, the sexual energy centres invite us into the deepest transformation; for they hold the power we have locked off through distorted beliefs and patterns. Our fears, doubts and beliefs held in the energy centres below the heart block our life-force. Their transformation is essential not only to our feelings of vitality and joy but to the release of creative power. To transform all the energetic vehicles of the body we need to get into the body. Sexuality is not the only route in, but it is a primary one.

Vesta's shadow is intricately linked to our relationship with our sexual energy. The power of this archetype spans our experience of sexuality from health to repression, from fear and feelings of inadequacy to over-indulgence and a lack of respect for our sexual expression. Vesta calls for sexual energy to flow, as its flow empowers the expression of our heart's devotion or service. If our priestess fire is locked away, we may engage our spiritual or worldly devotion and actions from the upper chakras alone, or only from the mind, taking us out of the body rather than deeply into it. This takes us out of this world where heart-based devotion is so needed. When we allow our self-expression or spirituality to be based only in the 'higher mind', we escape from the body rather than bringing our spiritual essence consciously into our physical realms. This is the outmoded model of spirituality, with its concept of physical life as 'an illusion'; it's the calling towards the heavens that is divorced from life here.

Transcendence is one aspect of the old hierarchical spiritual path. It is a legacy of the male way that denies the gifts of the body, our humanness and our Earth. It is relevant as one aspect of our evolutionary process, for to connect with the truth of ourselves as consciousness is profoundly real. But if spirituality is divorced from our humanness, suffering occurs. When we take the 'rise above' path (leaving the body, the challenges, our pain) into a serene but disembodied state of being, we not only forego a living spirituality, we deny our very human existence. We deny our bodies, the Earth and the Feminine aspects of the divine nature. We also abstain from our commitment to clear up the mess we have made on this Earth for our children and our children's children.

The energies of Vesta in our current collective culture call for sexuality and spirituality to be unified consciously. This is a vital act of empowerment. If we recognise that the priestess energy of Vesta has devolved into the role of the nun within our collective cultures, we can see how the totality of the Vesta archetype has been corrupted. The role of a nun is one of service to the divine, within community too, and yet the foremost aspect of the original function and sacredness of the priestess role has been lost. The celibacy of the nun utterly denies woman's function as creatrix within the Divine Feminine. This denial – in fact the labelling of sex as sin - has led to a dishonouring and distortion of women as equal but different from men. It's not just about the denial of sexuality; it's about the denial of women as the very vessel of physical creation. It is shocking to truly realise how much we have moved away from what is this very basic fact of life. Yet here we are.

Power and trauma

How did this disconnect from the truth of our nature happen? How could it happen when the truth of physical creation is so obvious? How has patriarchy actually managed to take us into the denial of woman's natural creative capacity as Feminine energy embodied? If we look into history, we might also see how the exploitation of women is a fundamental element of our disconnection from our Earth. It may be the play of evolution, but it is actually taking us to the brink of extinction. When you denigrate women, you

141

dishonour life and the source of life that she represents. Then life becomes a mind game for power. It's more than coincidence that as women have been controlled and abused so has the Earth. Disempowering the truth of our sexual energy is a major aspect of this denigration. Over eons the patriarchal need to have control has actively promoted the breaking of women psychologically and physically. For that control to be fully effective you must exert it forcibly, sexually and violently; for broken women do not protest. To disempower women, you damage the vagina. You imprint the female body and its psychology to be and remain powerless.

Our female bodies store what it is to be female. In their pure state they are the receptacle of life; the vagina as gateway and the pelvis acting as a creative bowl on every level of creative being. I explored this natural pulse of magnetism, attraction, fertilization and creativity in the Venus chapter. Vesta holds space for that creative process – however it appears - to be held and known in sacredness. When we are consciously in touch with both Vesta and Venus, we reconnect to our innate knowing of the body as the sacred instrument of the divine, with the vagina as gateway to the natural rhythms of life and death.

Just as the female body has a visceral memory of its experience, the vagina absorbs energy. One of the roles of the priestess was to serve purification through this intimate aspect of her sexual being. She would take in the lower frequency energies emerging through sexuality and transmute them through surrender, ritual and sacred practice. Just as the sensitivity of the vagina can serve divine connection, the reverse is true. Violation of the vagina can disrupt or sever a woman's natural connection to her divine nature. Violence to the vagina and rape imprint directly on the female brain, damaging the neural pathways up the spine that open the gates to ecstatic fulfilment and to union. Neurological studies now confirm how rape not only traumatises a woman, it activates the survival response within her vagina (fight, flight or freeze) switching her off from her connection to creative power. She becomes numb as her vagina freezes, or she becomes defensive and aggressive as a mirror of the force perpetrated on her.

Sexual violence also changes a woman's brain chemistry, affecting her capacity of speech and physical balance. Research has shown that a woman who has experienced sexual violence literally cannot hold herself upright; she lacks stability and grounding; she becomes a 'pushover'. Rape and sexual abuse, even sexual dishonouring, are the most effective control mechanisms, if control is your aim. They destabilise women. The same is true of our relationship to the Earth. Our rape and desecration of the Earth and her natural resources is destabilizing her delicate balance of eco-systems.

To state that a women's whole sense of self is rooted in the vagina seems extreme, but it is truth. The vagina is the doorway to the creative power of the womb. The womb is where the future of humanity is nurtured. It is also where we energetically incubate the next phase of life. When we disconnect physically and psychically from this inner place of potency, we not only walk this beautiful Earth asleep to our creative potential, but the whole of humanity also suffers. As women it is our sacred responsibility now, in partnership (and often in forthright honesty) with the men who come into our lives, to consciously address this imbalance. At the core of this response-ability lies our relationship to sexual energy; to dive and delve deeper in our understanding of what sexuality actually is as a sacred aspect of our being in human bodies on this beautiful Earth. It's to consciously engage and heal the sexual trauma in our bodies and the stored body memories from generations of women before us, with support, love and tenderness for ourselves in the rawness of what is uncovered.

For our world to change, the recognition of Woman as the creative vessel on Earth must be reclaimed. Vesta, woman as priestess, must be liberated. We don't know how this may look in our evolving culture, yet the fire in our hearts will guide us all individually to contribute and uplift our old paradigm wherever we are deeply called. It's clear the imbalance in our world – women as sexual objects and sexuality misused for commerce – calls for us all, men and women, to awaken, for the sacred nature of Woman to come alive. The Vesta archetype no longer lives in a temple or uses temple practices as her life expression, although that may be one aspect of this archetype's contemporary expression. She appears wherever we feel a passion to serve, to give our inner fires expression, to act on what's truly important to us, to utilize our capacity for focus and devotion in service to the heart's desire. She's alive when we feel the need to withdraw, retreat and replenish, and to create sacred space for our self.

For some women Vesta may involve the practice of sacred sexuality with different partners, for others it may be a lifelong devotion with one. For some women celibacy may be a conscious choice, yet if it's as avoidance of sexual desire, or of intimacy, Vesta is operating in the shadow zones. The patriarchal beliefs about woman as a madonna or a whore, or sex as sin, run deep. In reclaiming the Vesta archetype, this potent and very natural aspect of our being (whether we are sexually active or not) we are retrieving wisdom from deep in the female psyche; we are healing the split between soma and spirit. In reclaiming our own inner connection, our authenticity, our devotion to what is vitally and sacredly important within and the sacred nature of our female body and sexuality, we are taking the path of devotion and service that is Vesta. Our bodies are thirsty for her sacred revitalising essence. Our Earth needs us to take on her sacred role. It is time. It is beyond time.

Chapter 4
We Are the Cycles – Ceres

Tears
are the pearls
that water God's garden.
Let them flow
sweet woman.

Your grief
is the fuel
for Love's fire.
Your surrender
the gateway
to God's Heart.

Let the knife
cut deeper.

The wound
will open you
to purity and grace.
The fire
is the cleanser.
The water
the softness
of woman's healing.

Allow it all.
The one you have lost
is with you still,
his life is lives on
in Thee.
Cassandra Eve

Archetype: Earth Mother

Symbols: a sheaf of corn; sickle or plough; poppies; bread

Message: Life is change! When we flow with each season, we grow.

Ceres themes: connection to the Earth and its cycles; mothering and nurturing; food and its production; belonging; women's mysteries; love & loss; death & dying

Shadow themes: grief as endless suffering; the over-attached mother; powerlessness; the abandoning mother

How Ceres expresses Venus's energy: through learning to give fully to every season of life's natural cycle

Also known as: Demeter, Greek Goddess of the harvest. Her daughter Persephone is known in the Roman myths as Proserpina

Ceres is the great Earth Mother archetype whose capacity is one of unconditional love and nurture. She is the mother archetype and yet more than that; she is guardian of the processes of life, mother-child rearing and relating and women's mysteries. In her mythology Ceres was forced to learn through death, the letting go of life as it is and the journey into its gift of evolution. Ceres in us reveals our calling to embrace all the cycles of life and reap their harvest. She guides and teaches us to let go of what has served its purpose and move into the next season of life. She can reveal to us pathways through grief, to embrace the gifts of loss as well as the mothering qualities of nurture and abundance. She is the embrace of all seasons of life.

Her-story

The myth of Demeter/Ceres and her daughter Persephone is well known. Homer's 'Hymn to Demeter' relates the tale of love, loss and growth. Its echoes reach into our own times with its themes of abduction and rape, powerlessness and redemption. Behind the widespread myth is a deeper story; its meaning is connected to the cycles of life, death and rebirth within our lives and within all our human civilisations. The myth arises from a time when the Mediterranean cultures were being over-run by invaders from the north. The destruction and desecration of the Goddess temples that occurred at that time heralded the beginning of the patriarchy. Prior to the Olympian Gods Demeter was known and celebrated as a face of the Great Mother Goddess. Her meaning was to evolve, as is portrayed through her mythology. This evolution brought forth a deeper understanding of the processes of growth and evolution. Its gift to humans was freedom from the fear of death through the sacred rites and rituals of the Eleusinian Mysteries.

Demeter loved her daughter Persephone beyond any other. They loved to wander together in the garden of the Gods, sharing the beauty of nature. They were at one with each other, needing no other. Nowadays we might say they had a co-dependent mother-daughter relationship.

One day whilst in the garden with her maiden friends, Persephone spied in the distance a beautiful new flower birthed by Gaia. It was a deliciously fragranced narcissus, never seen on the Earth before. Persephone wandered off from her mother and friends to take a look at this new flower. This was the moment everything changed. Suddenly the earth cracked open. Hades/Pluto Lord of the Underworld appeared from this fissure driving his black chariot with six jet-black stallions. Here we find two versions to the myth; one tells us that Hades abducted Persephone, another that she went willingly with him into the underworld. However it happened, Persephone did shriek with fright before the earth closed over, leaving only a bunch of withered narcissi to witness her transition. Hecate, the Goddess of Magic, resting in her cave, heard her cry and noted it.

Meanwhile Demeter, feeling something was amiss, called out to her daughter. Hearing no response, she began to search frantically for Persephone. Fruitlessly she searched the garden, then the Earth, looking for her daughter. Wandering amongst mortals, disguised as an elderly woman, she roamed the Earth and she grieved. Persephone was nowhere to be seen.

Eventually, in her disguise, Demeter came to Eleusis where she became nursemaid to Demophoon, the son of Queen Metaneira. Loving the boy as her own, Demeter fed and anointed Demophoon with ambrosia by day and put him in the embers of the fire at night, with the purpose of making him immortal. She was trying to re-create her time in the garden of the Gods with this child. Yet despite her love of him Demeter still mourned her daughter.

One night Queen Metaneira discovered Demeter placing her son in the fire and screamed. She thought Demeter was trying to kill her boy. Demeter had no option then but to reveal her identity as a goddess. She threw off her disguise and stood in her power. Queen Metaneira and her household were in awe. The old nursemaid was actually a goddess! Demeter instructed a temple be built at Eleusis where in time her Eleusinian Mysteries would be celebrated. Whilst Demeter's true state as a goddess was now known and celebrated by all around her. Yet still nothing would console her in her grief for Persephone.

Eventually Hecate, realising Demeter's plight, came to her and shared what she had heard on the day of Persephone's disappearance. Together they travelled to the Sun God Helios for they knew he would have witnessed the events in the garden on his daily travels across the sky. Helios revealed the plot hatched by Persephone's father Zeus and his brother Hades, Lord of the Underworld. Together they had schemed to break Demeter and Persephone's bond and for Hades to take Persephone's hand in marriage. Demeter was furious. Nonetheless she pleaded with Zeus that she be reunited with her daughter. He would not hear her, so Demeter withdrew her fertility from the earth. It became more and more barren, cattle died and the people were starving yet still Demeter continued to dwell in her grieving. All the Olympians came down to encourage Demeter to let go of her grief but to no avail. Realising that all the animals previously available for sacrifice to the gods were now dying, Zeus eventually agreed to intervene. He sent Hermes/Mercury, the messenger god who could travel through all realms, to reclaim Persephone from the underworld.

Meanwhile in the underworld Hades and Persephone were getting to know each other well. Persephone sat on her throne as Queen of the Underworld with Hades by her side. Yet she pined for her mother and their time in the garden. As Hermes arrived in the underworld, Hades knew Persephone would soon leave him. Afraid she would not return to him from visiting her mother, he persuaded Persephone to eat some pomegranate seeds, the fruit of the dead. In this act he ensured she would come back as his queen.

Persephone was reunited with her mother Demeter. In their joy the Earth's fertility returned. The crops grew, the animals flourished, the people ate and sacrifice to the Gods resumed. Yet all was changed between Demeter and her daughter who had now become a woman. Having eaten the pomegranate seeds in the underworld Persephone had to return. So following the harvest every year Persephone is reunited with Hades. Nature dies back, the fruits fade and the leaves drop; just like Persephone, nature returns below ground.

Through Demeter and Persephone's experience evolution was accomplished. The natural cycle was fulfilled. They had come through winter and received a profound learning experience. In honour of Persephone's return each year, Demeter shared her mysteries as a gift to the people. They became known through the rites of the Eleusinian Mysteries in her temple at Eleusis. These rites helped to diminish the fear of loss and death in the people. The cycle of birth-life-death-rebirth was recognised and honoured in its entirety and its purpose. Demeter's grief had revealed its gift of growth and renewal.

Ceres's place in the Universe – Astronomy & Astrology

Ceres is the largest object in the asteroid belt between Mars and Jupiter. It is now classed as a dwarf planet.

The placement of Ceres in a birth-chart reveals our capacity for unconditional love and nurture. She opens up the wisdom from our journey through the cycles of life, particularly through the experience of death and letting go, whether that is the letting go of children to become adults, the ending of relationships or creative projects. As Earth Mother Ceres is the keeper of women's mysteries, she can indicate the gifts and challenges of menstruation, conception, bearing a child or menopause. Ceres is often highlighted strongly in the birth-charts of midwives, doulas and child-carers. Chefs or anyone connected with love of food, its production or distribution tend to have strong Ceres placements. Wherever she is placed there is a focus on nurture and nature, and the journey through loss into a new place of fertility and harvest.

My Journey with Ceres

My relationship with my son Matt was challenging and yet deeply loving. As a new mother, holding and caring for this baby came very naturally. I was blessed in the gift of immediate connection with this vulnerable child. Although I didn't know of her then, the Ceres archetype was expressing her sweet mother nurture in our connection.

Matt was always an independent boy. As he grew it became clear my nurture of him was only a necessary foundation for much more. At age eight he completely surprised me by declaring he was going to live with his father. No-one had talked about it; he had simply decided and so it happened. He now needed the experience of male energy and on some level he knew this. I let him go. Although I didn't know it yet, his soul was beginning to play the role of Pluto, Lord of the Underworld, to my mothering need. Despite my shock and grief, somewhere within me I recognised that truth. Matt was a soul on his journey doing what he needed to. Within a year he was home again.

As Matt moved into his teen years the challenges became greater. Aged sixteen he left home and spent time drifting between different relatives. Clearly he was lost on some level. As a single parent I was deeply challenged in trying to support him. We already knew the current education system was not meeting his creative needs. I knew, even then, he had to find his own path. How to find the balance between holding space and allowing independence was my constant question. I did not want to be an interfering mother. I had experienced parents who were overly controlling and in many ways was taking the opposite approach. I allowed him to be himself and couldn't find the right boundaries to support his growth well. One way or another he began to find his own path young as he was. Our relationship foundered but he was taking the journey into becoming a man. This was my only comfort.

Then Pluto arrived again, this time in the form of drugs. At first it was cannabis, then heroin. The underworld was pulling Matt in. Initially I did not recognise the signs. Perhaps some aspect of me didn't want to. Matt was living in Brighton now; occasionally visiting me, usually when crisis hit. Then he met his life partner, a beautiful Indian woman named Rohini. Soon they were pregnant. Rohini had been an addict and gone cold turkey to come off heroin. Her story gave me heart. Perhaps together they could make it?

After Curtis, my grandson, was born Matt & Rohini married. Events unfolded just as in the Ceres myth. On the wedding night Pluto charged in with his black horses. He took them down. This time he appeared as heroin, used with the excuse of celebration. Knowing Curtis was safe with me they had entered the underworld willingly. Chaos ensued.

After a night of little sleep, deep in the uncertainty of 'What can I do?' by morning it was clear. I knew the first step was to talk to Matt. Our conversation was honest. I had been through a marriage with an alcoholic husband, so I knew the traps. If Matt was not prepared to take full responsibility for his habit and recovery, I could not help. If I stepped in to support him, I was simply enabling. My love and concern for my grandson was overwhelming. Yet I had seen the soul strength in his little body. I knew he was a warrior in the making even before this latest episode in his parents' lives. I felt torn apart; it was agony. I wanted to help so much. Yet I knew the truth; I could not help without Matt and Rohini's acknowledgement and step up in responsibility. Our conversation revealed my son was caught between the habit and his need of me, yet he was not ready to stop.

After much agonizing deliberation I stepped away. It was heartbreaking for us all. One memory kept me sane. Matt had shared with me a meditation experience he had before using any heroin. He had experienced a deep opening into his true nature as consciousness. I knew that opening would grow in him somehow. It gave me hope that one day he would liberate himself and his family. Meanwhile I had to let go totally.

Despite my physical absence in their lives, over the next months I endeavoured to keep in touch with my son and his family. Every attempt failed. Eventually I discovered they had left their home. There was talk of drug dealing and other nightmare scenarios. No one knew where they were. It was terrible. My grief knew no bounds. Yet I knew, I had done what I could. Inevitably change would find its place in our lives. I had journeyed with Pluto too. I had come through. I prayed they would too.

Over the years as grief took me, its waves overwhelming, the only comfort I had was that my son, his wife and grandchild were following their soul journeys. Through blessed openings, it became clear that the grief I was feeling was not just personal. It was the grief of every parent who had lost a child to Pluto's underworld, to drugs or alcohol, mental illness or disease, abuse or rape, separation, or even death. Knowing that helped; it opened a door through which grief could be seen with clarity. I learned to simply allow it, knowing that my release was also a collective one. Knowing that when we are graced to love, grief is inevitable.

Eight years on, a door opened. Following a sudden intuition to call Matt's father I discovered where Matt was. They had just heard from him. He was clean. Matt's wife and child were thriving, but not with him. The journey of maturing had found its right place for them. Yet there is no happy-ever-after ending. He had not seen them for a few years and continues to follow his path of disappearing regularly. Like his mother, he is a gypsy; but unlike his mother he has no roots - yet. Perhaps his roots are in that wandering?

The full teaching of Ceres is to love and let go, to care deeply and let go, to nurture then let go, to allow the flow of a cycle to move naturally onwards. Pluto acts as the catalyst in this cycle. He takes many forms. He appears as the challenge of change and sometimes as life's most challenging experience. Ceres is the one who holds the aftershock. It is her role and her challenge to move it through. Her role is service to the continuation of the cycle, whether that's in nature or in our lives. She is the living experience of the knowing that life is moving on constantly. She reveals that in the embrace of all seasons, light and dark, our potential is evolution.

Not everyone's path with Ceres will look the same. Mine has been full of dramatic change. There have been many underworld journeys and much loss. We all face loss at some point. Its sting can be terrible. We may never get over it. But in some ways, if we are wise, if we allow it to open us, we learn to live with it. In embracing the winter of our grief, despite its cold, we live with the ever-present potential of spring. We are the cycle. Perhaps all that life asks is that we live it as well as we can. Through that we evolve.

Ceres Message: Message: Life is change. When we flow with each season, we grow.

Ceres as ancient goddess of the grain and the harvest represents the natural cycles of growth and abundance. Yet her mythology reveals a fact that is always present - the only certainty in life is that everything changes. Ceres and Persephone in the garden were happy, one might even say blissful. They were blissfully ignorant of their need for growth perhaps. Some myths state that Ceres was turning away suitors for Persephone's hand in marriage. Yet change was inevitable; they were powerless to stop it. Persephone wandered off from her mother. The new flower she saw was calling her; it represented the dawn of new experience. Persephone was ripe for change; perhaps she had the growing yearning for something new but was not conscious of it until Pluto appeared. She was the maiden ready for womanhood. Pluto and her father Zeus's plotting came at the right time. Pluto's appearance as the agent of change was evolution at work – whether Persephone went willingly or not. The next stage of maturity was upon her and arriving for her mother too.

Just like Ceres and Persephone we cannot avoid life's tides. The darkness is one with the light. The cycle is eternally moving, and our challenge is to move with it; change is unavoidable. Ceres, as a relationship goddess, was not made to stand alone. Her gifts were to nurture, to care, to sustain and to cultivate the harvest. Yet life brought her change and growth, as it does us all at times. As guardian of life how could Ceres not know death's sting and coldness too? In her aloneness and grieving of what was lost, the seed of new life was planted. It would bear a deeper, sweeter harvest grown through pain as well as love. It was the completion of the whole cycle. Ceres mythology shows us how we move through the entirety of a life cycle or a process: life and death, love and loss, pain and growth walking hand in hand. She reveals the gifts we may receive in what may feel like devastation. She reveals the mystery of life's eternal process to renewal.

Nature's seasons are this flow of life and death through emergence, expansion and contraction. Each day mirrors this. Every moment reveals a potential for expression and its demise. We cannot hold onto the pulse of life's expression. In truth the life that happened a moment ago is already becoming another expression. Some forms are here for a moment then fall away. Some forms last a season, a lifetime or a millennium. Eventually the cycle completes but Life remains. Ceres shows us how to meet each phase with grace and surrender to that truth and its flow.

The gift of nurture and bonding

Ceres primary quality is nurture. As mother her role is one of caretaking. It's an abundance of caretaking, not simply doing what's necessary. It's the maternal instinct that deeply knows what is needed, without thinking about it. Principally that nurture is physical, yet her care is expressed on every level. As Earth Mother she is responsible for the cycles of sowing, cultivating and tending that lead to the harvest. Often Ceres is depicted with a sheaf of corn, her abundant nature evident in the fruits and grains of the natural cycle. She is bounty manifested. She is generosity itself. Her beautiful daughter Persephone is the harvest of her care as mother.

Connection to others is a vital part of our being human. Our primary connection to our mother and the bonding she may offer during our first days in a body set the scene for our future relationships. Ceres is a relationship goddess, so her natural place is within the sphere of loving. She takes care of the process of attachment that is vital to our wellbeing. She is the one who provides, the full breast that satisfies or the bearer of the bottle that ensures we don't go hungry. In a similar manner, in her role as Earth Mother, if the seed is not sown and tended, there will not be a harvest. The foundation created at this first stage of the natural cycle sets the scene for what follows.

Ceres establishes our foundation in a body. Given adequate nurture during our early days we discover a sense of safety and security in being on the earth in a body. We grow physically and emotionally. We begin to develop a sense of belonging. At first that may be felt through mother's warm arms, or those of anyone who plays Ceres role. Then we expand out that sense of belonging to include others, family, friends and a sense of place in the world. As we mature, we may learn that we belong primarily to our self but that those around us are vital to our wellbeing.

In a healthy cycle of development love and care, nurturing and tending gradually give way to letting go. This begins shortly after birth when a mother first gives her newborn to another to hold. It may feel like a physical wrench to do so but it's a necessary shift. Detachment continues as the child matures and becomes more independent; it is necessary for growth to occur. What would happen if a mother does not allow her child to leave the breast, or to take the risk of walking? Nurturing has its small losses every day. These losses make way for growth and independence. In healthy mothering, nurture and attachment are combined with letting go to create a balanced relationship. Yet who amongst us knows this perfect balance? We tend more towards one than the other perhaps, depending on our own upbringing and emotional capacity. A mother's love for her child never dies but it must change and evolve. This is not an easy assignment. The bond that's essential at the start sometimes has to be broken.

The wheel turns

The myth of Ceres reveals to us the whole of a natural cycle. Spring's burst of life to summer's abundance to autumn's letting go to winter's quiet leading to rest and replenishment and the uprising of a new spring. If we look at the natural life span of a human being we can see this same cycle at play: birth and childhood as the physical growing phase of spring; summer as the fullness of adulthood; late summer revealing the potential harvest of a life well-lived; autumn as enjoying the harvest; then winter with its contraction and death. Just as nature sometimes storms and heaves itself into the next phase of life, the natural flow of a human life does the same. At times that flow may be interrupted. Life may not move to natural completion through a full cycle but move abruptly from any of its phases to death. We are not immune to life's processes; we live them. The fact that a human being may die at any time shows us we are not beyond nature; we are part of it. We are one with it.

We may see this same cycle in the inner aspects of a human life. Our emotions flow from light to dark; we are moved by life experience to know both joy and despair. One moment our mind is open to the possibilities of new perspective, the next it's locked down, rigid like the earth in winter. If we are in touch with our spiritual being, we will know times of immense faith and light, then times of testing. We may not have thought about it, but we know the flow of life's rhythms intimately, both inside and out. It is our very nature to express as the Earth expresses; to expand our creative expression, to birth new forms, to enjoy the harvest of experience, to let go, then rest and rejuvenate before arising with new creative potential. This cycle takes place over a lifetime, in our daily lives, even in every moment.

Ceres qualities of bonding, nurture and attachment are a necessary foundation for life. Yet they must give way to detachment in order for growth to take place. In a healthy development these phases of care, nurturing and independence walk hand in hand. Yet in Ceres's myth we see how life can sometimes tear apart our attachments. This tearing apart is actually an opening that provides the potential of growth for both Ceres and Persephone. Ceres moved through grief into an understanding of the full cycle of life. She was moving from the experience and archetype of Mother towards Crone, the elder wise woman archetype. Persephone's growth came from the innocence of maidenhood into the beauty of woman, in her case as Queen of the Underworld.

The truth is love and grief are intimately connected. Grief is the price we pay for risking fullness of life and love, for enjoying bountiful connection and intimate expression. To love fully makes one vulnerable to life's unpredictability and to the certainty of loss, at some point. The Ceres archetype represents this abundance of nurture and care that at some point must make way for the fullness of grief. It seems tragic yet it is necessary. John Updike wrote in his memoir, *"Each day, we wake slightly altered, and the person we were yesterday is dead. So why, one could say, be afraid of death, when death comes all the time?"*

Ceres reveals to us the necessity to adapt to the challenge of loss. The season of winter reveals this to us visibly. In our connection to nature we will recognise its necessity, even its bare beauty. In winter nature is stripped back to her essential elements, a skeleton devoid of flesh. The soil, broken up in the cold winds and frosts, is being made ready to release the nutrients that are necessary for good growth. The breaking of the old soil is part of the natural process of renewal, refining the land, making the soil friable, releasing nutrients that support seeds opening and young roots anchoring. Winter is a great power waiting to be liberated by the return of its source, the sun; the return of light awakening the earth's cycle of growth, flower, fruit and seed. We are the same. When loss walks with us, we long for the sun to shine on our grief. We await the return of hope even whilst denying its existence.

If we don't acknowledge or allow the experience of loss, we suffer. We may want to prolong the abundance of summer's love, yet we grow stale in avoiding the next stage of the cycle. The potential is that through our resistance to change we become stale and deadened to its gifts. Our struggle not to lose or change only exacerbates the pain of loss when it eventually arrives, as it must. Yet when we allow the whole experience of life, spring is certain. Life's calling to renewal is incessant. We are the life that will flow into newness - but only with our own willingness. We must learn to trust in the natural processes of life. We never know exactly how spring will look but we do know it is certain to arrive and that it brings a bounty of fresh new growth. It's the same with our lives.

When we allow loss, when we fully rest in its arms, the rejuvenation that follows is unquestionable. Yet we must wait. Just like Ceres in her quest to find Persephone, patience is required. We need to cultivate the capacity to willingly allow life's rhythm to deepen. We have to hold the knowing of spring; trust has to be called in. Ceres carries us through these hard times. Her journey through the whole cycle is our guarantee of emergence.

Just as nature veils the winter landscape Ceres was unaware of the purpose of her loss whilst in it. The next phase still had to be revealed. Here we see her

159

role as Earth Mother and guardian of women's cycles. Conception takes place in the dark, deep within the mother's womb. In the earth when the ground is bare and cold there is no sign of spring's new flowers. We know flowers will come but not in what form or abundance, or exactly when they will emerge. Loss requires we allow a space of unknowing, that we allow the inner conception of the new cycle to take place.

Letting the mystery of life have its way with us allows the magical places of renewal to ferment in the deep dark. We are simply required to develop the maturity to let go, to know winter's still space as an essential part of life's process. In truth we have no control over creation. We cannot avoid loss as we are participants in the mysterious natural process of life. Loss encourages us to rest deep in the Mystery from which we emerge and to which we will return.

Finding what we belong to

Returning to Ceres mythology we see the gift of life she reveals. On the completion of her trials and her reunion with Persephone she bequeathed the understanding of the whole cycle - life, death and rebirth - to the people through her Eleusinian Mysteries. Ceres had thought she belonged with Persephone but in losing her she found her deeper purpose. Isn't it the way of life; that in losing we open a potential of something more? For Ceres the evolution through loss opened the gift of wholeness. Not only was she the provider of food and loving nurture, she became the provider of spiritual sustenance. She brought that gift to her people through the Eleusinian Mysteries. These gave the people a ritual of recognition, a sacred sense of belonging to the whole cycle of life. Death (whether of the body or life circumstances) was being acknowledged not as the end of life but merely one of its stages.

The promise of loss is we may find we belong to the cycle of life itself and that, as Shakespeare so wisely said, "All the world's a stage, and all the men and women merely players." If we can relax into loss and its partner grief, despite its raw ache, if we can acknowledge that it is but one phase of a life's cycle, we may begin to connect with something beyond the cycles. A profound knowing of belonging, both to the cycles and beyond them, then begins to open. This belonging is our union with Life itself. We experience this first in the mother's womb and potentially at her breast. Through life experience we appear to separate from this initial knowing. Yet perhaps that seeming separation is simply to return full circle to where we truly belong. It's a paradox, held in Ceres mystery, that we leave, we detach and yet we return. It's the mystery of Life itself, unified and yet appearing in many seemingly separate forms. We believe we belong to the forms, or that the forms belong to us. Yet beyond that lies the truth; we belong to Life itself.

This sense of belonging is what is known when everything else disappears. It appears sometimes when all else seems lost. Some would call it Source. Yet whatever we name it, it is whole, fully inclusive of our humanness and its experience. It is not something we return to; it is what we are. When we belong, there is no separation between what we belong to and ourselves. Belonging is inclusive in a felt sense. We feel 'at home'. A baby knows this. It cannot name 'mother', or 'breast' yet it feels its comfort. A mother in her flow of nurturing knows this too. Yet we cannot stay in this space; life's forms move on. When what we think belongs to us is removed, we are called to look deeper. Loss compels us to ask, 'To what do I belong now?' and removes all the false answers. Perhaps in the end we come to know 'I belong to myself and something more I cannot name'.

When we truly open ourselves up to the experience of loss, we open the heart to belonging. Through 'being longing' - our longing for what has been lost, or for something to comfort us – life begins to move on. Potentially we discover we belong to something greater than the current experience, deeper than the anguish or despair that loss may bring. We encompass the fact that life gives and life takes away, and we are released. In the grace of that opening we begin to know we are held. Loss is still a challenge, yet we also connect to the unfailingly magnificent and abundant nature of life's flow towards renewal.

A deeper sense of belonging is grief's gift to us. Its potential is that it opens a belonging that cannot be removed from us. Perhaps nature's longing to express itself is what gives birth to spring? For it is our desire nature, our longing for something more or different, that will give rise to our next adventure, our next spring. Loss is both the training ground and the foundation for new life. Our surrender and tenacity through its rawness bursts forth in new life as the new cycle begins to take form.

Ceres's myth shows us that we are never far from loss. In the completion of her trials the loss of Persephone was still with her. That fact had not changed, as each autumn Persephone returns to the underworld as Queen. Ceres feels her grief anew, the land becomes bare; yet there is the promise of spring even in this starkness. Ceres reveals the integrity of the whole cycle. The reminder of loss may emerge in any season. Death is a fact of life. Underpinning the truth that we exist is the knowing that one day we will not. Softening to loss is opening the heart to that truth yet also to hope, to the promise of redemption and renewal. This is what the Eleusinian Mysteries revealed – the triumph of life over death, the living of the understanding that everything is both temporary and a gift. The price of life is always death. What expresses falls back to silence; what emerges or is given birth, grows, flowers and dies. The cycle is eternal. Our acceptance of this is a point of maturity that gives birth to wisdom. Ceres is our guide in and through every part of this eternal cycle.

Guardian of women's mysteries

Ceres, as guardian of the natural cycles of Earth and human life, also holds guardianship of the cycles of woman. The mystery of menarche, ovulation, menstruation, pregnancy, birth and menopause, are part of her mysteries, as are the challenge of their shadow energies: barrenness, abortion, miscarriage or the loss of a child.

The mystery of the female cycles reflects the pulse of life's natural cycles. They reveal the unity of the processes of life within women and the Earth. Each is a mirror. The ebb and flow of the tides, the cycling of the Moon, the pulse of night and day and the rhythm of the seasons; all is emerging, expressing, coming to fullness and completion only to begin again. Our lives as female reveal the innate rhythmic connection we have with nature.

Traditionally the Moon is seen as the guardian of women's menstrual cycle. Her cycle of waxing and waning to and from fullness connects intrinsically with our bodies' menstrual rhythm. As the Moon rules the tides of the ocean, she carries the tides of women's blood. Yet here we meet the Feminine nature of cycles within cycles, rhythms within rhythms, tides within tides. The Moon tides align in the same flow as the seasons, carrying the potential of life and its harvest, then its passing and renewal. Ceres is the same yet has one difference. Although primarily her energy holds the space of pregnancy and mothering, her cycle is evolutionary; it opens a new spiral of growth. Her cycle is going somewhere rather than cycling around in the same rhythm. Ceres opens and expands from the Moon cycle when there are evolutionary shifts for women within its flow.

Menarche, a girl's first menstruation, is the opening of the natural unity of the Moon and Ceres. It is the doorway to woman's role as creatrix of physical life. Menarche is an emergence; it's the promise of womanhood and the potential of becoming a mother. Yet menarche is a loss too. It's the loss of innocence. If not held well in its awesome mystery, it's the opening to the shadows of woman too – to shame about our body and its functions, to what might be seen as the inconvenience of 'the curse'. Resistance to the shedding that occurs at menarche reveals to us how collectively we have moved away from the 'letting go' aspect of the natural cycle. It shows us how disconnected we have become from our bodies, the Earth and her cycles.

Persephone as maiden is the guardian of the menarche aspect of the cycle and yet it is Ceres, the mother archetype, who either nurtures this transition in a supportive way or not. Ceres holds the space of bountiful nurture for the emerging woman, or as in her mythology, attempts to hold it back through attachment to her innocent girl. If we look back to our own first experience of menstruation, we see the differing responses of mothers to this transition;

163

the reaction of embarrassment or denial, the flippant or practical response, perhaps the clear explanation of what was taking place or a rare honouring of this step into maturity.

Pregnancy is within Ceres guardianship through its process of conception, gestation and the emergence of birth. Pregnancy is the blooming stage of the cycle, much like summer. Here Ceres abundance finds its natural purpose and fulfilment in the growing of a child. It's that feeling of being 'born to be a mother'. I recall feeling exceptionally well when I was pregnant despite relationship challenges; I simply wanted to stay in that state. Yet it's in pregnancy that we also experience Ceres in the losses connected with infertility, miscarriage and the death of a child at any stage of the cycle.

If we consider the myth again, Ceres adopted the care of Demophoon in her loss of Persephone, but it did not mitigate her grief. The anguish of not being able to bear a child or of losing one is perhaps the deepest form of anguish for a woman. Yet even this must find its way of balance in our lives somehow. Perhaps it only comes to rest in learning how to live with, and perhaps despite, such deep heartache. Did Ceres anguish subside when Persephone was returned to her? Perhaps for a while. Yet the knowing that her child was gone from her and emerging as a woman, meant there was no return from that loss, only a potential evolution. Just as autumn and winter storms come powering through clearing the way for new life, loss brings its own rhythm of storms and quiet, hope and renewal.

Every stage of women's cycles reveals the synergy of letting go and the arising potential. Childbirth is both a loss and the start of a new cycle. The physical unity of mother and child through pregnancy is emerging as a different form of connection. Birth brings its surging physical challenge of letting go, of the death of one's former self in order to become a mother. It is a huge transition. The birth of a child carries an enormous surge of natural power. It's painful, yet in the pain a profound understanding about moving through the natural cycles with power may be born. It's an opening to understanding the natural forces of creation. It is woman's connection to her natural unity with the Earth and its own heaving birthing processes. A woman loses her prior state of being when she becomes a mother. She goes through a huge learning curve about her power to move with the tides or resist them.

Every birth is different but just like spring it has one common thread: breaking through. In the process of birth, a mother potentially learns what breakthrough truly is and how to flow with it. If she tries to force her baby down the birth canal, she experiences pain. If she resists the power of the movement, she also knows pain. It's a lesson in life's natural rhythm and allowing them to carry you. Force means tightening in resistance, trying to achieve or get something completed, or struggling to avoid its full energy. Power means open active engagement and surrender in the same moment, riding and co-creating the movement of birth with the wave of a contraction. It is this openness to life's fullness of power that facilitates breakthrough. It's a power that births a child, yet also a new woman, a mother. This new phase brings deep learning about the qualities of selflessness and love, generosity and commitment. The woman who was no longer exists as the Mother archetype and its experience is born within her.

Just as in birth, a human being's impulse to grow and express is sometimes painful. We may have to break through the shell of our former self. Like the roots and shoots of new plants we may experience incredible tension as new life breaks through the earth of our old existence. In the discomfort of tension, the temptation is to interfere in the natural process: to try and push it, control or make it happen. Ceres teaches us to be fully with the process. This tension of birth may activate old fears and doubts, resistance to change, places in us that are uncomfortable with the uncertainty of new life. This is natural, for just as soil must move to make way for new roots, so we have to open and move for change to land in us fully. Soil has to give way yet hold firm, open yet nourish; so do we.

Just like childbirth stretches a woman's capacity to open, in our lives we are required to open and stretch for new possibilities to be born. We are called to let go and open to birth a new human being, whether that is a child or a new version of our self. It's this tension and calling to open however painful the experience that stretches our capacity as co-creators to walk the bridge between old and new, past and future self. It's a wonderful synergy of patience and readiness, letting go and moving forward with the wave of what's emerging.

Ceres reveals the synergy of loss and growth in every part of women's cycle, as well as its natural wholeness. Other goddess archetypes, as well as the Moon, rule the processes of a woman's rhythms and role as creatrix and guardian of life on earth, particularly Juno as the guardian of marriage and commitment within all relationships. Yet Ceres is the caretaker of each part of the cycle and its infinite spiral of evolution. In her loss of Persephone Ceres unwittingly entered the birthing pains of crone energy, held by the goddess Hecate. Similarly Ceres holds the transition a woman makes as she enters menopause, when the loss of physical fertility may be mirrored by the 'empty nest' of children leaving home, the loss of a job or business, or the seeming emptiness of the aging process. Her movement towards crone and grandmother energy inevitably takes us through an experience of psychological death.

Even where we have faced loss consciously before, for example, through the forfeiting of youth, through the process of mothering, or the loss of a loved one, menopause is a truly deep initiation. Just like Ceres, in menopause we are called to discover new meaning for our lives as women. For Ceres this new meaning emerged eventually as the expression of her Mysteries. She became a guide for the people through their ritual enactment of the natural cycles. Paradoxically through the loss of her main focus of love, as mother to her daughter, she actually expanded her mothering energy. She moved from personal mother to impersonal mother, the one who provides spiritual sustenance. She became the one who has a wider circle of arms for those who need her, who simply cares because she does, or who doesn't care simply because she doesn't, who is moved to express her creative nature in a deeper more soulful sphere. The potential of menopause is a rebirth where a woman not only loses who she has become but discovers the potential to move into a deeper sense of self and soul connection. Ceres is the bridge for this transition between the archetypes of Mother and Crone; a step over the threshold towards the wise crone energy held by Hecate and other Dark Goddess energies.

Ceres Shadow Themes

Grief as suffering

The potential of loss may arrive at any stage of the natural cycle, seemingly at random. Loss is inevitable at some point. Grief as a response to loss is natural; it's part of the cycle of change. Understanding the Ceres archetype is supportive in revealing to us how we react when faced with change. She demonstrates how to flow in conscious power and understanding, by allowing the process of grief to fully take us. To feel it is to heal it.

In its purity grief is not shadow energy; it's simply a release. But when we define our self by taking grief as our identity there's a different story unfolding. We enter a place of suffering. Suffering is different to grief; it may be felt as depression, lethargy and hopelessness, even despair. Suffering is not a release; it's a contraction of grief; it's a close down. When we contract or close down, we are hanging on to grief. We've become the dark cloud of anguish rather than letting the energy of loss pass through us in tears and roars of anger.

Suffering happens when we pull in and grip tightly. When we find ourselves fighting or refusing the fact of loss, hanging on to what was before, people we love, our roles and identity, we prolong the experience of grief. When we deny the fullness of our pain, we create suffering; we perpetuate the pain that we *could* deeply feel and let go. Suffering is a halfway house; we're no longer fully alive but we refuse to die to what was. We can see this in Ceres myth when she put Demophoon in the fire to make him immortal. She was endeavouring to replace her daughter Persephone and her former role as mother. She was trying to enter the immortal realm of happiness and bliss again. Although Ceres was clearly feeling grief, still she was resisting its fullness.

Creating a persistent sorry story from our pain creates depression. It's our modern epidemic, arising from disconnection to the natural flow of life from light to dark, happiness to sadness, love to disconnection and so on. No emotional state is eternal in the human realm, unless we cling to it. Perhaps it is partly fear that keeps us holding on to the memory of love or the good times? Sometimes it feels safer to hold fast to what was rather than fully feel its loss and then move on. Yet when we fully allow our feelings to arise, knowing that feeling is part of this life's human journey that has come to deepen and grow us, we allow our old story to gently dissolve. Then it can sit tenderly in our knowing of our capacity to love and be loved. Loss becomes as much a part of us as love is. We recognise we are always vulnerable in our humanness and that life's only constant is change. We become wise in knowing somehow the mystery of rebirth does arrive, in right time. Ceres brought this to life in human knowing in the rites of the Eleusinian Mysteries. Death became known as part of a constant cycle to renewal.

Sometimes renewal is just a matter of time. Sometimes it's about loving ourselves enough to *allow* growth through pain, or to recognise what we do to ourselves by holding on. Perhaps deep grief never leaves us, but the moving on is in learning to live with it well, in allowing it to flow and release as and when it arises.

The natural cycle of change has integrity. We can see this in our seasons. If we lived in constant summer the land would become parched and dry, unable to sustain life let alone new growth. We see this in our current cultures with its focus on constant expansion yet its lack of richness. In our own lives in not fully allowing the dark aloneness of loss we do not become whole human beings. Suffering consciously opens great gifts of humanity: strength to endure, resourcefulness, tenderness and compassion. When we grieve well, we do not suffer. Yet speaking openly about grief is not generally encouraged. The Irish culture gives us a pointer to the gift of loss, for their term 'wake' shows us death is an awakening point. Awakening to the calling to celebrate a life well lived. It is not to deny the darkness and pain of grief that follows loss; it is to embrace it, fully, as a part of life. In that intense embrace we may find self-compassion, we may discover healing even in the fiercest agony; we develop a wisdom that knows the eternal cycles and can flow from dark to light, pain to joy, loss to fullness. The Ceres archetype holds open the door, for us to know and embody the full cycle.

Attachment - The all-consuming mother

Was Ceres overly attached to Persephone? It's a strange paradox that the bonding necessary to raise a child well can become a hindrance to maturity later. Without doubt there was some resistance to change at play in Cere's refusal of Persephone's suitors. Perhaps she was trying to protect her child in keeping her safe. Yet when she rejected the natural emergence of the next stage of the maturing cycle, life came in however (in the form of Zeus and Pluto's plotting) and opened the door. Change often arrives in this way, like a storm. In this case it was masculine energy bringing the change. Yet perhaps that's often the way? Zeus and Pluto paid no heed to Ceres attachment to her daughter. It was time to move on and they were the agents for change. Ceres was powerless to prevent the loss of her daughter. Even in the light of her emerging knowledge of Zeus and Pluto's plot, she was still powerless to affect a return to what was before. The nurturing stage of life had been broken and rightly so. Masculine power to detach was pitched against Ceres's power to love and hold. Evolution was enacted in the experience of this meeting. What Ceres experienced as powerlessness over her own and her daughter's fate was actually evolution at play.

The journey of maturation requires a fine balance between connection and detachment. What is required in the early stages of mothering can be a hindrance to growth later. Attachment and the need to protect must evolve as a child matures. Our biggest learning through Ceres journey perhaps is in holding our children, or anyone we care about, fully yet lightly. Maturity requires the allowance of change and growth to occur and unfold naturally at every stage. This is where we see a paradox of unevolved Ceres; her very nature works against her when it comes to change. For she is naturally the nurturer. Yet she is the Earth Mother Goddess where all is changing constantly. It seems strange doesn't it? In the myth we see how her abundant capacity for mothering was holding back both her own and Persephone's potential for growth. Yet still life moved on.

In exploring Ceres shadow we see how an overly attached mother can be destabilising and disempowering for her child. Over-protection holds back development. Over-indulgence makes a child soft, lacking the opportunity to develop the necessary strengths that equip it to face life's inevitable challenges. If 'mother always does it' the child is rendered powerless in the name of love and actually exists in a state of co-dependence. The need to control or possess in a mother can be energetically paralysing for a child. It's actually destructive of growth. Dependent on mother's love, disempowered in developing its own resources, the child becomes stuck at a certain stage of development. We could see this as a psychological umbilical cord that passes the psychic energy of dependence between mother and child. One or both can feed from it in an unhealthy way, rather than cut the tie that binds to allow true freedom.

No matter how much the capacity for deep nurture there is in a mother, evolution must take place. Detachment is natural as part of a maturing cycle. Nature shows us this. Each year I'm fascinated to watch the development of gull chicks on the roof across from my lounge window. First these small grey bundles of fluff appear. Mother and father fly in all day with regurgitated fish for their two or three chicks. The chicks rate of growth is astounding. Within weeks their fluff turns to feathers. Father disappears; mother's visits lessen but when she does arrive a dance of bobbing and squawking ensues. As feathers grow, the chicks start to leap and jump. Testing their growing wings, they leap then hover for a few seconds, or peer over the edge of the roof as if they know this is a temporary resting place. Eventually mother flies off. The chicks are on their own. They have to fly, or they will die. Within a few days I notice one less chick; one has fledged. Soon the roof is clear; the play of maturing doesn't stop though. Walking on the promenade I see the chicks, still squawking, following mother. The bond is broken though; she turns her back whichever way they hound her. She keeps turning her back, minute on minute, constantly refusing their pleas for food. Persistent as they are, eventually the chicks get the message.

This example shows in many ways that we are no different to nature, except perhaps in our capacity to resist the flow of life. In the capacity of mothering it's essential to recognise the signs of the phase we're in and follow them. Have you noticed how insistently the two-year-old wants to do it for him or herself? That's healthy; it's essential, although at times inconvenient. Children, given a chance, will follow the natural flow of detachment, especially in their early years. A mother who's wise, who has her own sense of self, will acknowledge and empower this for her children for she knows we disempower both our self and others when we hold on for too long. We see this in women who care too much – the wives who mother their partners, those indispensable women at work, the interfering mother, the therapist who says 'yes' to just one more client when what she really needs space for self-care. What triggers this all-consuming need to support beyond what's appropriate? Is it truly love; or is it something else?

The inability to stay no, to set clear boundaries, to honour individuality, can be Ceres in her shadow of attachment. This over-caring, over-controlling aspect of a woman's nature has its basis in fear. Initially that fear may be about not being a good-enough mother, or fear her child will come to harm, yet at later stages the foundation of attachment may be based more on sub-conscious fears. When we stay involved for too long, we avoid having to face change that may be frightening. We avoid having to step into uncertainty. Whether we know it or not we derive a sense of power from occupying a certain position in life. It's not about the role per se; it's about attachment to security disguised as the role.

Ceres shows us how attachment of any kind held beyond its right time may render both mother and child powerless. Not only does the maturing adult remain a child, but the mother's role also becomes based increasingly on fear rather than love. There's a difference between sharing and caring from love and an agenda. We all know and feel an agenda when it's coming towards us. It's sticky; it can be interfering, out-of-place and inappropriate. It offers no value to giver or receiver. Ceres shadow can come disguised as 'love', yet its energetic hook is based in insecurity, moving from the fear of not being valued, the fear of being alone or unwanted, the fear of being rendered powerless. We may see this shadow in manipulative mothering, where a growing child (or even an adult child) experiences an unfair price to pay for maturity. It expresses in the manipulation and often unspoken threat of 'If you do that, I won't speak to you ever again' or 'If you leave me, I'll die'. The need of a mother to remain in her role can become an insidious, even vicious, compulsion to stay attached. As can the need to feel valued or reassured in all of us at times.

There is power held in our attachments. There appears to be power in the status quo. We feel safe when we know how life looks. We feel secure when we know the source of our love is assured by a relationship. Is this true though? Change is always imminent, even though we may deny it. The truth of attachment is it has a payoff — I am loved, I am valued and so on. Without doubt we all need to feel and know we are loved. Yet attachment soon grows stale, manipulates or disconnects when its needs are not met. Attachment, although essential at various stages of relating, is never fully satisfying, but love is. For love to remain fulfilling though, it needs space to grow and mature, to express in new ways. When we try to hold love in a certain place beyond its time, there is a potential that it dies.

As a relationship goddess Ceres's greatest fear is to find herself alone, unable to share her love. Ceres needs to nurture; she needs to care, even in her evolved state. So understandably she did not want to lose the object of her love, her daughter. Yet if love comes from fear of being alone, if co-dependence lies beneath our relationship connection, we will not reap the true gifts of loving. Ceres attachment to Persephone was fuelled by resistance to change, by fear of what that change would mean. A mother knows that one day she will face the empty nest her children grew in. The loss of her role may be both terrible and freeing. Yet all relationships must evolve. Terrifying as it may be, it is in standing aside from our former roles, when life calls it, that we open the potential for a new kind of connection, a new level of loving.

Throughout the course of a lifetime it's inevitable we will find ourselves alone. Perhaps this is the cruellest part of the natural cycle? Like the earth in winter life is cold. Yet our capacity to face the fact of our innate aloneness is to embrace the truth. This was Ceres challenge, to face her aloneness. Even in her attempt to make Demophoon a god it seemed she failed. Nothing would assuage her grief at Persephone's loss. Ceres had to learn that aloneness is part of the cycle. We are born alone; we die alone. We face this aloneness every night when, letting go of the day we have lived, we make the transition to sleep. We do this simple inner letting go alone, in the trust that we will wake. There is no guarantee however. Who knows what lies ahead in the darkness of the night's journey? We simply let go. We have no choice.

The abandoning mother

The attachment of mother to child is essential to a child's life in its first weeks. Ceres's shadow of mothering may express equally through the inability to connect and nurture however. Some mothers do not experience the natural post-natal bond. Birth can be tough; some mothers are simply too exhausted to connect with their newborn naturally. At other times a mother may be too unsupported to give any more. It's hard not to judge that aspect of our self that sometimes simply cannot cope. Mothers are supposed to cope says the belief system; mothers have endless resources say those soft photos of mother and children frolicking through a wildflower meadow. The ideal is utterly unreal yet it exists.

We arrive at mothering with the pattern of our mothering capacity set to some degree. We mother as we were mothered, or perhaps we do the opposite. Either way we may be out of balance. Some of us may not be equipped to mother well, if at all. We may not have the resources or the required strengths. We may not know how to love simply because we have not been loved. If we have not known the tenderness of nurture or

173

unconditional acceptance of our basic needs, we may not have a capacity for the same with our children, let alone our self. We may not know the selflessness that mothering calls forth. It's as if the mothering cycle gets stuck in winter. There is not enough bounty passed from the previous cycle of mother to child to carry through. The cycle repeats rather than evolves.

Ceres abundant loving nature in its shadow aspect can also give rise to a state of close-down, withdrawal and rejection at a later stage of the mothering journey. Anything may trigger this; life simply becomes too much. A friend of mine would lock herself in the bathroom for twenty minutes when her husband came home from work. She couldn't bear another minute of her toddlers pulling or climbing on her. She simply needed space. Yet sometimes withdrawal can become embedded in a mother's psyche. She simply cannot cope. This withdrawal may be depression; it may be anger at the demands of mothering turned inwards; it may be the neglect or abandonment of her children. It may be a sense of powerlessness over the simplest things, such as the needs of her own body.

If we look at the myth for clues about this withdrawal, we may see that in her grief Ceres natural abundance began to diminish. That is the natural flow of the cycle, when scarcity follows a period of growth and maturity. When Zeus refused her plea to release Persephone however, Ceres consciously withheld her bounteousness. She simply chose to withdraw. It was a way of establishing power where it had been removed. This withholding of her essential capacity for nurture of life was Ceres anger turned inwards. She became the destructive mother, refusing to express her abundant loving nature. In holding back her essential nature she was endeavouring to reclaim her sense of self as mother, her power and her need to bring back her daughter. It was a means to punish Zeus and also potentially Pluto. Yet Ceres's resistance was futile; her passive-aggressive behaviour although effective in Persephone's return, did not fully accomplish her desire. The old mother-daughter relationship was gone. Life had moved on. This was Ceres major learning. The cycle must turn; life changes. She could not redeem her love through going back to how it was before. She had to move on from the

174

Garden of the Gods. She was thwarted and yet paradoxically she was fulfilled. For in this enforced change her love found its new place, expressing as spiritual nurture of her people through The Eleusinian Mysteries.

The truth of Ceres's journey is that mother love has to become unconditional. It calls to evolve as our children grow. We see this play in nature. The trees don't hold their leaves in autumn; the buds don't fear to break into flower or to become the seed. Nature is unconditionally flowing. Ceres calling is always to growth through the darkness. Whether that shadow is our own inner world or external circumstances is immaterial. Ceres gift is in discovering the power to move *through* the cycle. In moving through it, no matter how forsaken we may seem, evolution is known. Love is rediscovered in another form. The capacity to nurture and care finds another landing place.

In truth, we are always being challenged with the seeming fact of our own powerlessness in the face of change. Ceres shows us how we react and hold on in the face of change yet how we have the potential to respond well to its inevitability. We are powerless to avoid change. Recognising this fact is maturity. Embracing change comes through living its flow. This is Ceres's ultimate gift. We are the cycle.

Chapter 5
The Call of The Wild – Artemis

Raw landscape;
mountains kissing sky;
light piercing dark clouds;
hawk resting on air,
still, watchful,
ready to dive;
vibrant liquid
turquoise lake,
mirror for light and form;
rock poised
at the brink,
as if to fall at
wind's breath
or earth's shake.
ripples of land;
soil, grass, stone,
Nature's golden sensuous
tear my heart
open
with desolate beauty.
Something in me
Screams
'Too much; too much'
Wild nature,
empty, stark
yet full of beauty.
Heart pierced
in tenderness
by this earth-shattered
Otago landscape.
Cassandra Eve
Written whilst living in New
Zealand following a series of major
earthquakes

Archetype: Big sister

Symbols: sickle moon; stars; a torch; animals - bear, horse, deer; Amazon warrior; the hunt; bow and arrows

Message: I am free; don't fence me in

Artemis themes: sisterhood; protector; competitor; a guardian of childbirth; independent feminine spirit; an Amazon warrior yet also a Moon Goddess

Shadow themes: vengeful; without mercy; independent; cool and aloof

How Artemis expresses Venus's energy: through protection of the young and vulnerable

Also known as: Diana (Roman)

Artemis is the Greek Moon Goddess of the hunt, wilderness, fertility and sisterhood. She is the twin sister of the god Apollo and one of the Greek pantheon who lived on Mount Olympus. Artemis spends much of her time in the forest and wilderness with her companion animals. Despite being a virgin goddess and having no children of her own she is a guardian of childbirth and protector of young girls, as we will discover through her mythology. Like all the Greek Olympian gods, Artemis was immortal. Her special powers included perfect aim with a bow and arrow, the ability to turn herself and others into animals and the gift of healing.

At a very early age Artemis asked her father Zeus for a silver bow and arrow (silver for the moon), fifty ocean nymphs, twenty wood nymphs and a pack of hounds to be her constant companions. She asked for the mountains as her realm and for her father Zeus to grant her eternal virginity. All her companions were virgins, so Artemis came to be associated with chastity. She was very protective of her purity and seriously punished any man who dishonoured her in any form. Her virgin purity hides a vengeful nature towards anyone, especially men or gods, who cross her or abuse those she protects.

Legendary Greek Homer, presumed author of the Iliad and the Odyssey, calls Artemis either "The Mistress of Animals" or "She of the Wild". Just like her brother Apollo, and representative of her function as a Moon goddess, Artemis is also known occasionally as "bright" or "torch-bringer."

Her-story
Whilst Artemis was a Greek Moon goddess, portrayed with the horns of the sickle moon on her head and often accompanied by a companion stag or dogs, her roots lie in ancient Asia Minor. One of the largest temples built in Asia Minor was the Temple of Artemis in Ephesus. This temple was so impressive that it was named as one of the seven wonders of the ancient world. Little remains of this temple that is now located in Turkey, yet it was clearly of great importance to this early culture, as was Artemis. It was a major place of worship and ritual for the Great Mother goddesses of more

ancient times. At Ephesus Artemis was worshipped as a fertility goddess, identified with Cybele the Great Mother goddess in those lands.

The statues of the Ephesian Artemis are vastly different from those of mainland Greece, where she is depicted as a young woman huntress with her bow and arrows. Those found at Ephesus show her as a mature woman standing upright with what look like multiple breasts on her chest. There are many theories as to what these 'breasts' represent. Some say they are breasts, others that they are a bull's testes - as bulls were sacrificed to her. It seems certain that whatever these shapes are, they represent fertility. Fertility was a function of the ancient Mother goddesses worshipped in ancient cultures, with their naturally intuitive connection to Earth as Mother. As the Artemis of Ephesus was taken on by the Greeks however, as with many other Greek or Roman goddess archetypes, her meaning changed. One could even say it was diminished as is the stature of many goddess archetypes under the growing patriarchy.

There are many myths involving Artemis some of which we will explore in the section on her shadow energy. We find the first mention of her in the Greek culture in a myth that relates to her birth.

Artemis was the first-born twin sister of Apollo the Sun God. The twins' mother was a nature deity named Leto and their father, Zeus, chief god of the Greek pantheon on Mount Olympus. It is said that Artemis was born in Ortygia on the island of Sicily. Her mother had fled there, afraid of the jealousy and vengeance of Zeus's chief wife, Hera (Roman Juno). After Artemis was born, she assisted her mother to flee to the Greek island of Delos, where she helped birth her twin Apollo. The birth took nine days due to Hera's vengeful efforts to thwart Leto's claim on Zeus as father of her children. Artemis's support of her mother during childbirth was a key foundation for her guardianship of childbirth and the young.

A second myth relates Artemis's role as protector, not only of animals, girls and women but of the gods. This myth relates how two giant brothers, the

Aloadae giants, grew so powerful they threatened the home of the Greek gods on Mount Olympus. The god of war Ares tried to stop them but was defeated and imprisoned for thirteen months in a bronze urn. Artemis was more tactical in her approach. She discovered the giants could only be killed by each other, so she disguised herself as a deer and jumped between them while they were hunting. Both brothers threw their spears at the deer, but she dodged them skilfully. The twin brothers ended up striking and killing each other.

Artemis's Place in the Universe: Astronomy & Astrology

Asteroid Artemis is a main-belt asteroid that was discovered by Canadian-American astronomer J. C. Watson on September 16, 1868, at Ann Arbor Observatory, Michigan. Artemis is known as a dark asteroid due to its carbonaceous composition.

In an astrological birth chart Artemis is a symbol of freedom and independence, sisterly love, and feminism. We might call her our inner adolescent or wild one. Her archetype is reflected in our psyche as the calling to the wilderness, our connection to animals and nature. Artemis placement in a birth chart often points towards where we crave freedom and have a reluctance to commit. She reflects where we seek independence beyond societal and social constraints, and where we will fight for that freedom. Yet she also represents what we seek to protect and defend, particularly those we see as vulnerable. Artemis placement may also be connected to where we 'hunt' or are constantly chasing something.

My journey with Artemis

My connection to the Artemis archetype involved both contradictory aspects of her nature in one experience. Her strength and fire, her numinous connection to nature, were both born over one summer's night on a Master's Course with my first spiritual teacher in the early 1990s.

We were in a Hamphire woodland, our venue for an overnight vision quest. The plan was to spend a day and night alone in the woods. Unlike the true vision quest where one would rely solely on nature for one's needs, we were well prepared, taking various means of support - a tarpaulin to make a shelter, pen and paper, a knife, water, a torch and a whistle (a means of summoning help in case of panic). As I entered the woods and found my spot, I felt I was ready for anything. We were to be without food for twenty-four hours however and that was certainly the biggest test for me at that time.

I had picked the darkest, most well-hidden spot that I could find for my quest. Surprisingly, as I did so, I realised that I felt no fear about being alone in nature, or even in the dark but I was also aware that could change. Who knew what the night would bring? I'd decided not to use a tarpaulin for shelter but be open to the night sky and the elements. The other eleven participants were located within shouting distance but out of sight – or so I thought. Our facilitator would be camping on the edge of the woods, well within earshot of a whistle. As each of us settled in we were left alone until the following morning.

I started my day with a strong sense of adventure. I was fairly certain that I could get through anything life would throw at me from the elements and was excited by what the vision quest might bring me. My space was nestled into a cosy hollow amongst a small group of beech saplings. I was exactly at the centre of a circle of trees. It was a perfect setting that offered me a feeling of natural protection. After settling in, I decided to meditate, to set my intent and ask for support and guidance through the quest. As I quietened and allowed myself to relax, I felt very much at peace. Stillness arose through my body. I felt at one with myself and all around me. It felt as if nature had opened her arms to me.

As I dropped deep inside myself in meditation, suddenly I felt compelled to open my eyes. It was as if I had been nudged from within. I surveyed the scene before me in amazement. The natural grace of the leggy beech saplings and scrubby undergrowth was etched with shimmering gold light. I witnessed a beauteous dance all around me as millions of twinkling rainbow lights flickered from the leaves and branches. It was as if all the elementals were dancing. It was simply enchanting. I felt the beauty I was witnessing dancing inside me, nature fully alive in my body. Such beauty; such bliss. Then suddenly it was gone, blocked out by my startled response to a shout from behind me. It was one of the male course participants and he was furious. As he approached my sanctuary from through the trees he was yelling "Get out of my space woman". His aggression catapulted me from the experience of beauty to one of fiery reaction. "It's my space not yours!" I responded vehemently. There followed an angry dispute about who should be where.

My course companion told me that he'd wandered off for a walk only to find me in full view of his camp on his return. He was adamant that I'd intruded and that it was not the spot I 'd originally chosen. I was happy where I was and knew it was the place I had picked. I was determined not to move and said so, despite my fear of being anywhere around such an angry man and very aware of my vulnerability in such a place once it got dark. Eventually, seeing I was not going to move, he went back to his camp. His return was not gracious however. At intermittent intervals I would hear angry mutterings thrown in my direction. Still I was determined not to give up what had become my sacred space. As the dappled sunlight turned to lengthening shadows, I prepared to dig in and defend what felt like my territory. "How dare he invade my woodland" I thought. Artemis had awoken.

The day passed with ease. I meditated, watched the changing light moving through the trees, wrote a journal entry, then I just sat. It was as evening approached and I began to feel genuine hunger pangs that I started to feel vulnerable. Nonetheless I reminded myself I intended to be here for the duration. I had the whistle to call for help if I needed to. As night drew in, I continued to sit. I listened and witnessed the subtle movements of nature around me. I meditated; I prayed; I wrote. I felt held by the presence of the nature; the land and the trees were my guardians. I was alert, awake to the smallest sounds, and as the dark surrounded me with its blackness, I felt safe. Not everyone did though. At one point in that long night chaos broke loose in the woods around me. A sudden screaming, a frantic whistle blowing, the beam of a torch through the trees, a crashing of footsteps, it appeared someone had had enough. I took comfort in the fact that help was indeed at hand if I required it. As the woods returned to their dead of night silence I gradually dozed off.

As the sun rose, I stretched on the damp earth where I'd eventually succumbed to sleep. Everything around me sparkled and glistened with diamond-like purity in the soft dawn light. The natural world smelt and looked so completely fresh and new. It was beautiful. I felt an incredible peace as I drank in the glory of being so connected to the natural world. As I sat, a young deer tentatively approached through the trees, pausing as he spotted me sitting silently nearby. We gazed at one another for what seemed an eternity. Then he moved, slowly picking his way through the trees, intent on some unknown quest. I felt so blessed in this animal connection. It held such a soft sweet natural beauty. Moreover, I had survived the night. Mother Nature had held me. In that recognition something deep within me shifted. I connected with the power of my own nature found and mirrored in the natural world. It was a moment of profound revelation. As I allowed this realisation to penetrate me, I noticed a figure approaching through the trees. It was my course companion; the angry one. Arms held wide he was grinning at me. "I'm sorry", he said sheepishly. We hugged.

Whatever had played out in that fight, was healed. Our night in communion with nature had transformed it.

Artemis message: I am free; don't fence me in

One with the natural world

Artemis has two distinct aspects to her nature. One is an inwardly orientated Moon goddess, at one with nature and its rhythms, the other is a wild and free spirit. As sister to sun god Apollo it seems natural that Artemis would be associated with the moon. This moon goddess aspect is connected to her virginity, much like the sickle moon represents the newly emerging maiden phase of the moon cycle. Artemis moon qualities are those of the sickle

185

moon, renewed from its meeting with the sun at New Moon. This phase represents what is emerging for the next full moon phase. One could call it a youthful moon; its qualities being subtlety, numinosity and intuition. This moon aspect is connected to the process of emergence in the natural world – seedlings, the birth of young animals and human children. At this time the new form is vulnerable, requiring protection. This is Artemis's role.

The sickle moon world is one of emerging light. In the natural world at night it casts a subtle light on the environment. This light is muted and mysterious; nothing can be seen clearly. Navigation has to be through intuition, sensing and feeling, allowing instinct to guide the way. Artemis represents these same qualities within. Like in the world of dreams we don't see the inner terrain with our eyes. When a new form of life or self-expression is emerging through us, we cannot at first know how it will manifest. Our need is to be delicate with this vulnerable stage of a process, to navigate by our moon nature, to protect the intangible form that is opening, to allow it to find its natural way of being. This phase of the moon, although emerging, also represents our hidden needs for seclusion and privacy. What is tender and budding needs to be safeguarded and held close. In her moon goddess form Artemis is protector of the newness of this budding moon. She holds that which is unseen, indistinct and intangible. She guides us to recognise our inner wild nature in its rhythmic connection to moon and natural cycles, the flow from silence to wild full chaos.

Artemis loves the wild places untouched by man's hand; the mountains and forest where her beloved wild animals are free to roam. She's wild and fierce like tropical storms yet deeply still and peaceful like a moonlit lake. Like nature's seeming cruelty – young chicks kicked from the nest or mature bear cubs driven off - Artemis's mood can turn in an instant. She is unpredictable in her impulsiveness and instability, instinctively attuned to the laws of nature not those of man. The natural world perfectly reflects her innately wild and free spirit, and vice versa.

Artemis is a virgin; her purity untouched by man's hand. Yet originally the term virgin had no relevance to sexual experience it simply meant whole. Artemis reflects to us that pure wholeness and unbound freedom we may experience before the onset of puberty, before awkwardness about our bodies or their rhythms hinder our openness. She is the female and moon phase that is whole in its own right before the next phase of blossoming into fullness. As a child she may express as a tomboy, climbing trees with dirty knees. We see Artemis in the intrepid backpacker spirit that loves to explore. The calling of uncharted territory is in her blood.

Just as indigenous cultures receive knowledge directly from the plant kingdom, Artemis is attuned to plant and animal kingdoms. She's equally alive in ecological activism, child protection or animal rights as in love of the wilderness. Her role as huntress was purely for food to sustain life and she actively hunted down those who tried to kill pregnant animals, because of its interference with the replenishment cycle of the natural world.

Artemis has many animal familiars; her hounds, the bear and deer being the most prominent. The bear is a fierce mother and symbolises Artemis intensely protective nature of the young. The gentle shy nature of the deer is suggestive of Artemis in her subtler realms, blending with nature's camouflage. Her silver bow and sandals (silver being the moon colour) suggest that even when Artemis is in her more active way of being, her motivations arise from her feminine moon nature. Knowing herself to be one with nature she is both its guardian and protector.

Big sister – A younger version of 'Mum'

When it comes to life's challenges, we all need someone to fight our corner at times don't we? The Artemis archetype is the one on call when we have a struggle or confrontation to face about being female. The protective nature of Artemis is one of her strongest positive attributes. She's the big sister who will sort it out or stand by your side when you need it. Artemis's companions were her sister virgins, nymphs and human girls as well as her animal friends. She has a clear affinity with innocence and vulnerability, shielding and defending those who need her shelter.

Our experience of sisterhood or lack of it begins in our family or childhood environment. Are you a big sister? A little sister? Or do you know sisterhood through friendship? These roles are very different, yet they all contain elements of the Artemis archetype. Sisters may support and advise, protect and guide or fight and fall out but it's a crucial relationship to our development as women. In the family it's a relationship where you experiment and learn about loving supportive connection and boundaries. The archetype of big sister acts as a role model one way or another. I remember how my sister would ask to borrow my clothes. I'd often say no then bump into her at lunchtime and she'd be wearing them anyway. She was repaying me for digging into her music collection without asking. We worked out our differences though, even sharing a bedroom without too many fights. In a healthy sister relationship, whether with a sibling or friend, we can test the edges of what's real and not. There's an opportunity to learn about conflict resolution. We can experiment; we can go places we can't with a mother, yet potentially we can receive an equally deep loving connection.

The oldest girl in a family often has to fight parental boundaries for her sibling. She's the tester pushing the edge of imposed rules, especially around socialising and dating. This is where Artemis comes out to play if she's a strong archetype. She stands up for what she wants, particularly for what's fair; she rebels; she questions and demands so by the time her sister reaches the same challenge she has an easier time. Both child and parents have potentially grown through the struggles and tests of the teen upheaval. Artemis's shoulders are broad. She can handle this 'buck the system' teenage role for its where her strengths and gifts may naturally accomplish change. Artemis likes a good fight or the struggle to change the status quo. Yet despite her strengths it's unsurprising that she occasionally gets frustrated, even enraged at always being the one to push for change. Perhaps, as we will see in the shadow section, this is when her extremes of cruelty or ruthlessness can more easily arise - when she has simply had enough. Perhaps it's just that her moon sensitivity simply gets overwhelmed, or in feeling overly responsible for fighting for others, she simply reacts.

Artemis moon sensitivity has strength within the family or a group too. When her sensitivity is strong (particularly at new or sickle moon) she may withdraw for a time, becoming absent or even aloof. Yet she will intuitively know who truly needs her support and when they need it. She's not fooled by the 'sad story' victim role but her moon sensitivity naturally recognises vulnerability. She will step in to protect and guide when there's a needed stretch beyond what youth or innocence is capable of. She makes a good listener, to the moon sensitivity within herself and as a trustworthy sister. Her intuitive knowing naturally recognises where the edge is, so this archetype is as likely to push the one she's supporting as to encourage her. At times her innate strength of will may take over but her intention is based in sheltering and safeguarding. There's no doubt that Artemis's protective big sister presence is felt wherever she's involved – as long as you don't cross her or push her buttons.

One version of the myth of Artemis and Iphigenia reveals this role as guardian and protector of young women. As the Greek army was preparing to set sail to take part in the Trojan War, Agamemnon inadvertently angered Artemis, by killing one of her sacred deer. In revenge, she caused the wind to stop blowing, so his ships would be unable to sail. To appease the goddess and undertake his quest for Troy, Agamemnon was advised by his seer to sacrifice his daughter Iphigenia as an appeasement to Artemis. Although he was initially reluctant to do so, eventually Agamemnon felt that if he was to reach the Trojan war, he had no option. He tricked Iphigenia to the sacrificial altar, yet Artemis substituted the girl with a deer just as she was about to be killed. She took Iphigenia to Tauris and made her a priestess of her cult. The second version of this myth has a completely different ending, shared in the Artemis shadow section.

Artemis's protective nature also extends to safeguarding the sexual innocence of the young, protecting young runaways, or those who live on the edges of society. Her feminist values grow ferocious when in the presence of abuse. Her moon sensitivity picks up the most subtle vibrations of sexual misalignment or intent. She holds the gift of a deep instinctual alertness that we need in order to survive. Her animal connection reflects how animal instinct is still keen within her. Like a lioness protecting her young, Artemis does not hesitate to act in defence of herself or her sisters. It's comes very naturally to her, and to us if her archetype is strong in us. This combination of sensitivity, alertness and ferocity are similar in nature to that of the animals she loves. It's the wild primal edge of our animal nature that civilization has called us to grow beyond and yet it's a quality we need. At times this animal nature in us is obvious, for instance when the hairs on the back of the neck stand up. Other times it's far more subtle and involves the psychic senses as well as the physical. It may simply be a feeling that 'something is off'. We do well to trust these subtle and not so subtle signals, for it is Artemis calling.

Several of the Artemis myths reveal her direct response to a clear danger or even a seeming threat to innocence. To see Artemis naked was to lose one's sight or life. Those who tried to seduce or rape her did not live to tell the tale. The myth involving Actaeon reveals her ferociousness even when the male protagonist was acting in innocence or quite naturally for a male. Artemis, unlike Venus or Juno, takes offence at any indication of male interest in her feminine nature or physicality, or that of those in her protection.

Whilst out hunting, Actaeon accidentally came upon Artemis and her nymphs bathing in a secluded pool. Seeing them in all their naked beauty, the stunned Actaeon stopped and gazed at them. When Artemis saw him, she transformed him into a stag. Then, incensed and disgusted at his natural curiosity, she set his own hounds upon him. They chased and killed what they thought was another stag, but it was their master. Actaeon paid the highest price for his interest in Artemis and her sisters. Artemis may be a protector and guardian archetype but when it comes to those who cross her boundaries there's no such thing as innocence.

Sisters are doing it for themselves

The Artemis spirit is pure independence. She is beholden to no-one, not even her father Zeus, as she had requested and received the right to freely roam her wild lands, with her animal companions and nymphs. This independent feminine spirit is whole. She chooses her own goals and causes. She epitomizes the concentration and focus required to send an arrow flying or to hunt. The Artemis archetype within us is active and self-sufficient, independent and undomesticated. She's glad to be female, values her sisters and will certainly hold feminist values. Her principles are autonomy, freedom and space to be herself, along with spontaneity and definitely no strings to constrain her. Competition is a natural aspect of her nature, simply in the desire to extend herself and her freedom. She will align herself with those who fight for the rights of the disenfranchised, yet she will always be herself in doing so. She knows who she is and what she stands for, her boundaries are strong. She doesn't suffer fools gladly and you will certainly know where you stand with her. Artemis is the natural archetype of the women's movement in terms of sister support, particularly in the arenas of rape, birth control clinics, midwifery and child protection.

On an inner level, the Artemis archetype's affinity with nature calls her to protect what is wild, innocent or natural inside herself or others against the restriction and suppression of society's influence to conform to its standards. She actively seeks out suppression in order to go beyond it. She will defy the rules if she sees they are unfair or dishonest; the rebel in her is active. Artemis's calling for psychic space is even stronger than the physical demand for freedom. 'Don't fence me in' may well be the most telling Artemis mantra. This applies to her inner space as well as her life. She is whole unto herself, not needing anyone, or anyone's approval. Her competitive spirit exceeds her desire to connect or belong. Even in female groups this archetype is to some extent a loner, definitely autonomous, authentic and free. She follows the call of her own integrity and may well be a pioneer, a voice in the wilderness that shouts whilst others are asleep to the issue that has lit her inner fire.

Artemis has long been linked with the mythological archetype of the female Amazon warrior. Many of the Greek myths speak of how the heroes of the day had to prove their worth by fighting the Amazon leader, women such as Hippolyta, Antiope and Thessalia. Homer immortalised these female warriors in the Illiad. Archaeology has now proved the mythological female warriors were real, through grave sites on the Eurasian steppes. These sites reveal small horse-centred tribes across vast areas from the Black Sea to Mongolia where women battled on horseback alongside men. Recent grave sites in western Russia reveal Scythian women ranging in age from early teens to late 40s, the eldest of whom was wearing a golden ceremonial headdress comprised of 65-70% pure gold. Myth speaks of how these women cut off their breast in order to wield a sword, but it seems this aspect of the myth is fantasy. Nonetheless it is perhaps indicative of an assumed loss of femininity or mothering instinct in these female warriors. In truth we do not know.

Artemis is always present when our warrior spirit is ignited. She indicates what we feel fierce and passionate about, what we fight for and where we hold a competitive non-conformist edge. She's different from the devoted mother archetypes in that her protection is ignited by injustice towards those who cannot speak or fight for themselves, or with regard to a cause, the environment or animal rights for instance. To Artemis injustice itself is the wrong to be put right; her demand for what's right is an impersonal quest. Although injustice may trigger personal feelings in this archetype, as we'll see in the shadow section, it's the principle rather than personal attachment that is generally a motivator. Personal attachment is anathema to Artemis. When just born she was assisting her mother to birth her twin. Aged three she was demanding from her father Zeus exactly what she wanted, her right to be free and have her own lands. Artemis knows what is right, real and true for herself, no question. She is influenced by no-one, attached to no-one. This lack of attachment or personal closeness with anyone apart from her brother Apollo, with whom she was equally competitive, leads us to into the question of Artemis and asexuality.

Abstinent or asexual?

Artemis clearly likes men. She is close to her brother Apollo and has a good friend in huntsman Orion, but whether she trusts men is another matter. Or perhaps it is simply she has no time or need of them? Being a virgin goddess Artemis is complete in herself. Her love of her companions, girl and animal, her love of wild places and her role as guardian and protector are fulfilling. She is not domesticated in any way. She needs no home other than the forest. Her interest in men is more friendly and brotherly, through a shared interest or a quest, than passionate or sexual in nature.

The twin archetype is key to the way Artemis interacts with men, more as sister or intellectual equal. She is not particularly interested in a man as a partner. It's as if the polarity of difference between brother and sister, Apollo and Artemis, sun and moon, repulses rather than attracts. The sun and moon's time in the sky is different with separate realms of day and night, with unique rhythms. When the sun is active in one place, the moon is active elsewhere. Day and night-time hold different activities, values and needs for us.

Some feminist circles equate Artemis with lesbianism. There is nothing in her mythology to suggest this. It's rather that her sexuality is undeveloped or lacking full expression, or more likely sexuality is on her own terms. Whatever the sexual expression of the Artemis archetype, it's clear that male-female relationships are secondary to her connection to the animal kingdom and nature. In many ways Artemis is asexual, balanced in her moon sensitivity and her earthy goddess of the hunt mode, accessing sensitivity or goal orientation and action as required. Being associated with chastity, and with virgin companions, Artemis is known for being chaste and protective of purity. Sexuality would seem to contradict her very nature.

The Shadow of Artemis

Our emotional thermostat

Artemis is a goddess of contradictions. As a virgin goddess, and as pure as she is portrayed to be, Artemis has a deep dark shadow side. As a moon goddess she is queen of the night; the time when shadows loom large. Much as with nature's storms she can shift in a moment from light to dark, from innocence to fury, from protective to destructive. When touched by innocence or purity, her protective nature flows – but not always so. When crossed, or even when the whim takes her, she can be vengeful and without mercy. Several of her myths point to this vindictive trait. None more so than the tale of Artemis and Apollo together avenging the honour of their mother Leto.

Niobe, a mere mortal, had boasted to Leto, the mother of the divine twins, that she had birthed more children and was therefore superior. Apollo was outraged at such an insult to his mother. The twin gods hunted down Niobe's children and shot them all with their bows and arrows. Apollo killed the male children and Artemis the girls. Niobe, now childless, turned to stone through her grief. In this case Artemis's naturally protective nature towards girls was relinquished in favour of defending her mother. Clearly this was a question of competing values and the stronger one won. Yet there is an obvious extreme in the twin's actions.

Artemis dealt equally harshly with those mortal men who did not revere her. Oeneus, King of Calydon, forgot Artemis in his harvest offerings. All the gods were given gifts except for her. Artemis was raging at this insult to her divinity, so she sent a monstrous giant boar to terrorise the king's lands, destroying farms and orchards, devouring the fruits of the harvest, sheep and cattle alike. The usual Greek heroes came to kill it but to no avail. Eventually it was mortally wounded by a female warrior Atalanta, whose arrow pierced the boar's only vulnerable spot, its eye. During the killing of this monstrous boar Oeneus's wife and son also died. Artemis was then satisfied. A personal sacrifice or death quells her rage at those who displease or anger her. Her fury is not assuaged through expression but through vengeance.

Artemis's fury at not being acknowledged by Oeneus is significant in that it points us towards imbalance in any fight for justice. A fight for rights can easily become highly personalised or motivated by revenge. Injustice doesn't just activate the fighting spirit it can trigger hostility and violence. It can precipitate extremes of destructiveness that go way beyond what is needed to make a point or assert a right. This then becomes counter-productive to a cause. Destructive rage is the product of years of power struggles, violence, humiliation and abuse. It is a self-perpetuating cycle, understandable on some level perhaps for unacknowledged pain breeds more pain, and yet it's certainly not constructive or creative. The myth of the Calydon boar gives us clues to what is needed when we experience or witness this kind of violent reaction in our self. The boar is on a destructive rampage. It has been possessed by aggression. Nothing will seem to stop it, not even the usual Greek heroes. Yet Atalanta is wise, she does not try brute force; she is cool and strategic. She looks, then she draws her bow. Her arrow penetrates the boar's only vulnerable spot, its eye.

What can we learn from this tale about the extremes of our own emotional reactions, particularly rage? Atalanta shows us; she shows us that we must confront our own destructiveness by calling on the perceptive part of our nature – the one that sees the vulnerable spot. Artemis has this perception in her moon nature. She understands the vulnerability of innocence. She is queen of the night shadows. Yet if this aspect of her nature is not sufficiently developed, or more importantly, if it is not honoured, destructiveness can take over the fighting spirit. What ensues is a rampage that may feel good initially but can result in shame or humiliation. It not only leaves oneself raw and exposed, it leaves the original circumstances unchanged.

It is very natural that when our values are thwarted or crossed, anger arises. How we energise or allow anger to take us over, or use it constructively, then becomes a primary focus and key for healing. Anger can be a strong motivating energy, but it is a poor master. The fight for right can easily become exhausting when we are taking it too personally. When reaction moves from being a motivating force to becoming the need for vengeance, the fight for right has become too personal. It is then damaging to the one who fights as well as the one who receives it.

How many of us know how to navigate conflict well? The very basis of conflict is different values or beliefs. For conflict to be addressed well we need Artemis's passion and fighting spirit. Yet for injustice to be addressed constructively we need awareness of where our passion becomes aggression. Aggression separates; it creates withdrawal or a matching violence that energises and escalates the potential for hostility. Healthy conflict skills involve bridge building. We may not want to build a bridge towards another who holds extremely different values from ours, or who we feel has wronged us, yet for change to happen it's an essential skill. Building that skill is an aspect of growing maturity. It's a measure of self-understanding and a responsibility towards conscious relating. Many human beings have a way to go with conscious relating and it's very clear what happens with this issue collectively. Yet individually we can all learn. Becoming curious about our over-reactions and emotional extremes is key. It's only in engaging these more challenging aspects of our human tapestry that we may grow.

Self-knowledge is power. If we're not aware of what's happening with our physical, mental-emotional and spiritual well-being, change is not possible. A simple example of this lies in connection to our bodies. For instance, when the body is over-heated, we naturally move to cool it in some way. We might remove a garment, take a drink, find a fresher place to sit or take a shower. It's key to the Artemis archetype within our self to understand how our emotional thermostat works too. What is the optimum temperature of our inner fire that acts as a motivator? When do we over-heat? What works to bring down over-heated reaction, the swing towards extreme that may become counterproductive, even destructive? These are all good questions. It is not that reaction is wrong; it simply happens. The way we respond to it is key as an avenue to discover deeper self-understanding and growth.

To become conscious an over-reaction requires cool assessment and sensitive perception without any judgment. It requires Artemis's cooler moon qualities of detachment, sensitivity and a knowing based on 'shades of grey and silver' rather than black or white. Nonetheless, even without judgment, when we've reacted, we may feel shame. We may feel we crossed the boundary of response-able connection with others. We may feel small and humbled. Humility comes from the Latin word 'humilitas', meaning of the earth or grounded. This touches the core of over-reaction and emotional extremes; we have basically lost touch with the ground of our being and our values. We've become incensed, consumed by the fire of our own passion. When we're consumed, righteous anger is natural; vengeance is not. It's a distortion that makes an issue only about 'you and me' and the need to inflict pain personally. It foregoes the bigger picture of injustice as a collective human failing. It lacks the understanding that we are all wounded in some way.

A fine line

The Artemis archetype is clearly a feminist. Her shadow energies reveal some of the darker elements of that movement too, for wherever women get together the play of patriarchy is with us, despite our denial of it, or our full-hearted desire to go beyond it. This is our healing evolution, as feminism moves through its waves, becoming refined towards greater consciousness. As we, individual women, move into the opening potentials for conscious engagement of life arising in our lives and through humanity. Undoubtedly feminism still has its place in our collective evolution. Yet more pertinently perhaps, these times are about the conscious empowerment of us all, man or woman. That's not to deny inequality. It is to recognise that we are all wounded and potentially powerless.

As we've discovered, Artemis is a protector, an advocate of sisterhood and a warrior; she has an independent spirit. In her shadow play however those qualities, when taken too far, can become disempowering or domineering. Artemis always means well; without doubt she's up for a challenge, especially on another's behalf. Yet it's a fine line between being a protector, an enabler and the one who takes over. It needs a conscious balance and awareness of the boundary between self and another that the Artemis moon nature may find challenging. Where to draw the line is a key quality to be aware of when this archetype is strong in us. As is wisdom about where the fight is no longer of use, when withdrawal is the wiser option. This is where the twin nature of Artemis calls us to growth in sensitivity; to discern, does this now require deeper reflection and a pause, or more focused action?

When we explore any duality, we might see a swing between extremes can always become a shadow element. The Full Moon shows us this; when the Sun and Moon are diametrically opposed, when ocean tides are high, we may be pulled into more dramatic behaviour. Artemis's need of solitude and quiet, combined with her independent nature, can also move into extremes. Independence can become aloofness that disconnects this archetype from her sisters. Her strong warrior spirit and competitive nature can separate her from the group, taking the role of a leader rather than a companion. Here one of the masks of feminism - we're in this together but don't you dare stand out more than me - reveals how competition still lies at the root of many sister connections. It's a legacy of patriarchy that's still healing. We see this particularly in the teen phase of maturing that Artemis so keenly represents. It lives in the need to have a special friend and/or a tribe and to exclude those who don't fit. It exists in the constantly changing alliances of adolescent female friendship.

Artemis's moon nature also reveals the potential for immaturity to shadow all her relationships. She represents Maiden Moon, the undeveloped aspect of the moon nature that's full of potential and potency yet lacks experience. She has no knowing of the mother or crone phases of life, the wisdom that flows from deep nurturing, caring, letting go and the 'hands off' detachment of a grandmother. The New Moon energies (Maiden Moon) always emerge as vibrant possibility. Artemis carries this fresh impulse and drive for newness that can become a forceful push for change if not engaged with awareness. How far to take this may be a constant questioning that grows us in this archetype. Artemis's twin nature of forthright independence and numinous withdrawal call to be constantly refined through walking the fine line of inner reflection and action. It is only in walking that line that we stay connected at the core, fueling our Artemis quests from deep truth, rather than simply looking for a fight.

Don't pin me down

We live in a world where material and emotional security are purported to be the raison d'etre to being human. Artemis challenges this vehemently. For her security lies in her beingness and her values. She abhors commitment or responsibility, knowing her only obligation is to be true to herself and to fight for right. She is defiant in her unwillingness to conform to tradition. Artemis lives on her own terms; she doesn't stand for anyone crossing her boundaries or invading her territory. Yet there is a price to pay for this way of being.

When we're unwilling to commit, or uninterested in close relationship, our capacity for intimacy suffers. Artemis is a virgin goddess. Much like Pallas Athena and Vesta this archetype is not made for relating. Yet Artemis is young, beautiful and athletic. It would seem, like her sister goddess Venus, that she would be involved in all kinds of romantic adventures but that is not the case. In many ways Artemis is the other extreme to Venus, hiding out in the woods, communing with nature, her animals and virgin companions. It may seem she's actively avoiding relationship. In her passion for independence is Artemis commitment phobic? Especially in relationship, or is it a question of disposition?

Artemis values equality, the right to be who she is; that is natural to her. It's relevant to relationships also, for without the capacity to be strong in oneself any relationship will be unbalanced. In any healthy relationship there's also the question of vulnerability. It's a quality that's essential to intimacy. One of Artemis's gifts is to protect the vulnerable, so she clearly knows what vulnerability is. Yet when it comes to connection with humans or gods, it seems she values her masculine energies more than her sensitivity.

Active in the hunt, loving the thrill of the chase Artemis is competitive, quick to take insult or exact vengeance. In relationships these qualities suggest the male role; more active, driven and potentially aggressive. As the huntress

Artemis is the one in control. This role reversal in relating may be exciting but it can depolarise relationship, especially where a woman's masculine energy is stronger than her mate's. Competitiveness in any gender makes relating a challenge and intimacy impossible. Who wants to feel they have to fight to relate? The need to win, or claim the kill, that is an active aspect of Artemis's love of the hunt, is the anathema to closeness. As is the need to run when faced with anything that inhibits freedom; or being solely focused in the passionate engagement of a campaign. Intimacy requires the time and space for closeness to develop; it requires willingness to engage with caring and tenderness at times. Perhaps Artemis simply does not care enough about one-to-one relating to go there? Or perhaps she likes being in charge too much or is it that she is not equipped for closeness?

Artemis's affinity with the moon holds keys to her lack of interest in partnership. The sickle phase of the moon is very cool; its colour is silver, lacking the warmth of gold. Gold is her twin Apollo's colour, for he is the sun. The sickle moon phase is quiet and subjective, connected to the inner world of dreams, subtle feeling and intuition. The tender intimacy of this moon phase is expressed through Artemis in a numinous connection to nature. It is moving towards expression of its feminine nature but it's not there yet. It's like the maiden energy of innocence; immature and sensitive. This moon aspect of Artemis's nature makes her distant and inaccessible. She may even appear aloof due to awkwardness about knowing how to relate. It's easier for this sensitivity in Artemis to connect where words are not required, with an animal friend or a tree. Or perhaps her coldness is simply a withdrawal from the responsibility she carries for protecting the young. It's a respite.

Artemis's coolness is the extreme contrast, even contradiction, to her active orientation where in her passion for a challenge or a fight action erupts from her and words overflow. This Artemis operates from instinctive sensitivity, much like her animal companions. She has heightened awareness of the subtleties of energy. Her instinct guides her well. She's like the deer in flight at the break of a twig, or a hound that snarls when you get too close. Such finely tuned sensitivity needs the protection of instinctual withdrawal. The protection that Artemis offers to others is also used well in protection of her own vulnerability. Lacking experience of intimate connection, it is easier for this archetype to leap into extremes of withdrawal, running or fighting than to find the middle ground of relating where authenticity and vulnerability meet in intimacy.

Here we come to the myth of Artemis and Iphigenia again. For the two different versions give us clues as to Artemis's contradictory relationship to vulnerability. I related how in one version of this tale Artemis saved Iphigenia by substituting her with a deer on the sacrificial altar at the last moment. In this act we see Artemis protecting the innocence of this young girl who has done no wrong other than being Agamemnon's daughter. Artemis then took Iphigenia to Tauris to be trained as a priestess in her temple.

In the second version of this myth Artemis demands that Agamemnon make the sacrifice. She has no interest in the innocence of his vulnerable daughter Iphigenia. It seems Artemis chooses who she protects or not on a whim. This suggests a contradictory swing between a protective and caring, or cold and merciless attitude towards her own vulnerability that we may witness in ourselves. In this potential imbalance, depending on Artemis synergy with other feminine archetypes within us as women, we may run similar extremes, either in relationship to our own sensitivities or those of others.

Without doubt Artemis is her own woman. She will never be anyone's else's, except on her own terms. That may be a good thing, or not. Artemis in you will decide.

Chapter 6
Guardian of the Sacred Marriage – Juno

He is here!
My heart rejoices
to see my Love,
True Man,
alive in form.

Every man
is in His Essence.
Every man
is in His Heart.
As my body opens
to His Love,
bliss enfolds me
in its most tender arms.

Bodies apart
yet souls entwined,

being in union,
I know
the truth of this Love.

I am One with Thee,
Truest Man.
I am Thee,
Pure Man.
'We' are not apart,
I am whole with Thee,
in Thee,
as Thee.

Union is known
in this flesh of earth.
in the glory of this Love,
I am free.
Cassandra Eve

Archetype: Triple Goddess, the wife or partner

Symbols: peacock; cuckoo; crown; sceptre; spear; rainbow

Message: I desire the sacred union here on Earth. I commit to its fulfilment

Juno themes: the guardianship of marriage and brides; the role of partner being one's main identity; relationship and its renewal; loyalty and commitment; sexuality,

Juno Shadow themes: Relationship power games; disconnection; separation; the wound of betrayal

How Juno expresses Venus's energy: through commitment to a partnership

Also known as: Hera (Greek) married to King of the Gods Zeus, Juno (Roman) married to Jupiter

Juno is Queen of Heaven, embodying the ancient triple goddess Maiden-Mother-Crone. Her role is sovereign, protector of women, guardian of women's sexuality and fertility, guardian of brides and childbirth. As such there are various titles and epithets given to her in Roman culture. Several of her titles name her as a light-bearer for women and children. She also holds guardianship of the wealth of the community, its calendar and politics.

In mythology Juno (Hera in the Greek pantheon) is best known as daughter of Saturn/Kronos (Greek) sister and wife of Jupiter/Zeus (Greek), king of the Gods. Yet as with many Goddess figures her origins remain hidden in the mists of time and may originate with the ancient Astarte or Ishtar of Mesopotamia, or the Etruscan Uni. Hera's temple at Olympus predates that of her consort Zeus, similar to her temple in Crete. She represents the fullness of the Feminine within partnership, with a complexity of roles and functions. Her most important purpose was as patroness of marriage and married women. June was Juno's most sacred month, giving rise to the phrase 'June bride'. She represents the longing for divine union to be known on the Earth and she expresses a deep commitment to its expression and manifestation. Juno is our guide through the wondrous potential and challenge of intimate partnership.

Her-story
Juno's story is best known through the myth of her Greek counterpart Hera. In the Olympic pantheon Hera was the sister of Zeus who desired his sister above all other women. There are two versions to the mythology. The first of these myths tells of a secret marriage between Zeus and Hera on the island of Samos, followed by a three-hundred-year honeymoon. The second tale features the common mythical themes of rape and abduction. It tells how Zeus spotted Hera wandering alone on Mount Thronax. First disguising himself as a cuckoo, Zeus conjured up a wild storm. Seeking shelter, he flew into Hera's lap, where he lay bedraggled and wet. Feeling pity for this poor bird, Hera wrapped him in her cloak and warmed him at her breast. Zeus at once resumed his God form and then he raped her. After this violation, chastened by his violent actions, Zeus married Hera out of guilt.

The mythic themes of rape or abduction are common in Greek mythology and may point towards the subjugation of the previous goddess-based cultures by the invading tribes of the north, as shared in the introduction. Homer provides clues to the status of Hera, both pre and post-wedding, calling Zeus "Hera's spouse" instead of by name. This seems to indicate her role took precedence over Zeus's within the Greek culture. As he was king of the gods this is telling indeed. It appears that the goddess took precedence at that time. Yet Zeus and Hera's marriage indicates the shift that was taking place. Patriarchy was taking hold. The goddess cults were being disbanded, whilst the sacred power of the Triple Goddess was being demoted to the role of a jealous wife.

Whatever the origin of their union and the concurrent shifts in culture, ultimately Zeus took Hera to Olympus as his bride where the gods and goddesses celebrated their union.

After their prolonged honeymoon, the mythology relates how Zeus and Hera's marriage fell into a state of competition and hostility. Her calling was to sacred union; his was to freedom. Zeus exercised this calling to freedom through love affairs with goddesses and mortal women. In her feelings of humiliation and rejection, Hera taunted Zeus and worked to defeat him, to subdue his arrogance. He responded by throwing thunderbolts at her and taking yet more lovers. Hera was faithful to Zeus yet through his behaviour, witnessed their union and her role as Triple Goddess dishonoured and her goddess cults destroyed. Forced into submission, her only means of expression for her rage was to take revenge on Zeus's lovers and their children. Eventually she retreated into herself.

There are many differing myths about Zeus and Hera's creation of children together, some contradictory as myths often are. Nonetheless after Zeus birthed the goddess Pallas Athena from his head, Hera created parthenogenetic children. These children included the giant Typhaon of Delphi, with a hundred burning snake's heads, God of War Ares and the crippled Hephaestus who became a skilled smith, artisan, and husband of Aphrodite/Venus.

Hera's relationship with Zeus's son Hercules in particular is the source of many of their myths. Hercules was the son of Alcmene, a mortal woman whom Zeus so desired he persuaded Sun God Helios to halt his stallions from their race across the sky, thus lengthening the night by three days. Zeus and Alcmene's lovemaking leads to the conception of Hercules whom Hera knew would mature into a hero of the growing patriarchy. In Hera's eyes this was not only another painful wound and reminder of Zeus's infidelities but a further shift away from her goddess culture. From the time of Hercules birth, the discord between Zeus and Hera escalated. She did all she could to ensure Hercules would not have a right to rule or fulfil his destiny. Conversely Zeus was doing all he could to make Hercules immortal. Initially Zeus tricked Hera into suckling the baby Hercules. When she realised who he was, she pushed him away from her breast. It is said the spurting of her breast milk created the Milky Way.

One legend tells us that eventually Zeus persuaded Hera to adopt Hercules as her own. A ritual took place whereby she held Hercules to her breast, then proceeded to push him through her robes as though giving birth. It seems that they were reconciled. The cultural shift from matrilineal to patrilineal descent and the subjugation of the goddess-based cultures was becoming established. The truth of what actually took place is lost in time, but perhaps Hera's goddess culture was alive for a time. It is said that her altars stood side-by-side with those of Zeus in the temples, as an honouring to both the god and goddess. Perhaps the sacred union she so desired was realised.

Juno's place in the Universe – Astronomy & Astrology
The asteroid Juno was discovered in 1804 by Karl Ludwig Harding and originally considered to be a planet. Juno was reclassified in the 1850s but is still the eleventh largest asteroid and one of the stoniest.

Juno's astrological placement in a birth-chart reveals how we relate within partnership and intimacy. She reveals to us how to mature in fullness of our Divine Feminine nature and to realise the potential of sacred partnership. Such a partnership requires that both partners being willing to transmute unconscious aspects of relating. So Juno reveals this synergy of the yearning for love and the transformative nature of this desire for union. She reveals where we are called to develop qualities such as forgiveness, strength and power, self-belief and understanding in our relationship journeys. Juno is often associated with female powerlessness and its healing, due to the nature of her marriage. She can pertain to any close relationship - business partners, guru-disciple, therapist-client or loving friendships - and its challenge of remaining deeply connected through the dance of love and its shadow.

My Journey with Juno

My mother's demand of my father to love her was compelling. Her frustration at his lack of connection to her and his brooding silences was tangible. It's not surprising that I inherited the desire for a deeply loving sacred partnership and yet also its shadow.

After two marriages and a long-term partnership, in my forties, I'd pretty much given up on relating. Then a series of inner awakenings revealed that a man who carried the potential for sacred union was arriving in my life. I relate that story in the Vesta chapter. Juno provides the next instalment in my journey with him, the Divine Lover (hereafter referred to as He or Him). My inner connection to Juno and Priestess Vesta archetypes was to take me deep into the knowing of union, within myself and in physical partnership. Juno is that potential of sacred intimacy available to us all, the truth of one essence in what seems to be many bodies.

The sacred union was not as I expected. How can anyone project how that might be? Yet it was real beyond any doubt. After our initial meeting (see Vesta Journey) He shared with me what the Circle of Woman is - a group of women living in the union of Divine Love, held within Realised Consciousness. Through honest, conscious relating, any separation would be transmuted.

Through the mirror of sisterhood, the Circle would move into the knowledge of One Woman - no competition, no jealousy, no conflict. In its place we would know love as One Woman. Our transformation of what that may bring up in terms of shadow energies, would ground Divine Union into the Earth. Moving through the unconscious patterning of man and woman into embodiment of that Divine Union, the personal and collective transformation of intimacy was opened. As He spoke, I knew without any doubt that this was the Truth; not just an idea of truth, the living of Truth. For I had been led to this doorway through my inner experience in meditation. The first indication of that Divine Union arrived on the inner levels too.

I was facilitating a weekend retreat. We'd shared a beautiful day, balanced male and female energy on the course, ages ranging from early twenties to eighties. All were flowing with the energy, sharing the beauty of touch and healing. As always it was amazing to connect so deeply with people I hadn't met before. That evening, feeling tired yet deeply still, and having come home to a beautiful message from Him on my voicemail, I was sitting quietly when I began to feel a change happening in my body. I allowed myself to go with it. An energetic expansion was happening in and through my body. I expanded out through the walls of my cottage, the village, over land and ocean, above planet Earth and into the universe. I flowed outwards until the Earth appeared as one tiny cell within my body. In that vast space everything was emerging from my womb – the whole of nature, humanity, enlightened beings, new planets and stars. It was beyond feeling; it was pure tangible knowing experience. Then I descended into deep blackness. Deeper and deeper I went whilst wave after wave of deep emptiness moved through. Graced by life, although there was no 'me' in that place, I knew I was being shown the profundity of the Great Mother herself. All sense of 'I' disappeared into that space.

The next day my body felt as though smashed into tiny pieces. Completely exhausted with a deep pain in my back, I felt as if I'd given birth. Yet on an inner level I was profoundly renewed. I knew life was gifting me a direct experience of the Divine Feminine. To be so graced was humbling indeed.

Surprisingly, in its wake came a longing to be completely with Him. I knew it as the longing to be in his form, in that place of love completely, yet I felt it physically, on a very human level too. The desire to make love, to be with Him totally was profound. All I wanted was to be love; to know love as the manifestation of my life.

Lying in bed shortly after this expansion I became aware of the energy of many Masters and Mothers with me. Then I felt His presence with me too. As I did so, the Divine Mother's voice came through me on the inner levels, "Step towards him. Be with him as man and wife", She said. Then a Master I had sat with, repeating her words "Step towards him. Be with him as man and wife. Open to him fully". As I moved in Being towards Him, I felt a flow of love pour through my body. In the sweetest ecstasy I found myself lifted up. I saw a six-pointed star, the symbol for the Heart of Life, the heart chakra, floating above us. As He and I merged energetically, this star descended, enveloping us in cosmic energy. I disappeared into its absolute bliss. When I returned to bodily awareness, I knew something profound had occurred. I knew also that it would come through physically.

Some weeks went by when I didn't have contact or see Him. Then one day I came home from work to find an invitation on my voicemail. It was to attend the funeral of a friend of his. It seemed a strange invitation, but I felt drawn.

As He and I drove into Torrington, a small country town in Devon, we heard a constant single drumbeat. The sight that greeted us was a rare scene in this rural community: a lone drummer, followed by hordes of brightly dressed individuals. Behind the drummer, on a simple cart bedecked with flowers and pulled by a donkey, lay his friend Wendy's coffin, gaily painted with stars, flowers, moons and silver spirals. As we passed, He threw a single pink rose onto the coffin. Then we joined the rear of this vibrantly alive procession.

The slow walk through this little country town was a profound experience. Led by the lone drummer, the donkey and Wendy's cart, all through the town people flung open their doors to participate. They threw flowers, bowed their heads in reverence and applauded. Many were visibly moved to see such celebration at a wake. It was a sight more usually seen in India than the Devon heartland.

Wendy's grave was in newly planted woodland to be named in her memory. It was a beautiful site, on a steep hillside overlooking a wooded river valley and surrounded by soft green hills. The burial ceremony was informal. When Wendy's coffin had been laid in the ground with private goodbyes from her family, we were invited to join in a spontaneous celebration of her life. There was poetry, drumming, chanting and poetry recitation, each individual who felt drawn honouring their kinship with Wendy in their own unique way. He spoke a few words, followed with a chant and we led the people attending in a spiral around Wendy's grave.

We left soon after the burial ritual was complete. Our journey home was a beautiful flow of sharing that continued as we arrived home and into the night. To say we made love doesn't begin to describe where life took me on that night. All I can say I knew the love of God come through my body. I felt the passion of man for woman and life for itself in form. Every touch was a prayer, every movement a deep stillness and a complete bliss. As I lay in His arms I knew myself whole in every sense and beyond sense. The blessing of receiving so much was a gift of Grace indeed.

On the next morning I found myself in a deeply nourishing empty stillness. As He was about to leave, we embraced. A flow of love moved through our bodies; it brought us both to tears. I felt my heart burst in utter fullness as a vibrant pink/blue light descended through us. Seeing the crystal six-pointed star hanging in my window, I sobbed. The 'as above, so below' of that star was grounded. My inner experience had found its places in bodies. Union was known.

Not long after this awakening my planned move into community happened. I had met my live-in sisters (His two existing partners) many times. We had shared a naturally deep connection. There were also other sisters not living with us who were in the Circle of Love. Although to be in such a relationship was strange to my human mind, I knew I was moving from inner truth in this move. I delighted in the newly discovered depth of connection. The love I knew was profound. Yet very soon the honeymoon was over. Isn't it true of all intimate relationships? The depth of love we reach opens the shadow. The shadow then calls for healing. Very soon I began to realise this is the purpose of deep relating – to keep opening in love through the shadows. Yet it was a big challenge. The honeymoon was over. I began to experience the pain of separation as 'not good enough', self-loathing and rejection arose.

Over the next months as I witnessed His love of my sisters, I felt my own lack of love surface. This was new and unexpected. There was no jealousy, just a desire to be loved for me, to be included physically in the love I saw around me. I knew in truth that I wasn't separate - my direct experience had taken me into the reality of love that I knew to be deeply true - but in my personal reality I was excluded. It was an old story from my childhood. He hadn't made love with me for some time. This only intensified the belief from my past that I was unlovable. He mirrored this shadow belief perfectly. When I accepted myself, He profoundly loved me. When I was struggling in resistance to pain, He reflected my own hardness with myself. It was tough. I was looking for security when truly there is none in love. I felt He was lacking compassion. Yet I was failing to see the mirror that life was offering me – my own lack of compassion for myself, for the shadows and pain of separation within me.

Despite the challenges, Grace was with me. Through talking honestly with my sisters about the pain I felt, I began to see I wasn't alone. I felt heard; I felt seen. My sisters knew well the flow from love to pain. They had felt it when I came along to join them, in the insecurity of change, in the fear perhaps of losing love. We were all going deeper. No matter how it looked, I learned that my sisters were also transforming their patterned beliefs. I saw the gift of growth and deeper connection through the pain we were all experiencing at times. It was challenging yet I knew it to be true. In truth I was being challenged to stay with the knowing of union I had already received. I was being called to live it. Juno had awoken. The divine union was alive in me. I simply had to claim it as constantly true.

Juno's message: I desire the sacred union here on Earth. I commit to its fulfilment

Juno's primary calling is to intimate partnership and its fulfilment. She is the guardian of the principle of conscious relationship. As Queen of Heaven, she's not interested in other aspects of life. Why would she be? She's already complete in herself and she is called to express that fullness on the earth. She innately knows the potential for sacred union as the peak of human expression. She has no doubt that is her purpose.

Relationship is not just Juno's purpose; it's her delight. She will give everything – whether it's her love or her shadow – for the sacred union to be known. Juno holds the pinnacle of love we long for. We see the archetypical Juno marriage played out in our culture through celebrity marriages with their apparent glamour and dramas. We know the pattern of falling in and out of love in our own lives. If Juno is strong for us as individuals, we yearn for the Beloved; we can't wait for him or her to come along. We are called by the potential; it's full of light and life. We may recognise the highs and lows of romance as the stuff of novels and films, yet we know they represent a truth too. Underneath our pain, cynicism or fear, we all long for love, whether we are aware of it or not. Somewhere in us we know love is always possible. Magic is always available. Relationship is always imminent. Juno's yearning for union mirrors our own desire – to deeply know love.

If we have this calling to partnership, we are wise to recognise that an intimate relationship requires commitment. Commitment is easy when we're in love's pleasure. When the shadow arises it's more of a challenge. This challenge is two-fold. Firstly, it is to stay connected to oneself in the darkness of conflict or pain. Secondly, it is to stay with the knowing of love within the relationship when it seems to have gone. Love's expression is just like the flow of seasons. Spring's blossoming gives way to summer fullness that falls in autumn as nature begins to draw in her bounty. Winter's quiet is a time of return to earth. In relationship we live the same cycle. The flowering of attraction, its expression through love and intimacy, then the disappearance of connection as challenge comes along. Inevitably we return to our self at some point, if just for a moment or two. This is the winter of love, the return to aloneness, perhaps to coldness. In the natural cycle the dawning of spring is assured. We don't know when, or how it will look, yet we know it will come. In relating the renewal of love is always a potential. If we winter well, spring is a promise. Its potential arrives in the embrace of the whole cycle. Juno reveals this cycle in relationship and guides us through it.

The commitment to renewal

Juno's gift, through her yearning for union, is commitment to love. It expresses as devotion to pass through the shadows, to claim the potential of love's renewal. When 'winter' appears in partnership – whether it expresses through storms or coldness - we enter a more challenging phase in the relationship cycle. This is where Juno's shadow arises (more on that later) but also where her gift of constancy appears. For Juno knows the sacred union is not found purely through romance, or through playing the field. Its potential lies in the deeper calling to love in and through the darkness. Hers is not an easy journey yet she doesn't need it to be easy. She's looking for the most profound connection. She's looking for the highest possible partnership and she's found him. The King of the Gods is her consort, even if he chooses to turn away from her. Her commitment is to go through whatever the connection with him brings, holding the possibility of living sacred union as her quest.

Juno's wisdom as Queen of Heaven holds her through the challenges of seeming separation. Just as Ceres/Demeter gains wisdom through the loss of Proserpina/Persephone, Juno holds the understanding of the whole cycle of relating and its purpose. Despite Jupiter's treatment of her and the ensuing pain and vehemence of her shadow, somewhere Juno keeps her commitment. She holds true to love inside herself and to its potential expression in partnership. In her constancy she is primarily committed to the knowing of love within herself. Yet she is energetically calling her consort to stop his philandering with goddesses and human women. She calls him to commit to a higher truth. Yet who's to say what that truth is for him? He is Masculine. He is King of the Gods; his journey is different. Juno cannot say what is right for him. All she can do is trust in her own and his commitment to the highest truth. In that trust the shadows burn.

Juno holds the commitment to love no matter what. That is her calling – with the one who is a match for her. For us as women, the play may look different. As we mature, we may express the calling to union with different partners at different times. In that journey, if we're committing to love at the core of our self, our consciousness grows. The potential is our expression of love through partnership grows too.

In our journey as women in partnership Juno is the archetype that holds us in commitment to the renewal of love. She guides us in the journey of deeply meaningful relating where devotion to growing love together is the primary connector. This takes dedication and a profound commitment to something more than a normal relationship, especially when the shadow emerges. It may seem foolhardy to hang in there when love disappears, yet wisdom shows us that is the natural journey. If real depth of love has been created when we first connect, that carries us through to the next renewal; and love does renew. Like the ocean its tides ebb and flow. The key is in knowing when the commitment is true enough and deep enough to flow through the darkness. We all know individuals who have stayed in a partnership when it's clear there is a lack of real growth potential. We may be one of them. We use a multitude of reasons other than love to stay together: comfort, money, fear of aloneness, to name a few. It is a sign of maturity to recognise when there's a commitment to love or an attachment to something other. None of this is wrong. We do what we do until we don't. Yet when loyalty to love as a principle reigns supreme, anything is possible. Renewal in some form is guaranteed. The truth and the challenge is that we have no control over how it appears.

Just as Juno guides us through the challenges of intimacy, her quality of devotion to embodying the finest frequencies of connection also carries us through other close partnerships. She's always involved where sex, money or deep transitions and growth are involved. As such Juno might appear in a business partnership, as a teacher-student relationship or as a guide through deep experience, such as a counsellor or mentor. This archetype's commitment to partnership empowers the growth of deep understanding that arises when we face life's shadows.

Commitment to partnership also runs alongside commitment to our own path. In the worst of her marriage conflicts, Juno simply disappeared. This reflects how in the winter phase of a relationship it is essential to reconnect with our true nature within; with the love within. Solitude brings the potential of rejuvenation. It strengthens our commitment to growing love within. Although it seems like retreat and may certainly be motivated by pain or conflict, this is a healthy aspect of Juno, much needed in partnerships, for it brings new life. Growing individuality is as much a part of union as togetherness. Juno carries this energy of togetherness and separation much as the natural cycles carry the energy of fullness and emptiness. In many ways Juno mirrors Ceres energy of the full cycle, yet for Juno it is expressed through the rhythms of relating. We seem to separate, to return to our self, in order to know the joy of re-union. It's a paradox; for in truth we are never separate. It's the great cosmic joke. The dance of separation and fulfilment is an illusion, yet it appears real.

The alchemy of sexual connection

As guardian of the principle of relatedness and the potential of sacred union, Juno is also a guide into the mysteries of female sexuality. Her calling to relatedness is the yearning to dissolve in physical union with her beloved.

Lovemaking opens the potential for unity to be experienced physically through orgasm. The potential is for separate selves to merge as one, if only for a moment. It's this merging that calls us deeply. To lose the self in an expansion into the wholeness we already are. This longing is Juno's realm within a committed partnership. Unlike Vesta, who understands sexual union as an impersonal pathway to the divine, Juno's yearning is to unite with her beloved. It's highly personal yet it also holds a potential for the personal to dissolve. Juno knows the energy of orgasm as much more than pure release. Its potency is not only blissful ecstatic union; it is transcendence. It is the end of separation. No wonder sexuality is so compelling. Aside from being a natural impulse of procreation its potential is our return to where we came from.

Orgasm is not only a highly enjoyable blissful temporary state. It holds the potential of form, the creation of children. It is where the creative power of the universe expresses through human beings. The moment of orgasm has infinite potential. It may be gathered to heal and rejuvenate the body. It may also be released towards conscious creation by bringing what is held in vision into form. Many years ago I was with a spiritual teacher whose lovemaking with his wife was always directed towards Earth healing. This is the alchemical aspect of Juno, where two become one and express pure creativity in flow. Juno's calling to fidelity was a desire to strengthen this capacity, that the Queen of Heaven and King of the Gods bless the earth and humanity in their sacred union and rejuvenate both. How different our perspective on sexuality would be if this understanding of the true power of orgasm were more widely available.

Everything comes from man and woman's lovemaking or sexuality. It's the origin of physical creation. It's where humanity starts. What we bring to love-making creates love or adds to separation. It's vital we understand the deeper energetic implications of sexual energy. It's essential we recognise our responsibility as women within sexual relationship.

Woman is the receptive and creative power as we have explored in the Venus chapter. Yet many of us do not understand this deeply or recognise the full consequences of our sexuality. When we take a man into our body, we take on his energy; all of it. Just as his penis penetrates the vagina, his energy penetrates ours on all frequencies. The recognition of this energetic transfer

218

has profound implications for our own integrity of relating yet also for the collective. We can create mayhem through our relationships. We know this. We know we disconnect from the heart through lack of discernment in sexuality. Yet perhaps we do not fully realise the implications for our self, or for our children and our world.

It's easy to see how the use of women's sexuality is rife in our world. We may condemn it, or campaign against it, yet the real responsibility lies with each of us to change this within our own lives. Every choice we make either adds to growing consciousness or to escalating pain. Every sexual choice either empowers us in love or pulls us apart in confusion and pain. Truly understanding this deepens our knowing of our creative power as women and our responsibility to make authentic choices in partnership. Making love with a deeply conscious man (or one of growing consciousness) can clear a woman's emotional pain; a deeply connected woman can heal a man through her love. It simply happens through conscious loving. Juno as Queen of Heaven holds space for this. Intimacy is the transformational field where this takes place. We open the potential for profound healing, or we feed the old attachments and separation within relating. We take on each other's energy, consciously or not. Recognising or knowing this opens the profound response-ability we have as women to be clear in our sexual choices. For the reasons we choose and who we choose has the potential to feed our children and the collective psyche with love. Isn't that what we want?

When deep love is flowing Juno is fully alive in relationship yet periodically, and very naturally, she retreats. It's part of her flow from fullness to emptiness, from summer to winter, from intimacy to aloneness. She is the Queen of Heaven. Her sacredness lies within herself and she knows this. Like Priestess Vesta, Juno holds an innate understanding of the deep inner connection needed to rejuvenate, especially when it's not flowing through intimacy. She is fullness in herself. It's her wisdom to return beyond all physical forms to her deep inner connectedness. In her authentic power, Juno is both alone and a partner. Yet her calling for divine union is ultimately compelling; she knows it is what she is here for. Unlike Vesta, whose sexuality is a sacred function of her role as priestess, Juno's choice is to a commitment in intimacy, to the full spectrum of relating and its transformation. Inevitably in that calling, the shadows will appear.

The Shadow of Juno

The games people play

Individuals have their own path in life and to create both a fulfilling individuality and loving partnership is perhaps the highest possibility for two people on Earth. All relationships are a synergy of the energetic fields of two individuals. There are places of merging and standing alone. There are spaces for togetherness and solitude, and of course any marriage calls forth an element of selflessness. The sacrifice of one's own wants and needs is sometimes essential for the good of the relationship itself. In conscious partnership how we create this dynamic interchange is the key to living sacred union. Relationship needs to be a living moving synergy for it to grow. There are always new challenges to communication and connection, negotiation and the occasional compromise are essential. Within that play, if we're awake enough, we get to see our positions of comfort or control, our subtle games and our ingrained tendencies. Relationships reveals the places we've grown familiar, where relating has become habitual, where love has lost its freshness.

Juno's mythology seems to suggest a complete lack of synergy in her partnership with Zeus. He did his own thing; she's the long-suffering partner who simply puts up with a bad deal in the relationship. That could be true, yet we must remember that she is Queen of Heaven, already complete in herself. The power games of the growing patriarchy were also at play in the myths. All is not as it seems.

Life and relationships always involve paradox. Juno's yearning is to partnership, yet the truth is, even as Queen of Heaven, she has no control over her consort. Nor would that be real. If she could control Zeus, she would not respect him. He would not be the strength of Divine Masculine presence she needs as a match. Does control ever work anyway? There's always a backlash. How may she create true partnership? The only way through is to walk the edge. She knows this. To stay connected to love within herself and her yearning for its expression; to stay available to love within partnership; to keep facing the shadow that arises when her love is not met. The relationship edge is that simple. It has no control yet is power-full in potential, precisely because of that. It is powerful in its simplicity and clarity. Yet such clarity is a challenge to our humanness, to our need for certainty or security, to our desire for knowing love through a beloved mirror. The crux is this: without deep self-connection we tend to get embroiled in relationship games. Even with it, the games are compelling. Precisely because we know their transformation is a way to deeper love.

We see the power games of relationship playing out in our world and we know them in our own lives. Even their subtlety doesn't mask them. Let's name a few: trading love for what's familiar, secure or financially stable; living through a partner, the woman who plays the power behind the throne; gaining kudos through a beautiful wife or successful husband; staying with a serial adulterer and gaining what seems to be power through being the 'good one' or the victim; sacrificing then manipulating emotionally. All these relationship games are based on powerlessness. When we feel powerless, we fall back on control, or manipulation, or some other game. These games arise in our relationships simply from not having the capacity or courage to stand up for love or step away into aloneness. We may not have confidence to feel we deserve more, or to assert our self. We may be afraid to leave, or that he or she will leave if we desire a different kind of relating. We may not realise what we're doing. We've become a relationship victim rather than a creator of love. It's not wrong; it's simply what we've learned. Yet the games are up now! Consciousness is growing. We're moving into more conscious relating where power games no longer work, where the shadows and pain of disconnection are rising in our self and in the world. It's the transition towards conscious partnership.

The game of playing the victim always carries false power. It's emotional manipulation. Yet if we've not been raised or haven't yet learned to stand in self-respect, we will try to find power wherever we can. If we've not been supported to know we're of value, simply through being who we are, then we'll try to find love in distorted ways. If we're not self-loving, we look for love in all the wrong places. We may be repeating a familial pattern of violence and abuse, or it may be subtler. Yet the distortion in our quest for love is endemic. In our culture, women have learned to trade their vital essence for what seems to be love. Yet in truth what is being given and what is being received? Is it love? Somewhere in us we know when it is and when it isn't. It is time for us as women to accept nothing less than love, a living sacred partnership; if that's real for you?

Human relationships often involve a trade-off of some kind. Yet Juno stands in her sovereignty. She knows in her bones that conscious partnership expresses a synergy of intimacy and individualism. She recognises that although she deeply longs for divine union on the Earth, it is also her greatest challenge. Maturity recognises that inevitably there are times in any relationship when the relationship synergy changes through necessity. There are times of busyness, stress and other focus. Then there are times when connection slips into old patterning. An innate imbalance looks different to a temporary shift in relationship engagement though. Ingrained beliefs and emotional patterns tend to express consistently; they're habitual. For instance, in over-giving we may expect love in return, because we're running on empty inside. In over-accommodating a partner, we may alternate being pushy for love with retreating in resentment. Perhaps one partner is more inclined to sacrifice personal desires than another. This is where Juno's desire for union can work against truly conscious relating. If we desire it too much, we can become appeasing, where compromise is an easy way out of standing alone, or it is done to avoid conflict. If one partner (Juno can be found in either male or female) is always accommodating in order to keep the peace, the relationship fails to thrive. Sacrifice can also be an agenda. Always being the one who is selfless, bestows subtle power. There are so many games we play in this dance.

None of these relationship games are wrong. After all, relating can be the most challenging aspect of our lives and staying awake can be difficult. They are simply games through which we may grow and mature. Juno is the fullness of the Feminine calling her Masculine to engage in conscious relating and transformation in human bodies. Even in her the pain of disconnection from her beloved manifests in the deepest of emotions – jealousy, rage, the desire for revenge. She is the both the heights and the depths of intimate connection and icy separation. Her and Zeus are the supreme game-players! Yet throughout all the games of adultery and humiliation, jealousy and rage, she maintains her commitment to love. She knows love is there underneath the play. She trusts that knowing. In truth she shows us where the true selflessness lies. It's not there in compromise, not even in collaboration. It lies in the dropping of our games into the well of love. From that deep well of love, growth naturally arises, for it is our true nature under all the challenges.

Love is a can-opener

When we give our heart in relating, when we open to another, we are at our most vulnerable. It's unsurprising then that we open up pain through our close relationships too. Love opens the door to all our un-love, the places we feel unmet, unheard, unaccepted. It's strange we don't recognise this as natural. Deep loving in this moment opens up the unresolved past in us. This is the cycle of healing growth.

In the tenderness of intimacy, it is natural that our fears and shadow energies arise. As human beings we want to defend or protect ourselves from pain. Pain is uncomfortable and emotional pain can feel devastating. We want to avoid it if we can, unless we're really awake. But maturity knows that when we love pain is inevitable sometimes. In the natural dance of connection and individuality there are bound to be misunderstandings, or even experiences we don't want. It's our response to these uncomfortable edges that both reveals and grows our maturity.

Pain is not always a sign that something is wrong. It can simply be a nudge to pay attention. Pay attention to what? Pay attention to what in us is calling for greater love. Pain is a sign we're going deep. It's an indicator that love is opening the self to what needs to heal. It's how we respond to the pain that is most important. Allowing our pain is a vital qualifier of real partnership. Not in the sense of inviting pain through disrespect or abuse, but in the knowing that disconnection is as valuable an aspect of relating as connection. It has a purpose – to open in us a fresh new loving potential. Without difference, without challenge, without disconnection, we stagnate and so do our relationships.

We make many different choices when pain assails us. We may close down; we may project it onto a partner in blame; we may deny or repress it; we may numb it with over-doing, food, drugs or work, or we may open to the bodily sensations of pain, feel to heal. The commitment to love works two ways. Juno shows us the commitment to deeper union with a partner and the commitment to open in deeper love within oneself. When we embrace our pain, when we don't make it into a story but feel it as sensation in the body, the potential is that embrace of self-connection may flow into relating. Yet it takes courage to face pain. It takes real honesty. This is where a deeper understanding of relationship alchemy is needed. Juno is that aspect of the Divine Feminine that will go through the fire of challenge and come out renewed. In the mythology her consort repeatedly humiliated her; she retaliated but she never gave up on love. She retreated to renew her self-connection. She revitalised her knowing of inner love then revisited her calling to relate, to express and know the divine union with her consort, her partner, her Beloved. She failed and failed again yet still was available. Disconnection led to renewed connection within which in turn led to the potential of connection in partnership; led to the potential of deeper union; led to disconnection. We know this cycle in relating, don't we? It's no smooth ride; but what relationship is? And if it is a smooth ride, is it truly alive?

In this dance that seems to go back and forth and in and out, if we're being conscious, we are developing muscles for deep healing and for love. To grow physical muscles, we have to use them. For a hand to be effective it must both open and close. It's the same in relating. The knowing of conscious relating truly arises in recognising that both the connection and the seeming disconnection are part of the whole picture of growth, that movement and change are natural. It goes against everything we desire as human beings – to constantly feel good; to know certainty, stability and security. Yet don't we also love the thrill of change, the passion of reconnection, the freshness of renewal and the return of love? The truth is that love never leaves, but sometimes we leave it. Our journey of developing relationship maturity lies in understanding how we close love down and how to open up through our difficulties.

The vital awareness when pain arises in a relationship is this: how far into disconnect do I go? Do I feed the pain through energising the story of it and then re-telling the sorry story to anyone who will listen? Do I hold the pain in and retreat, isolating myself in protection or defence against further heartache? Do I hold resentment and punish my partner through retaliation? Do I blame myself, moving further from love in self-judgment? There are so many games we play, none of which are wrong, yet it's clear to see some games further disconnect us from our self and our healing, some open a door into the potential of renewal. At times of disconnection, jealousy or hurt, we may retreat, with the intention of self-reconnection or merely to lick our wounds. We may rant and rage, storming at our partner, or we may open deeper in honesty, in raw connection. There is no right or wrong in this; it's the relationship game. If we can see it as such, the potential is we re-open the gate of love. We learn to have compassion for our humanness and to love it deeply, honestly, and in an authentic way. In that we may also understand and love another's humanity. It depends on our willingness, our commitment and on Grace.

It's natural in this play of connection and disconnect that fears and doubts arise. At times the question may well arise - Is he the 'right one'? Is he the one who will dare to go there? Has he the capacity? Is he true enough, deep enough? We could well ask that question of ourselves perhaps? Yet there is also the validity of a 'right match'. Not in terms of the 'shopping list' of what we think we want or need, but in terms of authenticity and commitment.

Here we need deeper understanding of the purpose of relating perhaps. To question; am I being realistic to expect constant loving? It's a bit like wanting constant summer isn't it? When we look, we may see that love's ebb and flow is through all seasons.

In the spring of love's beauty there's an attraction that calls us. We may not know exactly what it is but the attraction is enticing. In truth it's the match of mirrors – the potential for love and the particular patterns of shadow we need to face for deeper loving. This is the mystery of relationship, its perfect mix and its potency for alchemy. It's the unfolding of relationship evolution. Yet in that unfolding we tend to forget the growth part. We tend to want the good times to stay and the bad times to stay away. Often when challenge arrives so do the doubts. Yet the journey is simply to trust: to trust what is deepest truth in the moment and the next moment, and the next. It's about trust in oneself, trust in the process, trust in life and trust in the fact of change. In truth there is no certainty in relationship. If we are mature enough, we can trust this fact. This brings us to the challenge of trusting another.

There's no ownership in love

It's a challenging truth: there is no ownership in love. For how may we own another human being, or claim to possess an elusive yet tangible experience of love? What right do we have? Is love that personal, or is it a universal potential that anyone may know? Doesn't love come through Grace? The fact that love is a mystery is a clue that it arises from the Mystery. It is impersonal. Yet here's the paradox; when we open our heart in love with another it feels personal; it feels deeply personal. Because of this we are vulnerable; we want our heart to be held in love and in reverence and when it's not we face the deepest pain.

Infidelity is a core wound in a relationship. It might appear as a single betrayal of friendship through gossip, or a deeper deceit. Whatever its appearance, to the one wounded it is a violation, an abuse of trust or confidence. It hurts. It destroys, sometimes beyond redemption.

Infidelity seems to be about the betrayal of intimacy. But is it really? Can an experience of intimacy be lost? Can it be betrayed? Surely every experience is different. What I experience with someone else does not make my experience with you any less precious. Yet generally we feel it does. We feel demeaned when we're betrayed. Our perceived security in a particular form of love is rocked. We may feel we no longer matter, or that we're not truly wanted. Our trust in another may be shattered. Perhaps our trust in our self is broken in some way.

If we explore betrayal in a dispassionate way, we may see it always arises from a sense of breaking a boundary or perhaps an unwritten rule. Ideas like: 'If we're together we don't do this, or we don't go there; if we're together that means 'you're mine'. It arises from our beliefs, or perhaps our agreements, that 'relationship means....' It also arises from our beliefs about our self. If I was ...... enough, it would not have happened and so on. Whatever the story we tell ourselves about betrayal, there's no doubt that like love, betrayal is a can-opener. It reveals our innate lack of power to control a relationship. It makes us vulnerable; yet the truth is we are always vulnerable when it comes to the actions of others. The only real power we have is in our choices and in our response to their actions.

We see through the mythology that despite repeated betrayals, still Juno trusted in the potential for sacred union with her consort. Was she stupid? Some may say she was. Her commitment to love's full potential is without question though. She knew she had met her match. Her beloved was the King of the Gods; there was no finer possibility, even though his infidelities seemed to refute this. There are many myths centred on their marriage, with some surprising but revealing shadow themes that give us clues to the energies of the Juno archetype. They reveal that Juno mostly took revenge on the goddess or woman involved with her king rather than on him. Although there were occasions when she would mock him, or retreat from her marriage, more often than not she would project her dark emotions onto his latest lover, expecting her to pay for his infidelity. This archetype's shadow encompasses all the dark elements of relating such as possessiveness, jealousy, hatred and revenge. This begs the question why Juno would not express her hurt and rage to her consort. Yet it is also a clue to the distorted legacy of patriarchy, setting woman against woman in the growing dependency on men.

To turn one's focus for revenge on 'the woman' is not uncommon in our current times. It is a key Juno legacy still active in women as keeps the potential for dependence on a partnership safe to some degree. This is one aspect of our projective culture that also operates more generally, that seeks to blame rather than transform. This shadow of blame brings out the most damaged aspects of woman's pain within intimacy. Yet when we blame, we don't resolve. We merely push the pain away. Unwittingly in doing so we make ourself the victim rather than claim the power of self-transformation. Without doubt we feel like a victim when love is betrayed. We could say this is natural, yet infidelity also shows us the truth; that we cannot own love. The healing balm arises when we realise this, painful as it may be. Whilst the power of renewal lies in owning the pain arising from those actions that trigger us.

Juno was walking a fine line in her longing for the ultimate union. It brought her everything that seemed not to be love. Yet still she persisted. You may know this archetype in you and your relationships. Juno knew and held on to the potential, even through betrayal after betrayal. Some may question her self-respect. For how may we continue to open to one who betrays an intimate trust? To one who appears to abandon all intimate connection for lust? Yet here lies the paradox and the vital question. Was Juno committed to her beloved, or to her deep knowing of love and to its infinite potential for renewal?

The knowing of love cannot be betrayed. The knowing of love as one's true nature is the healing balm for betrayal. Its expression as loving union with another is always only a potential. It is always only temporary, although it may grow and deepen. Love is not guaranteed. It may be here one moment and gone the next. It may last a lifetime or just a season. It is Grace when we receive it, but we cannot hold it except as a knowing of our true nature. The truth of love is that no matter the shadows that appear, no matter their seeming strength and venom, love still remains. To stay with this knowing of love within oneself requires great courage, even greater humility. Yet love cannot be destroyed. No matter the circumstance it is still there inside. It may appear to die; it may turn to hate but it has merely changed its form for a while. The pain of betrayal may seem infinite. Yet to hurt is to know we're alive; to hate or to rage is to show we care. It is love's shadow. Yet where there is shadow there has to be light. Love is whole. It contains all.

Chapter 7
The Holistic Perspective – Pallas Athena

Like nature
we are patterns,
light and shade,
colour and hue,
every moment
a different tone,
unless we limit
and hold our self
tight
to one colour,
one tune,
and in so doing
fail
the unique artistry,
diverse creativity
of intelligence
being human
and beyond.

Cassandra Eve

Archetype: Wisdom Warrior

Symbols: serpent; owl; olive tree; spear; shield; golden armour; double-headed axe

Message: I see the whole picture. I act strategically from that place.

Expression: Creative feminine intelligence; strategy; reason and decision-making; the whole picture; guardian of the arts and artisans; healing; protector of the people; guide to the Greek heroes; the evolution of feminine intelligence

Shadow: the armoured Amazon archetype; Daddy's girl; supporting the patriarchal perspective; disconnection from the instinctual and emotional feminine; choosing achievement over love

How Pallas Athena expresses Venus energy: Pallas Athena expresses Venus's creative energy through accomplishment in the world, or through the creative and healing arts.

Pallas Athena (hereafter called Athena) represents feminine creative intelligence, a way of seeing that naturally knows the interconnectedness of life. Athena holds the gifts of intelligence and the quest for creative expression and contribution in the world. Strategist, advocate of justice, guardian and patroness of artisans, goddess of health and healing, Athena was a protector of the people and guide to the Greek heroes in their quests. Her capacity of intelligence is to see both the whole picture and its elements. She's highly attuned to differing frequencies of the mind. The Greek philosopher Plato refers to her as 'divine intelligence, she who has the mind of God'. Athena reveals to us the both the holistic perspective and the detail, pinpointing what needs attention or action whilst having awareness of far-reaching implications. This is creative feminine intelligence, living with relationship orientation and awareness of life's innate wholeness.

Her-story

Athena was a purely Greek divinity; no other culture had an equivalent goddess. She is one of the virgin goddesses, meaning she stands alone. In the Greek pantheon Athena was second only to her father Zeus/Jupiter. There are many myths that support our understanding of her and what she stands for in our consciousness as women. Her origins are lost in the myths of time yet there are pointers we will explore. Her birth myth is the most telling in terms of introducing her, her link to creative feminine intelligence and her role within evolution. In the Greek myth she was known merely as Athena at birth. The name Pallas came later.

In the most common myth of her birth it is said that Athena came fully formed from her father Zeus's head. Zeus had swallowed his wife Metis when she became pregnant, as he feared being overthrown by one of his children. This is yet another allegory for how the growing patriarchy were swallowing up the goddess cults. Shortly after this he had a terrible headache. He requested the God of the forge, Hephaestus, to cleave his head open with a double-headed axe. Athena sprang out fully formed, clad in golden armour, snake-headed Medusa on her breastplate and bearing a spear. The miraculous birth of this virgin goddess is wonderfully described by Homer in one of his hymns: 'snow-capped Olympus shook to its foundation; the glad earth re-echoed her martial shout; the billowy sea became agitated and Helios, the sun-god, arrested his fiery steeds in their headlong course to welcome this wonderful emanation from the Godhead.' Athena was at once admitted into the assembly of the gods on Mount Olympus.

As is often the case with goddess myths, Athena's birth also has more ancient roots. Her origins may be based in the Triple Goddess Neith (also known as Egyptian Mother Goddess Isis) of Lake Triton in Libya and Egypt. They may also lie in the tribes of female Amazon warriors who were the enemies of the Greeks. The Amazons lived in small tribes around the Black Sea and up into Mongolia. Although it is claimed they cut off their right breast to allow their sword arm freedom of movement, burial mounds containing the remains of warrior horse women reveal this is a fallacy. Nonetheless there is the connection with the strength and power of Athena as a warrior for wise action. Later adopted by the Minoans of Crete, we see Athena in the snake goddesses of that culture. The serpent association with wisdom and prophecy threads its way through all these expressions.

Despite the Greek perspective, Athena is not a goddess of war. Here we see the growing influence of patriarchy once more, where the expression of feminine energies became distorted. Athena's golden armour signified that her purity and wisdom were unquestionable. She did inspire, and even fight alongside, some of the Greek heroes but her support was synonymous with the virtues of justice and skill, whereas her brother Ares (Roman Mars) represented the blood lust of war. An exploration of Athena's mythology reveals that her main role was one of guide, protector and strategist, in contradiction to her brother who loved war for its own sake. Mainly Athena became involved in direct conflict only as the result of an order from her father Zeus, to whom she was a faithful wise counsellor.

The addition of Pallas to Athena's original name came through an early experience related in myth. After Athena was born fully formed from Zeus's forehead, Triton (son of Poseidon) acted as a foster parent to the goddess, raising her alongside his own daughter Pallas. Athena and Pallas loved each other dearly; they were bonded as friends, sisters and perhaps as lovers. The sea god taught both girls the art and strategy of competition. During an athletics festival, Pallas and Athena fought with spears in a friendly mock battle. Zeus, afraid to see his daughter lose, acted to distract Pallas. Athena, expecting her friend to dodge her spear, impaled her accidentally and Pallas died. Overcome with grief Athena took her friends name. She also carved a statue of her friend that was wrapped in the aegis (a shield or animal skin worn by Zeus). This statue was named the Palladium and came to represent the safety of the city of Athens whilst the aegis bestowed invulnerability on its wearer.

In yet another myth it is told that Pallas was a goddess of the invading Indo-European tribes. Her name was linked with Athena's, as were those of many other goddess figures, particularly those of the eastern Mediterranean areas such as Crete. In this way we see how the merging of two or more cultures was accomplished in a time of great change and growing patriarchy.

Following the death of her friend, Athena became protector of the state and stood for the maintenance of peace. Her temples were generally built on citadels, to enable clear views of the harbour and city walls and ensure the safety of the city. Athena's most celebrated temple is the Parthenon, on the Acropolis at Athens. It contains her world-renowned statue by Phidias, nine feet high, composed of ivory and gold, complete with spear and serpent, and second only to his statue of Zeus.

Athena's role as protector of the people of Athens finds it roots in her ancient position as the Minoan's household goddess. We see her in the Minoan snake goddesses found at the ancient site of Knossos. Here she was guardian of the family and of the palace, with her serpents as protection of the food supply. Her tools were the implements of domestic craft and utility: the spindle, the pot and the loom, along with the plough. The Minoan culture was very refined, creating the most intricate gold jewellery, flawless ceramics and sacred drinking vessels. Athena was the symbol of community and the

236

peaceable Minoan civilization reflects her gifts expressed at their finest. The snakes held by the Minoan Snake Goddesses confirmed her representation of the dark mysterious feminine and may also have symbolize a priestess or oracular role within the culture.

As Athena emerged in Greek culture her role transformed. This brought radical change for women. The myth of how she came to be guardian of the city of Athens shows us how the ancient goddess-based cultures were in the process of being overthrown by patriarchy. In a contest for guardianship of the city of Athens with the god Poseidon, Athena wins but the female gender loses its rights. This myth states that the Olympian deities chose Athena as city guardian as she had planted the first olive tree. The olive tree was deemed most useful to the citizens of Athens, providing them with olives, oil for lamps and wood for their fires. They judged Athena was better qualified for the role, as Poseidon God of the Sea, the only other contender, had brought only an ever-changing sea.

Following the Olympian deity's decision, the men of Athens agreed to accept Athena as guardian of the city on three conditions: that the women forego being called citizens, that they no longer vote and that their children be called by the father's name rather than the mother's. Women's rightful place within the culture was being systematically destroyed. As the dawning of patriarchy became more established women turned their need for protection away from their innate connection with Mother Earth, the rhythms of nature and each other towards men. Athena was a bridge between the old and the emerging new ways of civilisation, or more pertinently, what was deemed to be civilisation at that time. She was there as guide and guardian and so is an indicator of what was happening in evolutionary terms.

Over time Athena became the guardian of law and order and patroness of learning, science and art, presiding over inventions such as the plough, the use of numbers, crafts and artisans, spinning and weaving. She wove her own robe along with that of Hera, which she is said to have embroidered very richly. She also wove the hero Jason's cloak, for his quest for the Golden

Fleece. With her wide-ranging guardianship Athena was as strong in her influence on the advancement of culture as she was in her role as strategist and protector. She is a multi-faceted goddess as we shall discover.

Competition with her sister goddesses or mortal women and her support of the Greek heroes, namely Perseus and Hercules, is a strong theme through Athena's mythology. We see her first in competition with her fellow goddesses. It is a theme that runs through her archetype. For Athena's preference was for the males. The myth of The Golden Apple explored in the Venus chapter sees Athena at odds with the Greek goddesses Aphrodite (Venus) and Hera (Juno) who all hold different qualities and guardianship of feminine energy.

Another myth reveals more of Athena's competitive nature with females. Arachne, the princess of Lydia, who was a master weaver, challenged Athena to a weaving contest. Attempting to distract or anger Athena, Arachne wove images of the gods and goddesses in lewd poses. Seeing Lydia's weaving was superior, despite its offensive design, Athena shredded it. She could not bear to be beaten and in shame Lydia hung herself. Out of pity, Athena loosened the rope and Arachne turned herself into the first spider.

The most well-known of the Athena myths concerns her role in the slaying of Medusa, whose snake-entwined head is seen on Athena's breastplate. There are two versions to the start of this story; one in which Medusa made love with Poseidon in the temple of Athena voluntarily and one in which he raped her. These contradictory tales are common in the Greek myths, representing the transition to patriarchy that was happening at that time. Whichever way their sexual union took place when Athena discovered the desecration of her temple, her rage fell on Medusa. Strange that she should blame Medusa rather than Poseidon, or both equally, but here we see the play of Athena's shadow preferences begin to emerge. She turned the once beautiful Medusa into a Gorgon, with a swathe of hissing snakes for hair and the ugliest of faces. Furthermore, she swore that whatever living being Medusa gazed upon would be turned to stone. Medusa was doomed to remain in this state until the prize of her head was named as the goal of one of Perseus's quests. Athena was Perseus's mentor in this quest; we can see her role as both Medusa's captor and the means to her release. The story goes like this.

Perseus was the son of Zeus and Danae, a mortal. Tricked into his quest to obtain Medusa's head by King Polydectes, Perseus was unsure how to undertake the task without being turned to stone by Medusa's gaze. There are several long versions of this myth relating how he obtained winged sandals, the cloak of invisibility, a curved sword and a bag in which to put Medusa's head however Athena gifted him his best support, a mirrored shield. She advised him to hide behind this shield whilst using the mirrored surface to approach Medusa whilst she slept. This enabled Perseus to cut off her head.

Medusa was pregnant by Poseidon at the time of her beheading, so as her head came off Pegasus, a winged horse, and Chrysaor, a giant wielding a golden sword, sprang from her body. Eventually Perseus brought Medusa's head to Athena and her image was placed on Athena's breastplate. Some feminists see this as the ultimate insult to sisterhood, yet it could be said that Athena was honouring and releasing Medusa, recognising her as another aspect of herself; the dark face of female instinctual intelligence. The fact that her face sits on Athena's breastplate, over her heart, is perhaps a clue to a deeper aspect of Athena we have yet to discover.

Athena also aided her half-brother, the Greek hero Hercules, in his twelve labours. On realising he had become mad in his endeavour to gain immortality, she eventually killed him. Through all these myths we see her role as a major participant in the play of the gods and the heroes of the day. Athena's active role within their dramas reveals the growing emergence of new qualities of feminine intelligence at that time.

Athena's place in the Universe – Astronomy & Astrology

Athena is third largest asteroid in the asteroid belt and the second asteroid to be discovered, by the German astronomer and physician Wilhelm Olbers on March 28, 1802. It is named after the Greek goddess of wisdom.

Athena's astrological placement in a birth-chart reveals how an individual expresses and acts on their holistic intelligence. She shows differing styles of perception and its creative application and manifestation. We may see Athena signifying a capacity for craft or artisan work, healing, the arts, law or politics. She shows how we make our way in the world of work and grow our sense of purpose and accomplishment, with the journey of its seeming successes or failures. In relationship Athena reveals how we connect as a friend or ally, gender-based competitiveness and alliances, and has specific relevance to father-daughter dynamics.

My Journey with Athena

I grew up in a family where emotional expression was not allowed. Feelings were denied but intellect lauded. It's no wonder as a girl I felt as if I'd been adopted or flown in from another planet. I'm a full-moon-sensitive. Athena has her place in my self-expression but it took much life experience to recognise her fully.

When I reached the age of ten my father's focus on intellect and success began to dictate my fate. The journey to Athena was beginning. After I passed the eleven plus examination, I won a scholarship place at boarding school. I didn't want to board but it wasn't discussed. I was simply taken there and left. My parent's desire for me to do well academically was beginning to surface.

Boarding school was a nightmare for the fragile young girl I was. I found myself in a place where I knew no one. The denial of my need for home and family, my sensitivity and feelings were amplified by my parents' sole focus on achievement. As an adult I came to understand my parents desire for me to be the success they felt they hadn't attained for themselves. As a young girl I simply felt rejected. The need to have my feelings and my voice acknowledged was profound. Yet I couldn't really speak about how I felt. There was no space for it in our family. Inevitably I had to settle into this new way of life. The journey between home and school became just a transition from one place to another. Emotionally I was living in a desert whilst achievement became a measure of my value.

Over time it was discovered that I had a flair for languages so was streamed into Latin, French, German and Spanish. When I succeeded in passing all ten of my O Levels including four languages, I felt relieved. Surely this would bring the recognition I so desperately needed. Feeling I'd proved my worth intellectually, I asked to become a weekly boarder, spending weekends at home. I was longing to be part of normal family life and my growing and very natural need for a social life was strong. But my success in exams meant my father's dream of success had been ignited and I was refused. I assume my mother agreed but her views weren't expressed and so I stayed on as a boarder. Yet there was a change. I began to realise no one was going to support what I wanted; I had to look after myself. The fact that I didn't know how hadn't yet dawned on me. I didn't really know what I wanted, other than to be at home, be loved by my family and have a normal teenage life. Over the next two years I rebelled. I failed to work. I skipped classes. Friends and I escaped the boarding house in the small hours, roaming the village lanes. I became a rebel, up for fun rather than study. I began to smoke and drink. The desire for freedom was strong. I'd realised the only voice that might be heard was that of rebellion.

Rebellion has its price and its harvest. When I failed my A Level grades for university, I betrayed my father's dream. Yet it was the start of reclaiming myself. Despite my pain at disappointing him, and the deepening feeling of not being good enough, I was affirming my right to be me. Clear that I wanted to find my own path, I took a stand to do so. Despite my mother's pleas that I attend bi-lingual secretarial college, I found a job. The rebel came out of the closet in open defiance. It was a turning point in finding my power, albeit from a place of mutiny. Within two years I was married. There was truly nothing my parents could do... except silently disapprove.

No matter how strong a statement, rebellion is never a cure for lack of love. And perhaps lack of love wasn't the real issue? It's easy to see that with hindsight. My father's valuing of the gifts of intelligence was showing me something. It was his way of loving me. I wasn't mature enough to see it through. I simply felt rejected. My mother's lack of real engagement in my life was a clear indicator too. Athena's themes were emerging. Yet I could not see her then. I had to rebel to begin my own journey.

The years of my womanhood became an experiment in discovering who I was. It was a long journey that brought me through much experience into an inner synergy of feeling, intelligence and intuitive sensitivity. That road took me into the shadow realms. My rebellion against the gifts of intellect and rationale did not help. Yet I had to experience the whole realm of emotional experience in order to integrate my gifts. Twenty years with spiritual Masters and Mothers and living in community profoundly supported that journey. Eventually Athena began to come through consciously. The gift of creative intelligence expressing as wisdom is her expression.

Funnily enough, after many years I discovered that my father's dream for me had a hint of intuitive truth. He wanted me to be a diplomat or a translator. Strangely enough I am a translator, yet not of the spoken language. Since awakening in the late 80s this gift is what has been growing. I have been blessed with deepening into the multi-faceted nature of feminine intelligence. I have been called to fully accept my intuition, a sensitive embodied capacity to simply connect deeply and know, and an inner connection and teaching communication with Spiritual Masters and Mothers who are both in the body and not.

At times awakening took me into what seemed like intuitive craziness yet always I was held in love. Subtle levels of inner connection and knowing were shown to me manifest as I let go and embraced the depth of my inner experience. Now I acknowledge one of my major gifts lies in the realm of creative feminine intelligence, the translation of energetic frequencies, universal and cosmic, arising and expressing in the human realm. Athena's play and gift in that is clear. She is a strong placement in my birth chart. Creative feminine intelligence has found its place within my life.

What is creative feminine intelligence?

To discover what creative feminine intelligence is we first must step back in time. Looking at the evolution of male and female human beings we might see how intelligence has taken two pathways. Those two pathways are now available within either gender. Perhaps they always have been, but social conditions dictated differently, and experience was needed to bring them forth. If we go back to our earliest known beginnings, we may see what informed them originally.

In the times of the hunter-gatherer people men and women had vastly different functions. Man was the hunter; he had a specific goal that ensured the survival of the tribe, to catch and bring home the food. Men worked both alone and in teams to achieve this task. The honour of being the one to make the kill ensured also that each man was acting both alone and as a team member in pursuit of the goal. Teamwork and competition worked side-side by side. We can see this same play in our world now. It's much as a game of football isn't it? We might see it in the boardroom or on the stock market? It seems we've evolved yet perhaps not? The current focus may not be driven by physical survival but it's still on competition and winning. It's still on 'making a killing'.

Whilst men were hunting, women tended the hearth, gathering and cooking food, and looked after the tribe's children communally. They were the caretakers. They may well have assumed other roles, as would the men. Cave paintings suggest a sacred connection to nature and the animal kingdom. We would call that shamanism. Ancient goddess figurines suggest veneration of the female form was part of the culture too. Nonetheless in the more survival orientated aspects of life, men and woman held differing roles. When we consider the caretaking role, or relating, it's obvious goal focus has no place. A different aptitude is required when tending the children, watching the fire, gathering plants and herbs, cooking the meal whilst also listening for subtle nuances that suggest conflict or being aware of potential danger approaching the group shelter. Here we see holistic intelligence at play.

Holistic intelligence is spatial, subtle, aware; it's tuned in to people and levels of connectedness, and open to signals within the environment that indicate a vast array of potentials. Much like a web, this intelligence operates at a centre (the individual) and on its threads, radiating out through people and the environment, touching everything lightly and aware of the smallest signals. At that time it activated and expressed an instinctual response or reaction. It still does so now even though we've apparently become more evolved. In the everyday world of human beings now we might call this quality intuitive perception and it's linked to the survival response. A fairly obvious one is the skill of multi-tasking, the capacity to manage multiple strands of expression and action. Yet it is so much more.

Fast forward to current times and we can see the cross-over of roles in gender, and gender itself, evolving exponentially. It seems our capacity to know ourselves as human beings rather than as gender-based individuals is growing. Yet what about our brain wiring? What of our ancestral patterning? And what of our evolving consciousness? We are a multi-faceted and complex mix. If we look solely at gender, it's clear male and female have evolved to hold different roles within society and those roles are constantly changing, but are the male and female brain wired differently? Some scientists say they have discovered approximately one hundred gender differences in the brain. Others state that the differences are minimal. The dividing line is immaterial really for social conditions may well be the predominant factor in how male and female intelligence have developed. The need of the times, the tribe or family dictated the structure in the main (whether it was fair or balanced is another matter). There were always anomalies however, often hidden due to social mores.

All we can say with certainty about our evolving intelligence and its functionality is that change is ongoing. As we've emerged from the primordial soup of creation we have moved through many stages in the evolution of human intelligence. We have reached yet another now. Who knows where that is going in the 21st century? Perhaps 'male or female' is an inappropriate label now, yet when we speak about intelligence there is clearly a difference between goal-orientated or creative, rational or intuitive, reasoning or spatial. We know this as right or left-brain dominance. These differing expressions of intelligence are accessible within a male or female body. Potentially either one may be dominant.

What does right or left-brain dominance have to do with the Athena archetype? If we look at her role within the evolutionary context, we find she arises at the time of the changeover from the goddess based ancient earth-connected cultures of the eastern Mediterranean to the patriarchal world brought in from around 2000BC onwards by invading warrior tribes from the east and north. These warrior tribes worshipped a single male deity. Over time the goddesses of the earth-based cultures were either married off to the invader's god or subjugated, much as Christian churches were built on pagan sites. Athena represents a bridge in this cross-over period and the shift towards patriarchy. Being born from her father Zeus's head (the Godhead of that time) Athena signifies the emerging shift in female intelligence, also in how women were seen and treated. At this time women became subject to the rule of father or husband i.e., emerging from his head and his authority, not individuals in their own right.

As the Athena archetype was a bridge to the change towards patriarchy, I see she is also a bridge to an evolutionary shift unfolding now, our response and reaction to it, and the process of yet another evolutionary leap taking place. At that time Athena held the potential of an evolution, bringing not only reason but consciousness to the ocean of irrational-feeling-intuitive-knowing-sensing womanhood that had been dominant before. Athena represented a point of change expressed through the denial of the feminine as it was known then. The male was becoming dominant as was masculine linear goal orientated intelligence. Yet perhaps this was an essential change in terms of evolution, like the pendulum swinging from one point to its opposite before the falling into balance.

Feminists have denounced Athena as a traitor to her own gender and yet perhaps her role had a function on a much larger scale than has been recognised? For Athena is a major archetype in the evolution of female intelligence from instinctual and intuitive to conscious. Her holistic intelligence is needed particularly at our current point of evolution, as we navigate the play of both instinct and consciousness, dark and light frequencies at play in ourselves and our world.

Pattern recognition intelligence

The development of intelligence is not just related to what or how much we know, it's connected to how we process and connect facts, ideas and experience to other mental constructs. Pattern recognition intelligence was key to the survival of our Neanderthal ancestors, allowing them to identify poisonous plants, distinguish predator from prey, and interpret the signals of body language. The repetition of experience builds mental and habitual patterns; patterns that are essential for navigating our way through this world, yet patterns that must also evolve as times change.

We use pattern recognition intelligence in our lives every day without even realising it. Our lives depend on our capacity to join the dots of sensory input with experience and navigate our way through the complexity of multiple daily choices. Is it safe to cross the road? Shall I have this or that to eat for lunch? Is she telling me the truth? What do I need to do next? We make multiple decisions daily depending on sensory input, our inner landscape, past experience and natural tendencies; on facts, rationale or intuition, insight or knowing. This capacity to connect the dots will vary from one human being to another yet the ways we make these choices and the information we tend to favour will vary even more so. Head or heart? Logic or gut feeling? Intuition or fact? We all have a tendency to value one over another, perhaps depending on context but certainly influenced by our natural proclivities. So where does Athena come into this exploration? What is her role?

Athena reveals to us the map of intelligence. More than that, she is a map maker. She's the map in terms of our perception of the inter-connectedness and interplay of everything in our current life. She's the map maker in terms of how we respond to incoming experience and its potential influence on that map. She's our capacity to intuitively know and connect the dots in an intelligent, holistic way and then to respond with understanding of the potential implications. We do this naturally through pattern recognition intelligence. For example: I've done that before, and this was the result. Once we recognize the pattern, we can make conscious choices to go beyond it, because we see potentials for something new to emerge.

Another skill of Athena intelligence is to cross the bounds of time that bind a goal to the future. She sees through or pierces the linear time-frame. Her spear is a representation of her capacity to penetrate to the core of an issue. She holds the capacity of seeing both the entirety and its elements. With this gift, like an architect, she is constantly creating new interior structures and maps. We could see her as representing evolution at play through our capacity for intelligence. Creating new maps always involves an element of risk and courage, even strategy. Here we begin to understand Athena's key gifts, and her unique role as guide to heroes.

A woman in a man's world

Athena has many faces. Her gift of creative feminine intelligence means we cannot place her in just one sphere and despite her labelling in the Greek culture as Goddess of Wisdom and War she is so much more. What the Greek perspective denies is her rootedness in the ancient goddess cultures. That denial was necessary in order to establish patriarchy. The prevailing influence at that time was to sanitize and limit the mysterious sacred feminine realm, even to denounce it. One of Athena's symbols is the owl, a bird of night's darkness. Her connectedness to serpent wisdom through the Minoan Snake Goddess, reveals she is so much more than a warrior of intellect. Her battles

247

are fought through wise intelligence and the use of strategy. Her wisdom rises from ancient roots and encompasses expression as artisan, intellectual, diplomat, inventor, knower of life's mysteries, healer, seer, campaigner, politician, to name but a few of her faces but perhaps the Greeks had an agenda of making her a Goddess of War to fit the growing patriarchal world view.

This theme of change to suit the circumstances or desire for power wends its way through the whole Athena journey. In essence her journey parallels our evolution as women. It takes time for the fullness of a new archetype to appear through the collective, only appearing in a rare individual here and there. Athena's journey from primordial snake goddess to Greek warrior goddess links with the evolutionary journey of women from the late 19th century onwards. Until this point most women were powerless to develop their intellect, or if they did so they had to keep hidden for fear of censure and rejection. The gifts of feminine knowing, earth connection and healing were denied; hidden from plain sight on pain of punishment or death.

There are women, even in current times, whose gifts, discoveries and achievements have been used and usurped by men. Patriarchy has abused women and in the main, we have allowed that through fear. Female scientists, writers, artists, healers, educators and campaigners have excelled and yet not been given credit for their creative inventiveness or contribution. The take-over is still very much alive. We are claiming our right to be seen, heard, acknowledged and honoured, yet still we must be aware of it. Along with our own subtle yet insidious denial of the uniqueness and excellence of creative feminine intelligence.

Looking back in time we could see Greek Athena as the woman in the world of her time i.e., the Greek culture. According to their birth myth she had no living mother and therefore no female role model. Her early experience of female friendship, with her friend Pallas, ended in tragedy. The potential for her to experience sisterhood with other goddesses was marred by competitiveness. Her relationship to Zeus her father was the primary

248

connection. Athena bowed to his authority, in the main. She became an agent of his will. Nonetheless it was in how she executed his demands that we see the expression, use and development of her own holistic and strategic intelligence. In fulfilling her father's will she did it her own way. At times she even dared to disobey Zeus. In Homer's Iliad she is cited as being furious with Zeus's hardness and ingratitude. Nonetheless she is clearly afraid of his anger whilst mostly being aligned with him over what needs to happen to keep the affairs of both gods and humans in order. It is in the 'how' of accomplishment that we see Athena shine, for it's here her gift for holistic perception and strategy is revealed.

The Athena archetype now

We've given Athena context in her time and place but how does she express, develop and grow in us now? How does she signify the ways we navigate our place and purpose in the world?

The Athena journey begins through relationship to mother and father yet is emphasised particularly through our connection to male authority and role models. Each of us will have a unique Athena aptitude within her wide spectrum of creative activity. This may be brought out through education or work, or simply through experience. Through education we learn the use of the rational mind; we are called to develop discipline and the capacity to get things done. Through our working lives, even in choosing work that relies more on caring skills than rationale, we will have to develop Athena's detachment and decision-making capacity. It's a natural part of maturing. It's how we come to make decisions and how we learn to detach from our instinctual emotional responses that will signify our connectedness to Athena. Do we simply cut off from anything but goal focus to achieve a task? Sometimes that is a necessary strength. Yet if that becomes a habit, or our comfortable place, we miss out on Athena's broader inclusive perspective.

Through the Greeks Athena has been portrayed as an active archetype for goal-focused rationale. She is attracted to the world of men, the world of power. She wants to play the game. Many strong Athena women are also attracted to power, yet at what cost? Perhaps they have had to play the patriarchal way to find their place? Many women have become successful through using a masculine goal-orientated intelligence. It does not belong exclusively to men after all. Yet healthy intelligence is always about balance. Over-use rationale and we disempower our deeper more instinctual rootedness in feminine wisdom. Perhaps it's a price we have chosen to pay for what pretends to be liberation? Yet it's becoming increasingly clear that a strong woman in any worldly arena competing via the old paradigm is not liberated. She may have taken a brave step and yet it's not fulfilling. It may leave her dry and exhausted. The need to achieve, to fit in and yet beat the system play against each other. How much of herself does she have to forego to wield the influence she desires? What other aspects of her life pay the price for her collusion or fight with the patriarchy? It's a different and difficult compromise for every woman. Yet the winds of change are stirring. Our deeper calling, along with the necessity to think differently about the personal and collective cost of success, is becoming clear.

Athena is an evolving goddess archetype, and we are still growing in the acknowledgment of her gifts. Our need to value the synergy of rationale and intuition as wisdom is essential, not only to ourselves but to our collective survival. Without doubt our cultures need to hear and value the unique perspective of the disenfranchised sectors of society, particularly the women, our earth-honouring tribal cultures and our elders. It's clear we need to fully acknowledge and change our relationship to the earth. We need to recognise the potential impact of every choice we make, through the interconnectedness of life. This is Athena's realm when she is in balance. She sees what's needed for the whole. We're at the centre of the web of creative intelligence and intimately connected with everything on it.

This capacity for seeing the whole and diverse aspects of a set of circumstances made Athena a valuable mentor or friend to the Greek heroes. Her intelligence was used in their service. She could see what they couldn't. She is also known for following her father's lead. Yet this perspective is only partial. A woman's capacity for reasoning and decision-making, strategy and action, although valuable, does not fully actualise her depth of knowing. It's like looking through glasses with only one lens. In her full archetype Athena reveals that the 'how' of action and its potential impact at every stage of a process is as vitally important as the vision or goal - as is our capacity to live with uncertainty or to acknowledge our intuition, gut feeling or womb knowing. Wisdom grows through the bringing together of all these elements of intelligence. If our Athena intelligence is strong, we know that in any endeavour the process is as important as the goal, if not more so.

Process orientation is an Athena intelligence; it does not deny goal focus but expands on it. This all-inclusive view expresses wholeness as a vital aspect of any endeavour and more importantly at every stage of any endeavour. Wholeness is authenticity; for without this holistic view, we may be avoiding or denying aspects of a situation that have vital value. If we don't realise, or if we choose to deny, the interconnectedness of life within the manifestation of a vision, our web of life suffers somewhere. This is plain to see, both personally and collectively, especially in these times. The price of goal focus personally might be lack of time for deep relationships, damage to our health, or leave us feeling over-stretched and stressed. Collectively the cost is our relationship to each other, a true sense of community and the desecration of our earth. Linear perception has its place for it's how we reach, strive, grow and evolve. Yet the healthy Athena archetype reveals the linear perspective can become disconnected from reality and relatedness, dry and hard, lacking real life because it lacks real connection here and now. It's based on a projection of achievement without real presence or accountability.

Women's full embrace of the gift of Athena brings strength, the wise holistic perspective and capacity to speak and act from that place. It's about an ability to perceive what's evident and what's intangible and to be in the world from a new place of consciousness, as warriors for the deep sacred feminine. It's engaging the fight for what is right for the whole. It is time now for feminine intelligence in women and men to stand and speak what they know so the culture will hear. For women in particular this is what it means to be a woman in a man's world now. It's no easy task but it's surely a worthwhile one. It takes a heroine to truly value and be herself, to follow her knowing, to stand for that and to risk all. Women's role in the world has changed dramatically over the last fifty years. Many women have entered the world and played the patriarchy at its own game. The game is evolving though and it's becoming more necessary for feminine intelligence to be claimed if we are to survive. The potential is that we're stepping into a higher activation of Athena energies now as more women learn to stand in that core feminine intelligence for their self and for their world. But it is up to the individual.

The Athena archetype is a vital guide to us in these changing times, for without our feminine intelligence, the heart's desire may not be fully perceived or actualised. The emergence of female world leaders, environmental activists and other pioneers who guide with forthright service-orientated expression and action, reveal this 'new woman of the world' is coming to life. To be a new woman of the world now requires that we honour the feminine perception of right relationship and interconnectedness. That is right relationship to the aim, to how we achieve it, to the cost of every element, to the personal and collective impact, to the environmental implications. This need for change is not about making our global culture a woman's world. It's about bringing new life to our world through feminine seeing, insight and wisdom. It's about the voice of feminine holistic intelligence being heard, acknowledged and honoured. That starts with each one of us discovering the courage to acknowledge our unique gift of intelligence and to make our voice heard. In that quest, we heal personally whilst contributing to collective change.

The demise of goddess and community-based cultures brought a power shift. The politics of power was born in its place. In her time Athena entered the world of politics. One of the Cambridge Dictionary definitions of politics is this: the relationships within a group or organisation that allow particular people to have power over others. This is the prevailing issue in the collective right now. The healthy Athena political perspective is not about 'power over', it is about alliance; it's about 'power with' or 'power alongside'. It's about what serves the task and what serves the whole. Our cultures, particularly the political aspects, are starved of Athena's gifts. Yet she is alive, mainly in the background. She's here in the environmentalists, feminists, educators, campaigners, artists and artisans. Yet the value of their differently edged perspective is not seen, heard or valued in a world based on consumerism and expansion. Perhaps we need to shout louder? Without doubt we need to understand the value of this archetype more deeply and embrace Athena's gift as bridge-builder.

The weave of life

The predominant view on Athena as a Greek goddess of war does not recognise her role as a bridge between ages and cultures. Much of her-story is lost in the mists of time yet if we look at the supreme artisanship of the Minoan culture it is clear several aspects of the Athena archetype were thriving within that ancient civilization. Although she may have been named differently then, what we know as Athena's gift of guardianship of creativity is very alive. Perhaps she was also muse, priestess, goddess, guide into the serpent mysteries for the Minoans. Their snake goddesses signify an ancient connection to feminine wisdom. Despite her later portrayal as a goddess of reason by the Greeks it's that capacity for wise understanding that Athena brings to their culture. Her connection to craftsmanship also endured.

The vision to create a beautiful ceramic pot does not take form without a deep understanding and connection to every part of the process, whilst the necessity for presence and perspective in each part of a process in undeniable. Skip one element and the possibility of an aesthetically pleasing manifestation falls away. Every true artisan knows this fine balance of focused attention yet openness to far-reaching vision. Every true artist knows the artistic process has its unique journey beyond his or her own agenda. This is the serendipity of connection, how together the energies of artist and the process combine to make artistry, how the mind must be open to receive differing frequencies of creative process and craftsmanship at different times.

True artists fall into the timeless when they are in creative flow. This reveals a surprising numinous quality to Athena we have not met before where she calls us into the experience of life as a mysterious melee of interconnected energies and potential. The mind tries to make some sense of this. It does so through excluding some inputs and engaging others. Yet the creative process opens up channels of the mind that are not ordinarily engaged. It can literally take us beyond our self. Whether it's through the composition of a piece of music, a complex mathematical problem or sitting at the potter's wheel we move into a field of potent open creation. What we see in artistry is this play of potent creation, of wholeness, appearing through process. It's almost as if the pot or painting is already complete somewhere and merely has to appear. This is the alchemy of creativity and its potential for magnificence.

Athena holds space for this potency of artistry. We could say she represents the intelligence of the web of frequency and its potential manifestation. Whether the creation is a new structural framework for a business, a colourful handwoven carpet or a gourmet meal, Athena perception sees both the parts and the whole, with its potential manifestation and evolution. This capacity of creative intelligence does not stop at the goal or hold it as the only possibility. It's open to the constant arrival of new elements. Much as a mother preparing a meal must have on ear open for her sleeping child, this intelligence is actively looking and listening for other potentials to emerge whilst also fully present with the current template. It's open and connected to the ever-flowing, ever-expanding weave of life because that is its very nature.

If we consider Athena's guardianship of healers, we may see similar threads. A healer has the aim of bringing health to an imbalance in the body-mind system. Whatever tool or system they are using, awareness is always in the wider field of perception, feeling into the differing elements of the imbalance. Listening for subtle body or energy signals, tuning into unacknowledged aspects of the imbalance, the healer's skill lies in broad holistic perception. This requires both depth understanding and the capacity to let that go in order that new information may present itself. It's in the synergy of both parts and whole that the healer discovers, or perhaps more appropriately is led to be a catalyst for rebalancing. Does the healer act on his or her own? Are they operating in a vacuum? No, they are simply a catalytic aspect of a whole process with many parts, Athena at play.

The whole picture

The Greeks viewed Athena as the voice of reason and strategy. She was her father's daughter in the main, compliant to his world view. To the ancients the Athena archetype is rooted in serpent wisdom, right-brain intelligence rooted in the Mystery. In truth her perception is the whole picture – or as much of it as one has the capacity to perceive at any one time. That is where we are evolving now. Athena is connected to the vision or goal and the multi-faceted strands that may bring it to life. Her intelligence is like the web of connections through the brain yet it's also a frequency receiver that expands way beyond the brain. In an individual's life it's an ever-expanding subtle awareness of oneself (and one's choices) at the centre of one's web of life. All its creation is laid out on that web, whilst also interlinking with the whole web. Like the universe, where's the edge? Just like a spider's web one touch on any part of the individual web activates change in the whole of one's life whilst also affecting elements within the wider web. Everything has influence or impact. And that's just looking at it in two dimensions. What about the influence of our unseen dimensions: our thoughts, our prayers or our soulfulness? As you may see, Athena is a multi-faceted goddess, yet every aspect plays through intelligence.

Seeing in this way clearly opens us to the broader implications of everything we do as individuals. It takes more than courage to acknowledge this; it takes true recognition of oneself as a creator, with all its inherent responsibility. Athena reveals the weave of life from the exquisite beauty and symmetry of a tapestry, to the diverse elements that make up an illness, to the political games within our relationships or in the wider world, to our connection with our self, each other and our Earth. To engage her fully requires that we open our minds to so much more than our known patterned existence. It asks that we deepen our understanding and engagement of creative feminine intelligence.

The Shadow Energies of Athena

Whose authority?

Athena was undoubtedly her father Zeus's favourite child. She was the one in whom he placed his authority, and the Greeks reflected this honour. This father-daughter bond is a key element in both her expression in the world and to her shadows. It draws her into the world of men and that is where her learning and growth take place. The influence of her father is significant to her unfolding in that world, as is the input of each of our own father's ideas, beliefs and shadows to our patterned consciousness. Athena's connection to her father was one of daughter to God. What more complex relationship can one have? He had swallowed her mother Metis whole to avoid losing power to his offspring. What more powerful symbol of patriarchal take-over can one find? As girls the connection to our father (or whoever stood in that role) may be similarly power based. It is about our relationship to what we perceive as authority.

Archetypically the father role teaches us how to be in the world. It is a powerful influence on the innocent nature of a child. As Zeus's aide, Athena identified herself with his power of direction, even command. She values what he stands for. But was that real power? Real power is rooted in connection to oneself and one's divinity, in authenticity and integrity of action. As head honcho of the Olympian deities Zeus held absolute power but tyranny and true power are entirely different. On some level Athena recognised this, for she made her own choices in actualising Zeus's commands. Rather than use force (as her father and brother Ares did) she discerned how best to take action to accomplish the goal. She used strategy and made wise choices. Athena even disobeyed Zeus when her integrity saw the situation differently to him.

If we are to engage Athena's gifts fully, we also need to extricate ourselves from the distorted influence of the male authority figures in our lives – whether they're alive within us, in our patterned beliefs, or are external sources to which we give power. This attempt to extract our self from paternal influence may involve out-and-out rebellion, a quieter withdrawal into self-discovery and empowerment, or a mix of both. Rebellion doesn't always serve as it's reactive, nonetheless it is an essential and powerful reclamation of oneself on the journey to becoming whole.

The claiming of Athena intelligence is an essential aspect of mature individuality. It lies within our valuing and expressing the qualities of reason and detachment, in partnership with intuition and wisdom. In Athena's shadow we may over-value the patriarchal energies of goal-based cool detachment and control in order to achieve; decision-making may come just from rationale rather than the holistic perspective. Or we may be afraid of using the mind intelligently, of challenging the status quo with our wisdom and give way to any male influence of false power or force. The role models of father and mother (or in Athena's case, lack of that) make her what she is. It's the same for us. The process of developing holistic intelligence as we mature gives rise to two potential Athena energy imbalances; the hardened 'Amazon' warrior archetype along with its opposite: 'Daddy's girl'.

What price success?
The Athena energy, whatever its mode of expression, calls to be active in using creative intelligence in the world. Her capacity for both intuition and reasoning, subtle creativity and logic, process and decision-making needs to be expressed. Our skill with her energy lies in being conscious of which particular aspect of intelligence is relevant or potentially fruitful at any given moment. When we're tuned into her energy within ourselves that happens very naturally. It's fairly obvious that intuition plays no part in doing the annual accounts for a business and that logic has little value when creating a piece of art. Goal orientation clearly has value in our lives, as does process, along with our capacity to flow into unknown realms of creative potential. Left and right hemisphere intelligence has its place. The evolving Athena archetype has access to both.

Despite this creative synergy of right-left brain perception the Greeks have depicted Athena mainly through reason and strategy. In their myths she is seen to be motivated by achievement or winning. We may be similarly motivated, yet we all know accomplishment is a moveable feast. It will mean different things to each individual. Athena's definition of success always sits in the worldly realm. When we experience the desire to be purposeful, expressing through intellectual or productive excellence, we are connecting with her archetype. The Athena archetype in us wants to see the tangible results of creative intelligence, as do we. That may be through the harvest of our strategic intervention, or through the application of our healing skills or creative ingenuity. Tangible results may equal success. It depends how we measure them. Yet whatever the measure success always has a cost. That cost is reflected in how we achieve. The 'how' is where we may find evidence of both the healthy and shadow expressions of Athena energy moving through us.

When we set out to achieve something there is a fine line between staying connected to all aspects on our web of life and becoming focused on just that goal. Women are said to be the masters of multi-tasking (clearly an Athena quality) and yet, as we well know, the danger of becoming scattered, stretched or unbalanced is always present. The Greek portrayal of Athena was certainly unbalanced. They emphasised her role as a warrior goddess and her compliance with Zeus's commands. We could say they made her a servant of patriarchy. Yet paradoxically this was what was needed to birth a new faculty of feminine intelligence - the qualities of reason, decision-making and strategic influence. The feminine intelligence was expanding even as it was being denied.

In the Greek world Athena's armour was a symbol of her status in the world of mind and men. Her mythology shows us she never lost her cool head or her heart. To enter her rational strategic mind Athena had to cut off from the feminine aspects of nurture, instinct and love in favour of authority and alliance. This armoured archetype still plays out in the world now. Many women have had to take it on in entering the world of work. The danger is in putting it on we cannot take it off. To be in the world of work many women have needed to protect their sensitivity in order to be successful. Of necessity we have had to move from belly and heart orientation to head. In doing that we may have become lost in the drive to achieve and succeed. Perhaps we try to play the men at their own game, either by becoming the master of efficiency, competing and fighting to be a success, or through covertly winning by using manipulation? Either way the gift of our feminine intuitive wisdom is lost, simply because we are not valuing it. The importance of how we accomplish goals gets lost in the process. We may have denied aspects of receptive feminine within us that are not acknowledged in our current cultural climate in order to achieve. In developing the incisive skills of rationale, drive and detachment, some women find their armour has become a strait jacket of limitation. What feels like a protection actually leaves us dry and unfulfilled.

The power games of our world bring out the worst excesses of Athena. Her naturally competitive streak that is effective in meeting a challenge can become a drive to win at any cost. We see the shadow of Athena as the Amazonian women: the strident feminist energy in politics, law, campaigning or the corporate world that is a powerful voice where change is needed. Yet in excess, Athena's need to make a difference and to bring justice, can create a disconnection from the very cause she is advocating. Withdrawal from feeling the vulnerability of our humanness can generate a harshness that does not serve the task. In the shadow of this role 'getting the job done' precedes personal relationships. Athena's critical eye becomes like the gaze of Medusa where those around it can feel 'turned to stone', disempowered and without worth. Athena's lack of a mother can mean sensitivity to others is unavailable. At its worst Athena's disconnection from the inner world of feeling makes her cold and dry, an efficiency machine that runs from rational mind and has little or no heart. We see this particularly in the world of politics and big business. But it does not have to be so.

The world can seem to make us hard. It seems to require we protect and defend what is right and good. That we must fight for what is right, let alone any values connected to a more holistic collective perspective and sometimes we do. Yet if we are unaware of the danger of Athena's armoured shadow, we may simply create more alienation. The purpose of armour in battle is to protect oneself from being wounded. Yet when we keep protecting, we will eventually stop feeling. We lose our empathy, our passion, our intensity and our capacity to be moved by the mysterious and mystical. Athena lives in her mind and certainly it's essential that we embrace her and the gifts of her particular intelligence. Yet in calling on her qualities of purpose and achievement we need to also honour the capacity for less rational aspects of mind. We need to honour our instinctual roots and the input of other goddess archetypes. According to the myths this was something Athena could not do, preferring the role of competitor with females. Like her, without these deeper aspects of our feminine nature the danger is we fail to be in our body. The danger is we disconnect from the heart. It pays us to explore what armour we pull on when entering the fray of the world. Simply to see; will this really accomplish the task?

As awakening women we're becoming deeply aware of how imbalance in our world affects our feeling feminine orientation and vice versa. Our current culture does not support the deep sensitivity of our feminine knowing or its emergence as female wisdom. Because of this we need the Athena warrior to be alive and active within us and yet we also need to take off our armour. This is where deep awareness of how the shadow of armouring actually does not protect us is essential. It's actually cuts us off from our inner world and each other. Yet awareness of where we need to be strong and centred in expressing our values is key. It is a fine balance. We are learning to be warriors for feminine knowing without being steel-clad.

The Athena archetype is still evolving, for women are evolving in fully claiming their place in the world. We are still discovering how to navigate an increasingly mental and technological landscape with integrity. We are constantly discovering how that looks, both individually and collectively. It's an experiment; a vital one. Athena's birth and calling to live in the world of the mind means we are also discovering how to be in that, not by over-using masculine rationale, but in fully being the intuitive sensitive wonder of the Sacred Feminine that we are.

The shadow energy of the Athena archetype values career or creative accomplishment over relationship every time. The price of her success will be, at some level, separation from the more sensitive intuitive aspects of self, her heart and feelings. Similarly, in chasing achievement the desire to prove our worth may be masking a sense of helplessness and exquisite sensitivity. These qualities are unacceptable to the Amazon archetype yet may erupt at different times in her life. For many women, the armoured Amazon aspect holds within herself a fragile yet disempowered girl. Every time we disconnect from our feelings, especially our vulnerability, and go up into the head, we strengthen the shadow of this archetype. Every time we attempt to fix something about our self that we don't like, we strengthen the Athena shadow of coldness and detachment. Rationale will never heal our pain. Yet paradoxically the fullness of Athena's creative intelligence in us knows exactly what's needed to facilitate wholeness. When she's emerging and alive in us as creative feminine intelligence we naturally move towards healing and wholeness.

Daddy's girl

A young girl needs to feel the loving protection, strength and integrity of masculine presence in her life. A father may provide this, or some other strong male in a girl's life. If we have received strong loving empowering masculine role models in our lives, we are blessed indeed. As adults we no longer need this physical protection, yet we may still long for it, albeit subconsciously. For how many of us feel truly at ease in a world based on the distorted use of power? The growth of power games and abuse is a cancer affecting us all. We need the presence of strong masculine and feminine beings in our world. We need to reconnect with the truth of Sacred Masculine and Sacred Feminine frequencies. Perhaps unknowingly, we are learning to be this presence. In this process of conscious reconnection, we are all, male and female, parent and child, healing the wound.

The epithet 'Daddy's girl' probably has meaning to most of us. It seems to be the opposite of the Athena 'armoured Amazon' shadow yet the wound is the same. It comprises a lack of self-knowing and trust. This 'Daddy's girl' shadow archetype is based on admiration of the masculine, or masculine qualities and a desire to emulate them. We see it in girls who become 'one of the boys'. It expresses through a disconnection from being female, or through the desire either to emulate or please. It arises through the need to win the approval or love of male authority figures. This shadow of Athena is revealed through the well-behaved daughter, the submissive partner, the power-behind-the throne wife or via an inauthentic response to any male authority figure. It's all about power. Beneath this shadow lies a fear of being oneself and the need for approval from the significant male (or indeed any male) in one's life. Without that male approval the Athena girl-woman is on unsteady ground. She is effectively lost. She hasn't developed her own strength of will or sense of creative purpose.

Whereas in the Greek world Athena represents the power of reason, the 'Daddy's girl' archetype expresses disempowerment. She expresses the opposite of the armoured Amazon shadow. For this shadow aspect it's easier to play the game of passivity or compliance than to stand out. It's seen in the woman who's afraid of failure so doesn't try, who self-sabotages because she secretly feels she doesn't measure up to the current worldly values (even if they're not her own) or who plays small in order not to stand out. Even now women may be taught that to be successful can be a threat to a man, particularly one not strong in his own masculine presence. The belief that it's somehow 'unfeminine' to be strong, capable and effective in the world is dying now nonetheless deep with the psyche there is an insidious schism between being successful and being loved. It's a key dilemma many women need to face. Depending on what we value most, we choose to be 'our own woman' or to play down our gifts and strengths in favour of approval.

Athena's gift of strategy carries this shadow aspect most obviously. Feelings of powerlessness often lead to manipulation. It's one way to achieve an end, albeit a distorted one. Athena's gift is to see the route less travelled but then to act on it effectively. When this gift is distorted it works behind the scenes. It might play out through attention-seeking behaviour or taking a particular role we don't truly enjoy; it might express through dismissing our intelligence so as not to be a threat; it might distort through being disingenuous. Whatever the appearance at its core the gift of strategy is being distorted in order to win what seems to be love. But do we feel love if we are not truly being our self? How may we feel loved if we're being inauthentic? Truly such games are an abdication of power. They're often a habit, a manipulation to avoid facing disapproval or anger. Behind the 'Daddy's girl' shadow lies a deep fear of being and asserting oneself. This shadow is caught in the web of paradox: attraction to what males may provide in the form of validation, and to their apparent power to give or withdraw love. Beneath it lies a deep-seated fear of simply not being good enough.

The 'Daddy's girl' shadow aspect of Athena may be deeply connected to her gifts but she's choosing not to use or express them in her own unique way. When we deny our deep feminine knowing in favour of another's perspective about what's right for us, we're playing this game. Whenever we're seeking approval, we're playing this game. At times we all experience the fear that causes us to disengage from effectively expressing our creative wisdom. It's how we transform or energise that fear that reveals Athena's strength or lack of it. Is it held in the knowing of the whole of one's strengths and gifts, and merely as a passing experience? Or is it allowed to dominate our inner world? There are times we may desire the strength of a physical male reflection to hold a strong space for our deep feminine. It's natural to want the reflection of others to support our self-expression and creativity. Maturity realises we won't always have that though, that sometimes we need to choose to go against the grain. When we do this, we activate and strengthen our connection to inner power – the power to be our unique authentic self. Authenticity is natural power. Self-honesty is naturally powerful. If we view power as something other than this, particularly something external, we will always remain invalidated.

What we see as representing power is unique to each of us. In truth real power is known through inner connection and support of our own values and expression of our authenticity, but there are many pretenders such as money, position or status. In a healthy role the energy of father or male authority teaches us to be our own power and authority, to fully become our self. More often than not we are taught to give power away– to a person, a belief or idea – and not to trust our own deep knowing. What breaks the insidious bond of this archetype is the rebel, the fight to be oneself, to discover one's own inner fount of wisdom. To be free we're required to break free from attachment to father's or any external authority's influence and develop our own wisdom as a source of power.

Rebellion is complex. It's a necessary stage in the maturing process of oneself yet like any phase of growth it can become a habit rather than a transition. If rebellion is simply a reaction, an "I'll show you', the wound remains. We may swing fully from disempowerment to force, to trying to prove our self. We may appear to have it. We may find our place of creative achievement in the world, but if Daddy (or any other significant male) doesn't recognise that, it may have no value in our own eyes. We cannot see our self without his validation. We're still 'Daddy's girl', trying to retain or win love and approval. Our achievements, fulfilling as they may seem to be, have an edge of emptiness. It's the need for love or approval that sits in the core of this wounding. And because the wound can be deep, even when love is given, we may not see it. Athena's lack of connection to her sister goddesses and to female friendship adds to this wound. Her relationship to females was based on competition. She lacked the reflection of a mother and loving sisterhood, and so naturally in her shadow the search for validation continues.

The woman who acts as 'the power behind the throne' or who allies herself with powerful men expresses this Athena shadow too. She may even defend patriarchal rights, because that is where her second-hand power comes from. The myth of Athena's involvement in the trial of Orestes is a pointer here. Those who know the myth sometimes see it as her final betrayal of her female gender and women's rights. The myth goes like this. In a complicated tale Orestes was on trial for the murder of his mother. Under ancient law killing someone unrelated by blood was no crime so having killed his mother (related by blood) he was guilty without trial. Fleeing the scene, Orestes was pursued by the Erinyes (the Furies) to face responsibility for this act. Seeking sanctuary at the altar of Apollo, both Apollo and Athena became involved in the debacle. Athena arranged trial by jury; Apollo became counsel for the accused, Orestes. In his speech Apollo claimed a mother was not a true parent to the child but merely a nursemaid, yet the father was essential. He used Athena's existence as proof that a mother was unnecessary. When the jury was tied in their decision, Athena had the casting vote. She chose in favour of Apollo's theory, thus validating male superiority. For she had indeed been born without the need of a mother to do that. This sealed the emerging trend to patrilineal descent. The fact that Athena did have a mother, who was swallowed whole by Zeus, never seemed to enter the debate. The emerging patriarchal worldview was being established. Athena's actions in this case show her support of male right and might at that time.

To transform the shadow of 'Daddy's girl' we must claim Athena's courage and take the journey to authenticity. This means breaking free. Athena teaches us how to fully claim our self-integrity and authenticity. We have to reach for it, as much deeply inside as in the world, if not more so. We must get behind our self with support and respect for our unique capacity of intelligence. We all have an Athena gift. How that expresses through you will be different to any other woman. We may have to dig deep to truly find it, to discover the true Athena within who knows the value of her unique expression of creative feminine intelligence and expresses it as a unique and valuable contribution in the world. We must claim her. I feel this is a journey many of us are still accomplishing. The Father wound is deep. As is the Mother wound. We are all healing.

Where is the love?

Athena's ancient roots lie deep in the instinctual and sensual feminine. Strangely perhaps love played no part in her life, yet she's directly connected to serpent wisdom and the mystery of birth, life and death. When we explore the Greek version of Athena, she has lost her rootedness. Her apparent birth from Zeus's head disconnects her from mother and feminine. It's a sorry tale created for the purposes of patriarchy and yet with hindsight we may see it's not without worth, for it indicates the processes of evolution and the potential for a full embodiment of being female that includes the expression of mind.

Despite the Hellenic perspective if we look deeply into her pure archetype Athena does not lose her connection to the ancient serpent power, she merely uses it differently. The creative power she bears does not express through sexuality or as love but goes into her intelligence. It arrives in the role of guardianship of the people of Athens, through the arts and healing. Athena bears no physical children, but she manifests creatively. She bears creative children and in her connection to the welfare of the people she is caring for all children. Nonetheless Athena's evolving alignment to serpent power can come up strongly within her shadow. If Athena is living solely from mind, as is suggested by the Greeks, and if we are doing so in our lives now, what of relationship, what of love?

Athena's primary relationship connection (apart from to her father) was through her role in the lives of the Greek heroes. Her capacity of mind to see holistically was a powerful tool to support them. Perhaps in her guise as mentor and guide, Athena was also the friend of heroes. We do not really know. Yet clearly her calling is to companionship rather than intimacy. As her father's daughter Athena is not made for relationship. It is not her field of expression. She channels her sexual energy into creative and strategic endeavours. The pure Athena archetype has no need of a man. Yet without doubt she is drawn to powerful males. She respects masculine energy. If Athena is strong in us her energy will influence our relationship choices. We may choose not to marry, or to remain celibate. We may marry for strategic reasons, as a way of advancement to position or power. We may choose not to bear children. Whether married or not, whether Athena enjoys intimacy is questionable. Many women would say that the energy required to be successful in the world leaves little space for intimacy. It's a dilemma that requires conscious choices, with particular awareness about our pain and shadows of relating.

The full engagement of our creative lives, whether through work or artistry, hides the potential guardedness of Athena's shadow when it comes to intimacy. Being busy can an avoidance of relationship. Living in the head can become a habit, switching it off a challenge. Athena was never valued simply for being a woman. This is key to her archetype. It many ways she is androgynous. Her sense of self comes from her purpose and involvement in the world. If we're attached to this aspect of life as our identity, there may be fulfilment at some level but difficulty in love, even more so in self-love. Love requires that we feel and that we connect with another through openness, vulnerability and trust. A strong Athena shadow may be in control and effective in the boardroom yet avoiding the chaos of emotion, or the sometimes-messy-yet-alive power of sexual connection. Choosing a career or creativity over love is easier for some of us. It can be an avoidance of intimacy with one's own frailties, potential failings and the vulnerability of relationship.

In her darkest shadows the Athena archetype appears untouchable. She's deeply disconnected from her feeling self. She may give off the vibe of not needing anyone or anything and she may even believe she doesn't. If we are imbalanced (and potentially armoured) in our Athena expression, we may appear invulnerable too. We may think we don't need anyone. When we're fueled by creative fulfilment, we may feel complete. Living in the mind may be satisfying on one level but ultimately is disconnected from Athena's roots in the instinctual feminine. Being out of touch with the body, cut off from the full range of feelings and emotions may seem to be easier to this shadow aspect of Athena. Lack of body and emotional awareness can be deeply unfulfilling; some would say it's unhealthy. Here we see Athena's link with Medusa from another perspective. Medusa's head was placed on Athena's breastplate, protecting the heart. The head disconnected from body, guarding the heart. No wonder Medusa's gaze turns people to stone. When the mind rules this is the danger. We disconnect from self and from others. We become numb to our mind's dominance over our body and the impact of our cool detachment on others. When that gaze is turned inward it may turn one's own heart to stone. Such invulnerability does not make for healthy relating. To compound the theme of coolness Athena's relating with females was disconnected. At her worst she was dismissive of qualities such as beauty or tenderness, her female relationships fueled by competition.

When Athena is strong in us (and she's there somewhere in every woman) we need to clearly define where she plays. Athena was never a child. Born an adult she entered the world of politics immediately. To be in our wholeness we need to be clear about when and where Athena is appropriate. If she's alive in the bedroom rather than the boardroom it's likely that the attraction of polarity will suffer, especially sexually. This is where our strength of intelligence and effectiveness in the world can become a failing. What place does the mind or creative strategy have in intimacy? Intimacy requires polarity of energy. Intimacy requires willingness to be vulnerable. If we have a fear of vulnerability, we may use Athena's efficiency, strategy and strong work ethic as an escape from the openness of true connection.

Despite Athena's portrayal as distinctly rational, her energy may be seen to symbolise androgynous qualities. As we connect deeply and come into balance with her energy, we bring together inner masculine and feminine. Along the way we may tend to an over-balance in one or the other. This is our journey of evolution. Athena's calling to the use of strategy provides clues to her calling to balance and harmony. In that urge for integrated wholeness the shadow aspects of Athena, particularly in relating, have need to remember and reclaim Metis, her mother. This need to reconnect to her ancient roots, to the dark mystery of the feminine, to feelings and intuition, to nurture and nature, brings Athena full circle. In that place of wholeness, she gently holds the web of intelligence, intuition and instinct.

Athena wore Medusa on her breastplate. Aside from the mythology, she clearly is of importance to this archetype. The question is why? Is she honouring her connection to the deep mysterious feminine or is she merely representing her victory over the chaotic forces of darkness? We can explore the same in our own relationship to Athena and her qualities of creative feminine intelligence. Do we use the mind to over-ride our body, our deeper darker feminine energies? Do we live intelligently and wisely, honouring all aspects of the feminine as representative of her differing faces? Do we detach in order to avoid the vibrant yet uncontrollable encounter of powerful emotional and sexual forces within our self and within relating? An integrated Athena archetype will flow with intelligence through intuitive and instinctive expression, will recognise when to speak out with strength and when to listen, will know how to utilise the best qualities of awareness yet also come down from the mind into the wisdom of the heart, feelings and the body. Athena is our guide to living our fullness. Our connection to her takes us beyond what we already know. She is creative feminine intelligence evolving within us.

Introduction to Book 2 in the Sacred Pathways series
Embracing the Dark Goddess Archetypes in You

"The spirit of the valley never dies;
This is called the dark female.
The doorway into the dark female
Is called the root of heaven and earth.
It is there within us all the while;
Draw upon it as you will, it never runs dry."

~ Tao Te Ching 6

When we look at the night sky, we may gaze in awe at the light emanating from stars and planetary bodies visible to the naked eye. Just as the stars, planets and asteroids are held within the black backdrop of the universe, the Sacred Feminine also has dark archetypes holding and informing her expression through us. Not unlike the universe these archetypes are shrouded in mystery, hidden from our rational perspective, yet they hold a deeper wisdom of life in a body, keys to the split in our consciousness between spirit and matter. She holds core energy essential to evolution and conscious embodiment. When we face the raw energy of the Dark Feminine and our misguided beliefs about Her nature, we discover the power to be more fully present in all of life's chaos here on Earth.

Book 2 in the Sacred Pathways series takes a look at the archetypes sitting behind the Sacred Pathways Mandala. We'll explore the myths and stories, energy, shadows and gifts of Queen of Heaven Inanna, her dark sister Ereshkigal and Goddess of Discord Eris; Crone Hecate; Queen of the Underworld Persephone; Sedna who inhabits the icy waters of the north; Black Moon Lilith, first wife of Adam; and snake-headed Medusa.

The Dark Goddess has no reference points; She is the Mystery itself. Nonetheless we can discover pointers to her numinous qualities through myth, ancient writings, astrology and our own experience as women.

Embracing the Dark Goddess Archetypes in You will be available in early summer 2021.

Glossary

Archetype: a model or pattern of a particular way of being, held within the human psyche

Being: one's essence

Body-being: the whole of one's nature – body, emotion, will, mind, soul and spirit

Chakra: Invisible energy centres within the body. See Subtle Body

Collective: whole of humanity

Conditioned self: the ego; the identity we believe our self to be; the result of our childhood programming and experience

Cosmic Egg: Current cosmological models maintain that 13.8 billion years ago, the entire mass of the universe was compressed into a gravitational singularity (an extreme concentration of a huge mass). This is the so-called 'cosmic egg' from which creation emerged, mentioned in the stories of ancient cultures.

Creatrix: as opposed to Creator i.e. Feminine energy of creation

Crone: wise woman aspect of the goddess

Dark Goddess: the goddess archetypes that carry our shadow energies

Dharma: a Buddhist term meaning true behaviour, action or way of life

Divine Feminine/Goddess/Deep Sacred Feminine/Feminine: interchangeable terms for the receptive, nurturing, loving aspect of the divine expressing through women and men; Shakti

Divine Love: love beyond our human capacities

Earth Mother: the innate intelligence in the Earth, Gaia

Eleusinian Mysteries: rituals enacted in ancient Greece to honour Earth Mother Ceres and to reveal to the people the natural cycles of birth, life, death and rebirth

Enlightenment: a state of oneness with the Divine

Feminine/Divine Feminine/Goddess/Deep Sacred Feminine: interchangeable terms for the receptive, nurturing, loving aspect of the divine expressing through women and men; Shakti

Form: physical object or manifestation

Gaia: Planet Earth, the spirit of the Earth

God-head: Supreme deity

Goddess/Deep Sacred Feminine/Feminine/ Divine Feminine: interchangeable terms for the receptive, nurturing, loving aspect of the divine expressing through women and men; Shakti
Grace: divine intervention

Great Mother: a Universal or Cosmic Goddess symbolising the fertility and abundance of the Earth, out into the Cosmos, and encompassing all other goddess archetypes.

Her: Divine Feminine energy or archetype

Her-story: past events and knowledge as portrayed through myth and story, art, music, culture, tribal and oral traditions as opposed to the supposedly factual accounts of history (his-story)

Individualised: of each and every individual

Kali Yuga: The age of strife, discord and conflict in Hindu philosophy, spanning 3102BCE to 2020CE

Knowing: our non-rational connection to what is deeply true

Kundalini: spiritual life-force within the body. See **Chakras, Subtle Body & Sushumna**

Ley lines: energy lines within the Earth that are said to act like meridians connecting different ancient sites and temples

Mandala: a patterned representation of the connection between different ideas, concepts or archetypes; or simply shapes

Masculine: The masculine frequency of the Divine; Shiva consciousness; presence of stillness

Masters and Mothers: Divine beings

Matrilineal descent: ancestry traced through the mother's line

Mystery: life in its unknown quality

One: a state of unity

Pantheon (Greek or Roman Pantheon): collective noun for the gods, goddesses or deities of a particular people or culture

Parthenogenetic children: children created out of one's own body without sexual union

Participation mystique: a term introduced by philosopher Lucien Lévy-Bruhl to describe a psychological connection with objects, people or ideas where the subject cannot clearly distinguish himself as separate but is bound by identification. The relationship is both unconscious and undifferentiated.

Patriarchy: a system of society or government in which males hold the power, the father or eldest male is head of the family and descent is reckoned through the male line.

Patriarchal: pertaining to patriarchy – a goal oriented linear process

Priestess: a woman devoted to serving the Divine in whatever form is sacred to her

Realisation: a profound life-changing opening into the truth of our divine nature

Realised Consciousness: consciousness opened to its true nature as divine

Self: the divine within as opposed to self: ego

Shadow: unhealed aspects of self, often suppressed, rejected or unconscious. The disowned self—the parts we think are unlovable, unworthy, unacceptable.

Source: Life as divine energy

Subtle Body: psycho-spiritual or energetic constituents of living beings, according to alternative health, esoteric and mystical teachings. Each subtle body corresponds to a subtle plane of existence, in a hierarchy of being that culminates in the physical form.

Sushumna: an energetic channel that connects the subtle bodies with the physical along the spinal cord

Tantra: the embrace of every part of life, including sexuality, as sacred
Tarot: a system of divination using a set of Tarot cards

That: our divine nature

The Collective: the whole of humanity

Transcendence: moving beyond the normal or physical level of existence or experience

Triple Goddess: Great Mother Goddess with her forms of Maiden, Mother & Crone

Woman: the archetype of consciously awakened Sacred Feminine energy in women's bodies

Yin & Yang: the twofold nature of universal energy: expansive and contracting, seemingly opposite or contrary forces that are actually complementary, interconnected, and interdependent

Yogi: Hindu holy man

Bibliography & Suggested further reading

These are books that have informed, inspired and enlightened my journey with the Divine Feminine Archetypes. I honour the wisdom they carry.

Astrology
Gainsburg, Adam – *The Light of Venus*

George, Demetra & Douglas Bloch – *Asteroid Goddesses, The Mythology, Psychology and Astrology of the Re-emerging Feminine*

Guttman, Ariel & Kenneth Johnson – *Mythic Astrology*

Massey, Anne – *Venus, Her Cycles, Symbols & Myths*

Myth & Woman's Journey
Bolen, Jean Shinoda – *Goddesses in Every Woman*
Bolen, Jean Shinoda – *Goddesses in Older Women*

Estes, Clarissa Pinkola – *Women Who Run with the Wolves*

Kempton, Sally - *Awakening Shakti*

Monaghan, Patricia – *Encyclopaedia of Goddesses & Heroines*

Small, Jacqueline – *Psyche's Seeds*

Stone, Merlin – *When God was a Woman*

Wolkstein, Diane & Samuel Noah Kramer – *Inanna, Queen of Heaven & Earth*

About the Author

Cassandra Eve is an astrologer, soul coach, women's facilitator and writer. She has been sharing astrology and women's wisdom internationally since the early 1990's.

After experiencing a complete life breakdown in the late 1980's Cassandra serendipitously met an astrologer in a café. This was the start of her journey in conscious awakening. Shortly after she trained in astrology through the Mayo School and as a counsellor with a women's Rape & Incest Crisis Line. Training in other healing modalities followed. In 1993 Cassandra began her twenty-year journey with two different healing communities, spending thirteen years in an evolutionary Tantric community in the UK and New Zealand during that time.

In 2009 her first book 'Total Embrace – fully being human' was published.

Cassandra is utterly inspired by the possibilities of our healing journey to awakened consciousness both personally and collectively. Her life is dedicated to walking side by side into healing and deeper embodiment with those who are inspired by her sharing.

Discover more: www.beingwholewoman.co.uk

About the Illustrator

Pauline Burnside is an artist from the Scottish Highlands with a finger on the creative pulse.

As well as a great love for illustration and specialises in Sound Therapy.

Pauline says, "When I engage in the creative process, for me, it's about taking the plunge into trust and surrender. I find when I let go of expectations and outcomes something truly beautiful can arise. Creating a work of art can draw the viewer in and spark an emotion, a memory or a story within them. My role as an artist is to be able to create a bridge for the viewer to cross over and immerse themselves deeper into the story.

This collaboration with Cassandra has been an important part of my journey. This has been voyage of discovery into ancient knowledge and I am blessed to have collected many pearls of wisdom along the way."

Discover more about Pauline's latest creative endeavours and projects: Facebook: Pauline Burnside or Instagram: hive1spirit.

Printed in Great Britain
by Amazon